THE 100 GREATEST PHOTOGRAPHS OF THE PARANORMAL

FROM THE PUBLISHERS OF
Exploring the world of the unexplained
Paranormal

WRITTEN BY
Janet Bord

SIGHTINGS COMPILED BY
Mark Fraser

EXPERIENCES EDITED BY
Richard Holland

ART EDITOR
Gareth Evans
gareth@jazzpublishing.co.uk
Telephone: 01244 663400 ext. 204

GRAPHIC DESIGNER
Lindsay Burdekin
lindsay.burdekin@jazzpublishing.co.uk
Telephone: 01244 663400 ext. 226

PRODUCTION MANAGER
Justine Hart
justine@jazzpublishing.co.uk
Telephone: 01244 663400 ext. 235

ACCOUNTS & ADMIN MANAGER
Emma McCrindle
accounts@jazzpublishing.co.uk
Telephone: 01244 663400 ext. 207

ADMINISTRATION
Jan Schofield
jan@jazzpublishing.co.uk
Telephone: 01244 663400 ext. 219

Katie-Marie Challinor
katie@jazzpublishing.co.uk
Telephone: 01244 663400 Ext. 220

CREDIT CONTROL
Pam Coleman
pam@jazzpublishing.co.uk
Telephone: 01244 663400 ext. 215

ADVERTISING ENQUIRIES
Richard Davenport
richard.davenport@paranormalmagazine.co.uk
Telephone: 01244 663400 ext. 304

CIRCULATION & PROMOTIONS
Katy Cuffin
katy@jazzpublishing.co.uk
Telephone: 01244 663400 Ext. 237

PUBLISHER
David Gamble
david@jazzpublishing.co.uk
Telephone: 01244 663400

MANAGING DIRECTOR
Stuart Mears
stuart@jazzpublishing.co.uk
Telephone: 01244 663400

PRINTED BY
Warners Midlands plc

050 SPIRIT PHOTOGRAPHY
056 ECTOPLASM
060 MATERIALISATION
066 EXPERIENCES
078 POLTERGEISTS
084 STRANGE POWERS
094 RELIGION
106 EXPERIENCES
116 MONSTERS
126 UFOS & ALIENS
134 EXPERIENCES

FOREWORD

BY

RICHARD HOLLAND

When I was about 16 years old, I picked up a paperback on a second-hand bookstall for 65p. Contained within it was a heady brew of folklore and antiquities – subjects I was becoming increasingly interested in – which sparkled with speculative theories regarding earth energies and old religions, enlivened a spicy dash of the paranormal.

I was hooked. That book led me down all sorts of strange, dark and twisty paths, and I never looked back. It led to me writing my own books on folklore and the supernatural and becoming editor of *Paranormal Magazine*.

The book's title was *The Secret Country*. It was the second book by Janet and Colin Bord on the strange and mystical locations of the British Isles. I lost no time in seeking out the first, *Mysterious Britain*.

A couple of years later I started university, by coincidence in Leicester, Janet's home town. On my first or second, rather nervous, day I explored the university bookshop and there discovered another book to tempt me: *Earth Rites*. 'Hey,' I thought, 'it's another book by *them*.' Indeed it was and I have fond memories of taking my copy back to my room, my homesickness forgotten thanks to my immersion into the world of pagan rituals, green men, enigmatic carvings and holy wells.

One of the great strengths of the Bords' books is the extraordinary wealth of photographs and illustrations which illuminate the informative and engaging text. Colin is a talented professional photographer. Generally speaking, this husband and wife team share the work in the books that bear their name: Janet writes the text, Colin takes the photographs and handles the illustrations (but there is some overlap, of course).

The vast majority of classic photographs showing paranormal phenomena are owned or licensed by the Fortean Picture Library.

Travelling up and down the length and breadth of the British Isles in their old mini during the 1970s, the Bords began to amass an unrivalled collection of photographs of ancient and mystical sites. They also started to accept images – and video footage – from other photographers and also first-hand witnesses of strange phenomena. Photographs of UFOs, ghosts, poltergeist activity and strange creatures – all the fascinating subjects covered by this book, in fact – found their way to the Bords' home in North Wales. In this way the Fortean Picture Library was born.

Chances are any illustrated book on the supernatural you have ever read contains imagery from the Fortean Picture Library ('Fortean', of course, refers to the philosopher Charles Fort who spent a lifetime amassing thousands of references to inexplicable events and published several seminal books on the unexplained). The vast majority of classic photographs showing paranormal phenomena are owned or licensed by the Fortean Picture Library.

Now you have the 100 best of them in your hands.

They say seeing is believing. Here are 100 of the most startling or intriguing photos you are ever likely to see, and they may well have you believing in the paranormal (if you don't already believe, that is!). They cover the entire range of the unexplained, all the subjects we hope you have enjoyed reading about in *Paranormal Magazine*, from possible spirit manifestations and psychic powers to UFO landings and cryptozoology.

Very recently, after Janet Bord had finished compiling this book, one photo (I'll leave you to find out which) had serious doubt cast upon it. It's possible others may one day also be shown to be less than authentic. But the vast majority have been defying explanation for decades and will have you wondering, too.

Janet and Colin moved near to my home town some years ago and I have had the privilege on many occasions of visiting the the Fortean Picture Library, marvelling at the racks upon racks of carefully labelled boxes of prints – 'Loch Ness Monster', 'Kirlian Photography', 'Psychic Surgery' and the like. It's like an Aladdin's Cave of weirdness.

It must have been a tough job selecting the 100 greatest photos from the thousands of candidates in their vast collection, but Janet has succeeded admirably.

The 100 Greatest Photographs of the Paranormal from the Fortean Picture Library is a book you will return to again and again. It will endlessly fascinate you. It may not contain the absolute proof of the paranormal, but the pictures contained in this volume are about as close to proof as you can get.

Richard Holland
Editor, *Paranormal Magazine*

INTRODUCTION

This collection of 100 intriguing and mysterious photographs comes from the Fortean Picture Library, which was started by Janet and Colin Bord in 1978. (The name 'Fortean' refers to Charles Fort (1874-1932), who paved the way as a collector of weird and wonderful facts relating to events outside the realms of conventional science.)

Over the last 30-plus years we have collected together literally thousands of images relating to mysteries and strange phenomena, though a relatively small proportion of them show actual phenomena in progress. That is because not many such photographs exist – and of those that do, it is virtually certain that many are hoaxes, or sometimes misinterpretations of natural phenomena.

However, we cannot always be certain which ones are mundane rather than mysterious, because although it is easy enough for someone to claim a photograph to be a hoax, it is usually very difficult to prove it. So these pictures come with a warning: some may be hoaxes, some may be misidentifications, and some may be genuine – but which ones?

The range of topics covered by the Fortean Picture Library is surprisingly large, and encompasses everything that is considered impossible or inexplicable, from toads in stones, through spontaneous human combustion, to vampires and zombies. Ghosts and spirits are the phenomena that have been most often successfully photographed (again with the warning that hoaxing has been rife!), and the photographs we have showcased will give a good overview of what has been obtained down the years.

Also well represented are strange powers such as levitation and psychic surgery, monsters such as the Loch Ness Monster and Bigfoot, religious phenomena, and UFOs. We hope that you will find plenty here to puzzle you, and to set you thinking about what is possible in this strange world of ours.

Great ball of fire
This photograph may have captured the rare phenomenon known as ball lightning, and so is a good contender to be genuine. It was taken during a thunderstorm by Werner Burger from his home in Austria. He set up his camera to grab some shots of the lightning, and was lucky enough to obtain this – which experts have stated does not show a firework, meteor, or normal lightning. Ball lightning has only been accepted as a genuine phenomenon in recent years. It can be anything from 1 inch in diameter to the size of a football, and moves through the air sometimes with a buzzing or hissing sound.
[© WERNER BURGER/FORTEAN PICTURE LIBRARY]

'Over the last 30-plus years we have collected together literally thousands of images relating to mysteries and strange phenomena.'

The man who lost his head
A few of the images we receive at the Fortean Picture Library fit no clear category. One puzzling, and rather amusing example, was sent to the library by Mr Vic Burnside. Mr Burnside took two self-portraits in 1986 while he was attending a meditation course. At the time he had in his pocket a book with the title *On Having No Head,* a popular work of Zen philosophy in which author D. E. Harding encourages his readers to lose their sense of self.

It's difficult to determine why Mr Burnside has literally lost his head in the second of the two photos – at the very least, it's a remarkable coincidence.
[COINCIDENCEHEADLESSMAN - © VIC BURNSIDE/FORTEAN PICTURE LIBRARY]

The Cottingley Fairies

Although many sightings of real fairies (or the Little People, as they are sometimes known) have been reported, including by level-headed people not normally prone to fantasizing or hallucinating, there are no convincing photographs of them. The five pictures known as the Cottingley fairy photographs were for a long time believed to be genuine, but are now known to have been hoaxed by the young girls who took them between 1917 and 1920, because they confessed in the 1980s and showed how it was done.

Elsie Wright and Frances Griffiths, two Yorkshire schoolgirls (aged 17 and 9 respectively in 1917) took the photographs in the woods by the stream behind Cottingley village, near Bradford. They fastened cut-out drawings using hat-pins, and their stated intention was to illustrate the fairies which they said they really did see down by the stream.

In fact, although admitting their fakery, they continued to maintain that the photograph which shows the fairies sunbathing in the bushes (reproduced here alongside two of the faked photos), was genuine.

Ghosts

Ghosts have a long history: they were reported as far back as the first century AD, when Athenodorus, a hard-up philosopher, rented a house in Athens, which was cheap because of its eerie reputation.

Sitting working late at night, Athenodorus heard the rattling of chains and then, suddenly, the horrifying figure of an old man appeared before him. It beckoned to him and, although Athenodorus tried to ignore it and get on with his work, it refused to let him, rattling its chains so that he couldn't concentrate. So Athenodorus followed the ghost into the garden, where it pointed at a spot on the ground and disappeared.

Next day, a hole was dug at the place indicated by the ghost and a human skeleton with chains still around it was discovered. After the remains were given a proper burial and the house purified, the haunting ceased.

This was clearly a ghost with a purpose, but usually the reason for a haunting is not clear. There have been a few modern cases where ghosts seemed to have a message, such as 'crisis apparitions' of a person, seen by close friends and relatives at the time of his or her death, an event unknown to them until confirmation came later.

However, in many ghost sightings, the apparition seems purposeless and its identity remains unknown. Many of the ghosts which pop up in photographs were not even seen at the time the picture was taken, and such appearances therefore seem to be totally accidental rather than purposeful.

Menacing figure

Unsurprisingly, numerous people claim to have seen or sensed ghostly presences in many of England's ancient churches – the smell of incense, the sound of the organ, voices singing, knights dressed in armour, and so on – but no one has ever claimed to have seen the ghost of Newby church in North Yorkshire which revealed itself on a photograph taken by the then-vicar, Reverend K. F. Lord.

The Rev Lord was a keen amateur photographer and one summer afternoon some time in the early 1960s he decided to photograph the interior of his church. There was no one else there with him except one friend, and neither of them saw anything untoward in the church.

Some time later, when he made some prints from the negatives, the Reverend Lord discovered the ghost on one of them. Standing beside the altar is a tall (possibly 9 feet) menacing figure, wrapped in a long, dark cloak, with its face apparently covered by a white cloth with eye-holes.

The church only dates from the late 19th century and was not known to be haunted. I maintained a long correspondence with the Rev Lord from around 1971 until his death in 2000 aged 86, and he remained firm in his belief that the photograph was genuinely mysterious.

Sightings

Taken from the pages of
Paranormal Magazine

GROWLING: A strange, eerie growl has been heard by several witnesses in a ruined church along Cold Christmas Lane, Thundridge, Herts. The building attracts 'devil worshippers' at Halloween, and has long rumoured to be haunted. A recording of the growl has been made. But locals Bernard and Marion Hill, who have been in the area for the last 30 years and walk their dogs through the ruins twice a day, say they have never seen, heard or experienced anything out of the ordinary. (SOURCE - EAST HERTS HERALD).

HIGHWAYMAN: Helen Coughlan says she has encountered the ghost of highwayman Bill Saunders on several occasions in Epping Forest and that he has told her he was hanged for a crime he did not commit. Apparently, Saunders, part of Dick Turpin's gang, refuses to pass over completely to the other side until his name is cleared in a gang murder. Mrs Coughlan said: 'There was a stench of rotting flesh whenever he was close. While highwaymen were buried in consecrated ground, murderers were hung and their corpses allowed to decompose until they were nothing but bone. He spoke to me and said that he had been staying around the place as he didn't want to cross over as a murderer, as he was innocent of the crime. We performed an exorcism which involves the last rites, so now his soul has been commended to God and he seems feels a lot freer now." Rev Spencer Hayward performed the exorcism with his wife Janet. (SOURCE - THE GUARDIAN).

19th CENTURY GHOSTS: In January, English couple Tony and Doreen Galbraith were holidaying in CO Fermanagh, Ireland, when they had an unusual experience. Mr Galbraith reports: 'My wife and I decided to take a walk. We went to an area known as Cleenish Island, a very rural setting with many deserted dwellings near the village of Belnaleck. We drove our car across the bridge onto the island and drove about a mile further down the twisty narrow road, where we decided to stop and take a walk to where we were told there was an old graveyard. The area was so quiet and peaceful it made for a lovely walk, even though it was cold and getting dark. The closer

In the Outback
Little is known about the circumstances in which this photograph was taken, other than that the photographer was a clergyman by the name of the Reverend R. S. Blance. It was taken in 1959 at Corroboree Rock, Alice Springs, in Australia's Northern Territory. This place was once of great significance to the Aborigines as a cult site and initiation rites may have been performed here. It is now a 'conservation reserve' visited by tourists and hikers.

Not much detail of the ghostly figure can be made out, but what you can see doesn't look much like a Native Australian, so perhaps the ghost is of an early 20th century tourist who strayed off the track and was never seen again (except as a ghost).

In the street
Brenda Ray took this photograph in Tutbury, Staffordshire, on 4 March 1993. At the left, between the cars, is what appears to be a figure in a black cape. Brenda did not notice the figure at the time, and it does not appear in the next frame taken seconds later. Tutbury has an impressive ruined castle, which can be seen on the skyline, where Mary Queen of Scots was imprisoned for almost twenty years in the 16th century.
[BRENDA RAY/FORTEAN PICTURE LIBRARY]

we walked to the graveyard, the more old empty houses we passed, the more myself and my wife began to become spooked. It felt like we were not alone. As we passed the house, my wife claims someone walked past the window. Although she only caught a glimpse, she says that she saw a man wearing clothes like from the 19th century period. I walked into the house but could not see anyone.' On their return they had another odd encounter, as Mr Galbraith explains: 'We approached the old graveyard and both saw a lady standing amongst the gravestones ruins. As we approached closer, we noticed she too was wearing what looked to be clothes from the later 19th Century. She smiled at us and I said, "Are you alright?" As I said, this she walked in amongst the trees and disappeared. (SOURCE - FERMANAGH HERALD).

IRISH WHITE LADY: As reported in last month's issue, the curious have been flocking to the Mullaghmoyle Road near Coalislan in Northern Ireland for a glimpse of the 'white lady'. For the last four weeks cars have been lined up nose-to-nose, people arriving armed with cameras and camcorders in the hope of catching a photographic image of the ghost with the sad face. Raymond Bell, who owns a pub nearby in Brackaville, said his 17-year-old son Ryan had not believed in ghosts until he saw the 'woman' several times. 'My son says he has seen the shadowy figure on numerous occasions and others have seen it, too – it is the face of an elderly lady wearing a long white dress with a long white cape,' he said. People are still coming in their droves to see her. They come when it gets dark at about 4.30pm and they stay until after 1am. It is only about 400 yards away and I have tried to get down there but there are just too many cars. It is all that anyone is talking about.' (SOURCE - THE TELEGRAPH).

HAUNTED HIGHWAY: 'It's a stretch of road, up north in Maine that's never ever, ever seen a smile...' so goes the 1965 song A Tombstone Every Mile by Dick Curless. Route 2, which locals refer to as Haynesville Woods, in Ohio, has long had a sinister reputation

Ghost in the gallery

On 15 May 1982, Chris Brackley took a photograph of the interior of St Botolph's church, Bishopsgate, London. After the photo was developed he spotted an eerie figure in the gallery, top right (see close-up).

Mr Brackley explained: 'My wife and I arrived early to photograph a wedding and decided to take some interior shots of the church. The caretaker unlocked the church and let us in (empty, apart from the three of us). As the interior was dark, we set the camera up on a tripod and used a lengthy exposure – after which we exited the church which was once again locked. The unexplained image was only noticed some time later in the wedding proofs.'

The figure appears to be dressed in Tudor costume. Although the current St Botolph's dates from the 18th century, it was built to replace a medieval church. After the photograph was reprinted in a book, a heating engineer got in touch to say that he had had to knock down a wall leading into the crypt as part of his work and had found a number of old lead coffins, one of which contained 'the well-preserved remains of a person' who closely resembled the figure, 'both in dress and appearance'. It is hard to imagine how the face of a corpse could remain in recognizable condition after 400 years, however.

for ghosts and strange accidents. A woman in white is said to haunt the highway: she would appear suddenly in front of a vehicle and ask the driver for a ride, saying she and her husband had just been in a wreck. The woman would, of course, disappear from the vehicle suddenly, leaving the startled driver with 'a cold and terrible chill'. Other witnesses have reported a red flashing light that comes nearer and nearer to their vehicle, until it turned into a white cloud that then follows them along the highway.
(SOURCE - MIKE CONLEY, THE MCDOWELL NEWS).

HITCH-HIKER RETURNS: The ghost of a girl dressed in a short white dress is supposedly causing the deaths of motorists in Guadalajara, Mexico. She has appeared on several highways in the area in the past few years; motorists swerve to avoid the apparition causing several deaths. People in the area believe it is the spirit of a hitch-hiker who was violently murdered and who has now returned to have her revenge.
(PHANTOMSANDMONSTERS.COM).

BOLLYWOOD BREATHER: Mreenal Deshraj, while playing the part of a ghost in Mumbai, had her own encounter with the unknown. She previously did not believe in the supernatural, until she stayed in the Palace Hotel. At 04.30hrs she at first heard heavy breathing as though there was someone beside her asleep in the bed. She said: 'After some time the breathing became louder, scaring the Bollywood actress who then, in her night clothes, fled the room. The hotel reception staff did not believe her.
(SOURCE - INDIA TIMES).

GHOST SCARES ALIENS: The cast of Glasgow's Alien Wars are terrified of the spectre of a young girl. As the staff try and scare punters when they are queuing up to pay, they in return are being frightened by the apparition of a 'wee girl'. Show creator Gary Gillies said: 'My guys can't do their jobs because they're being distracted by this ghost. A wee girl wearing old-fashioned clothes has appeared during the show. She sees the alien and then starts screaming blue murder before disappearing into thin air again. It's playing havoc with the production. My aliens — who are meant to be invincible killing machines — are squeamish about spooks! We're also concerned about the public seeing the ghost during the show — the last

Sightings

thing I want is for somebody to have a heart attack.' Psychic detectives are being called in to find the cause of the haunting. It is rumoured that a little girl was murdered in the area 200 years ago.
(SOURCE - NEWS OF THE WORLD).

FERRY TOLL PHANTOM: What was believed to be an apparition was spotted in Fife, on Rosyth's Ferry Toll, in early August. The witness who wishes to remain anonymous said: "I saw a youngish soldier wearing army fatigues with socks and boots as if combat ready and he seemed to be trudging along on the pavement He was fairly small-built with short crew-cut hair and I would say around 18-years-old. I registered him but did not take any particular notice. Then, for some reason, I looked into my mirror – the soldier had disappeared. I turned round to see nothing. It occurred on a straight piece of road, there were no turnings off and not enough time for him to turn off and go in another direction.'
(SOURCE - DUNFERMLINE PRESS).

DEAD RINGER: Jen Bowman, landlady of the Prince of Wales Feathers in Kendal, Cumbria, believes she is haunted by a man in an old photograph that is hanging on the wall of the pub. Many people, including customers, have seen the spectre, who is said to be a friendly soul. Jen said the phantom regularly emerges from behind locked doors. The ghost is described as being short, dressed in a shirt and tweed trousers, and said by Jen Bowman to be "the dead ringer" for former landlord John Nowell. He has a habit of lifting up the toilet seat to let them know that he is around and turns the television on and off at her request! On one occasion when Ms Bowman walked into her bedroom she saw him sitting on the end of her bed as plain as day. She reports: "I was looking down when I went into my room. I saw a pair of shoes moving around the floor. I looked up expecting to see Tom, but it wasn't. I screamed, threw my coat at it and ran off, but he's been seen so many times now that it doesn't faze me at all."
(SOURCE - THE WESTMORELAND GAZETTE: 26TH AUGUST 2009).

BACK ON THE BEACH: Another photograph on Scotland's Saltcoats beach has come to light, this time seemingly of a male figure who posed for the photograph. Charlene

The Belmez faces

The mystery of the Belmez faces is one of the eeriest in the paranormal literature and has never been solved satisfactorily. It began on 23 August 1971, when Maria Pereira, a peasant woman living in the Spanish village of Bélmez de la Moraleda, found a face that had apparently been painted on the kitchen floor. This odd event drew unwanted attention to the family, so six days later they dug up the kitchen floor and replaced it with fresh concrete.

But a week later, another face appeared. The face remained for several weeks and slowly changed as if it was aging. The floor was dug up again, and an excavation revealed human bones – it turned out the whole street had been built on an old graveyard. Two more faces appeared on the new floor, and a professor who came to study them ultimately counted eighteen. He was even able to watch a face forming.

Intensive work and analysis by a number of researchers has failed to ascertain how the faces were formed, though inevitably some have suspected a hoax. One possibility is that Maria was a psychic (she died in 2004, aged 85) and the faces were a thoughtographic phenomenon which she unintentionally 'thought' into being. The faces continued to appear over a period of thirty years, until she died.

The Black Abbot
The village of Prestbury, near Cheltenham in Gloucestershire, has a reputation for ghosts, one of which is known as the Black Abbot: a hooded figure in a black cloak said to walk through the churchyard. One lady who had seen the ghost said that it appeared to walk below the current ground level, because the ground in the churchyard had been raised over the centuries.

Photographer Derek Stafford (now deceased) was in the churchyard on the night of 22 November 1990, taking photographs of the floodlit gravestones. He told me that he chose that particular day because it was very foggy and he hoped for some interesting effects. The ghostly Black Abbot showed up on his very last photograph, but he saw nothing strange at the time.
[© DEREK STAFFORD/FORTEAN PICTURE LIBRARY]

Wieringa, who took the photograph, said: "We were down at the beach because some friends of ours had come over with their camper van. We had a bonfire and my partner Scott took a picture of the girls and we didn't notice anything. It wasn't until later when Scott was going through his phone deleting pictures that he came across it again and we thought we could see something. Scott thinks its smoke from the fire but the girls and I think it looks a bit like a Scottish soldier.' Several people from the local area have contacted the Ardrossan Herald with similar pictures that feature uninvited guests in the background.
(SOURCE - ARDROSSAN HERALD).

MORE CAUGHT ON CAMERA: Security guards at Liverpool's Croxteth Park have yet again seen the phantom thought to be former resident Hugh William Osbert Molyneaux. The guard said: "I was only covering for someone who was off, so don't usually work in the park – it's all a bit spooky." A picture described by the Derry Journal as "a ghoulish apparition" was taken of a shadowy figure on the steps of St Columb's Cathedral in the Irish Town of Derry, in early September. As usual the snapper only noticed the figure after developing the film and saw nothing at the time. Spalding Paranormal Investigations claim they have caught the apparition of Catherine Bystock on camera at the former RAF Metheringham near Lincoln. Airwoman Bystock was killed whilst a pillion passenger on her boyfriend's motor-cycle during World War 2. It is believed her ghost often frequents the area. She has been reported flagging down motorists in full uniform, asking the drivers to help her injured boyfriend.
(SOURCE - LIVERPOOL ECHO, DERRY JOURNAL, ARDROSSAN HERALD, THIS IS LINCOLNSHIRE).

CIVIL WAR: Strange things are happening down at Port Columbus National Civil War Naval Museum in 

The Guildhall spectre
Professional photographer Haddon Davies was undertaking a routine assignment on 22 January 1985, when he went to the medieval St Mary's Guildhall in Coventry to photograph the Coventry Freeman's Guild dinner. He climbed up into the ancient minstrels' gallery and set up his tripod and camera among the suits of armour, swords and pikestaffs. A ten-second exposure was necessary because of the dim lighting in the large hall, so Mr Davies waited until everyone was standing up to say grace before he took his photograph.

Later, when an enlargement was made for the Lord Mayor, a strange figure was noticed at the end of the top table. The Lord Mayor, Walter Brandish, described it as having 'a skull-like face and clothes of armour of mediaeval character'.

Despite much discussion, no one could offer any logical explanation for the figure. Mr Davies checked the photographs he had taken both before and after the chosen picture, but the strange figure was nowhere to be seen. The Lord Mayor had a guest list and was able to account for everyone except the enigmatic visitor, and the people sitting in that area had no recollection of seeing it.

Staff at the 14th-century hall were not surprised by the suggestion that the building might be haunted, however, and, as Mr Davies commented, 'It seems that just as I had felt, the Hall was no place in which to work alone after dark.'

[© HADDON DAVIES/FORTEAN PICTURE LIBRARY]

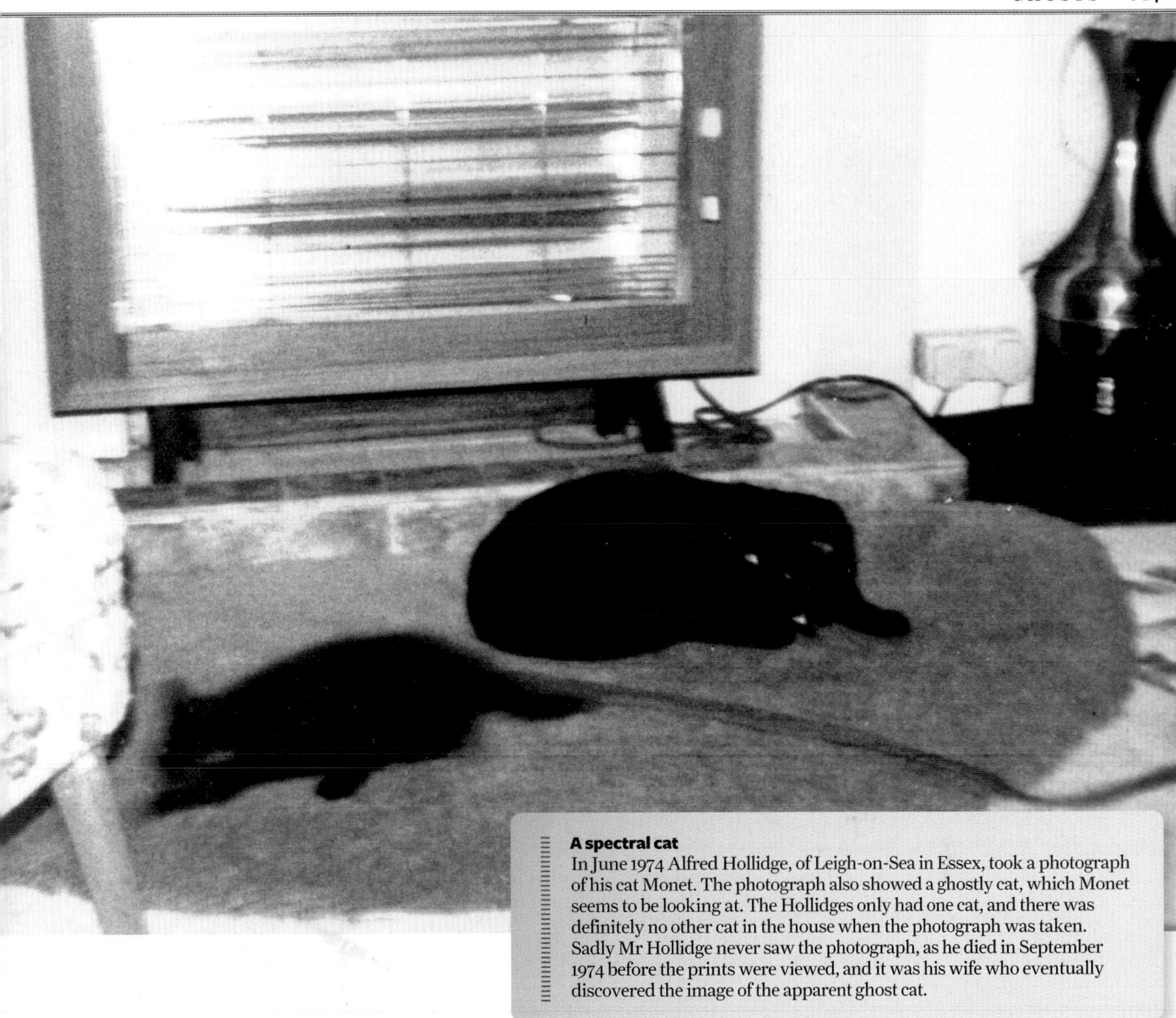

A spectral cat
In June 1974 Alfred Hollidge, of Leigh-on-Sea in Essex, took a photograph of his cat Monet. The photograph also showed a ghostly cat, which Monet seems to be looking at. The Hollidges only had one cat, and there was definitely no other cat in the house when the photograph was taken. Sadly Mr Hollidge never saw the photograph, as he died in September 1974 before the prints were viewed, and it was his wife who eventually discovered the image of the apparent ghost cat.

the USA. An invisible something is throwing books at visitors and staff alike, one book landing squarely in the back of a bemused patron, who then looked accusingly at a nearby member of staff. Books are landing up to seven feet away from their original position, sometimes landing standing straight upright. Staff are used to this and say it is a regular occurrence. Bruce Smith, the museum's executive director, said: "We have these continued unexplainable dumping of books on the floor. ... We don't know what the deal is. We've looked, and we can't figure it out. We think we've got these things anchored pretty good, and the next thing we know, crash! And there's nobody in the store."
(Source - Ledger Enquirer: August 2009).

TIME TO GO! The Venetian Theatre and Bistro in Oregon, USA, is haunted by a punter who is reluctant to leave after closing time. Staff have seen a tall grey-haired man several times in the back row of the seats after everyone else has gone. When he is told it is time to go he simple disappears. Staff have heard "unexplained footsteps, lights turning on and off by themselves." Unexplained water leaks have occurred, music playing, and one member of staff saw a grey/dark mist rush by him and the word 'stop' was heard; the staff member went no further.
(Source - oregonlive.com August 2009).

FAINT SPIRITS: In Japan the word for ghost is yurei, translated as 'faint spirit' and they usually remain in the area where they died. Their military establishments seem especially susceptible. The ghost of a marine has been spotted many times at the Atsugi Naval Base wandering aimlessly from room to room. One hangar bay on the base has its doors constantly slammed open and shut, as well as "disembodied red eyes" that float around the building. Military police at the field hospital in the Sagami Depot are spooked by ghostly footsteps and objects moving around when there is no one there. They are also baffled by

Is this Lord Combermere?
Sybell Corbet took a photograph of the library in Combermere Abbey, Cheshire, on 5 December 1891, the day of Lord Combermere's funeral. It is thought to show the ghost of Lord Combermere himself, sitting in his favourite chair, on the left. Miss Corbet said that no one entered the room during the long exposure. She did not see anything untoward herself, but when she developed the glass plate she found the apparent ghost. The figure seems smaller than he should be, and also has no visible legs. Lord Combermere's daughter-in-law said that none of the servants resembled the figure in the chair, but all his children were convinced it was Lord Combermere.

the doors and windows that have the ability to unlock and open by themselves.

At room 301 in the Iwakuni Barracks soldiers are terrified by the ghostly face of a man who stares back at them when they look in a mirror. It is believed the phantom is of a man who broke a mirror in a fit of rage, then used the broken glass to slit his wrists.

At Camp Hansen, Okinawa, World War 2 soldier covered in blood appears at Gate 3. The gate has now been closed because of this. The ghost of a Samurai warrior haunts the Yokusha Naval Base and has caused several accidents when seen by shocked motorists. The list goes on, but perhaps the most chilling of all is the voices in Hiroshima and Nagasaki that can be heard at twilight screaming for help!
(SOURCE - WEIRD ASIA AUGUST 2009).

NIGHT VISITOR: In the small village of Kilmaurs on the outskirts of Kilmarnock, Scotland, a middle-aged couple are experiencing odd sensations that are seemingly on the increase. At first they put it down to imagination, but now they are not so sure. In addition to doors opening and shutting by themselves and unexplained bangs in the night, phenomena include objects being moved from room to room, the strong smell of cigarette smoke and gusts of wind passing by them while they're sitting in the lounge. The most disturbing is hearing the crunch, crunch on the gravel as though someone is walking by the side of the house, hearing the back door open and close and footsteps on the stairs; no one is ever found and all doors are securely locked.
(SOURCE - MARK FRASER BCIB OCTOBER 2009).

KING OF ALL WITCHES: Witch Magus Lynius Shadee claims he has conjured up a demon to prey on the congregation at the Church of Our Lady and the English Martyrs in Hills Road, Cambridge. Magus, who claims to be the king of all witches, claims to have summoned the evil spirit to reside in the church and 'cleanse it'. He said: 'It's an elemental, a hunter that will attach itself to an individual, either send them insane or make them depressed. The worst is to cause them to take their physical life.' Fr Dick Healey called Shadee twisted and added: 'He should be reported

Sightings

to the police. It's as if someone came into your home and performed some sort of magic trick without your permission. He's obviously a bit twisted to perform witchcraft in a church. We will not be performing an exorcism, but I will consider reporting him to the police.'
(SOURCE - CAMBRIDGE NEWS: OCTOBER 2009).

THE ENCHANTED FOREST: Sarah MacKessy filmed her baby while on a visit to the Enchanted Forest Nature Reserve in Tunbridge Wells, Kent, and thought nothing more of it until she played it back later after returning home. As her baby stares at the screen a voice is clearly heard saying 'I'm alive.' Mrs MacKessy said: 'The only people around at the time were my partner and the two children, who were about 10ft from me. All the other members of the public had gone as it was nearly closing time. The ghostly voice sounds as though it is directly next to me and is very loud and clear on the video.' You can view the video at http://www.thesun.co.uk/sol/homepage/news/article2657764.ece#ixzz0TeZzIfLx
(SOURCE - THE SUN 28TH SEPTEMBER 2009).

FOOTSTEPS: Karen Griffiths, curator of the Howard County Museum, USA, knows the sounds an old building can make after everyone has gone home, but it is the footsteps that she has heard on many occasions that still perplex her. She said: 'I have never felt afraid, really. But I will hear a strange noise now and then and it

His dead pet?
This family group, of a lady and her two children, was photographed at Clarens, Switzerland, in August 1925. The boy is seen with a toy animal in his left hand. His right hand is held against his midriff but appears to be enclosing a white kitten whose face is quite clear. In fact, there was no kitten present at the time. However, some weeks before the photograph was taken, the family had owned a white kitten that had died after being mauled by a dog. Was the tiny animal still keeping its young owner company, but in incorporeal form?

Tara and Kathal
Lady Hehir was photographed while taking her wolfhound Tara for a walk in 1926. When she saw the photograph, Lady Hehir saw that Tara appeared to have the head of another dog on her rear end, and recognised it as the head of a Cairn terrier puppy she had recently owned. The puppy, named Kathal, had died six weeks before this photograph was taken. Lady Hehir said that Tara and Kathal had been inseparable, eating, playing and walking together. The place where the photograph was taken had been a favourite spot to walk the dogs. Had Kathal returned from Puppy Heaven to enjoy another walk with his best friend?

surprises me more than it scares me. I still hear the footsteps now and then; I don't like to be the last one around to close up.' No one is ever found when she investigates the empty building. Cool blasts of air rushing by her and her printer often turning itself on of its own accord are other things that make Ms Griffiths feel she is not alone. A recent night's investigation by Colin McGuinn of the Greater Maryland Paranormal Society did not produce any evidence for a haunting while they were in attendance, however.
(SOURCE - EXPLOREHOWARD.COM).

DOGS TAKE THE LEAD: For the past three years Tom and Deborah Weaver, of Cleveland, Ohio, home claim to have been 'visited by spirits on an almost daily basis'. Tom Weaver said: 'It seemed to start with one spirit, and then progressed to the point where we identified seven of them. Our dogs were the first to notice that something strange was going on in our living room. I was really sceptical, and I really didn't want to believe in any of this. But after enough stuff happened to me, I had to admit that something very special is going on here.' Deborah continues: 'It started with our dog, Trouble, barking and chasing something we couldn't see in the living room. We actually took her to the vet because she was acting so strangely. She would start to stare into space and start pawing at something that we couldn't see.' Then the couple began seeing and hearing unexplainable things in the living room and hallway. Laura Templin, Deborah's sister, was an unbeliever until an unseen someone touched her head and shoulders. She ran out of the house.
(SOURCE - WYKC.COM 7TH OCTOBER 2009).

NEW NAME, SAME OLD GHOST: The Victory Bar at 118E Sixth Street in Tucson, Arizona, is now called Gooch's Grill, but all patrons know of the ghost that lurks in the rooms whatever the sign says outside the door. After closing time 'bottle caps are flicked by unseen fingers, the swinging saloon-style doors that lead up to the second floor office will swing back and forth for no apparent reason [and] lights turn off or on by themselves.' The ghostly figure of a woman is also sometimes seen and crying can often be heard. Although the ghost is well known throughout the area, no one knows its identity, although the present owner, Lon Wirtz, believes

Angelic apparition
Silvio Mayer started bending metal using only psychokinesis after seeing Uri Geller doing this on the television in 1974. He lived in Switzerland, and one day after the death of his mother in 1978, he went for a walk in the woods and saw a luminous ball. He photographed it, and in the picture it appeared as a yellow circle with a luminous angel-like figure inside it.
[© DR ELMAR R. GRUBER/FORTEAN PICTURE LIBRARY]

that a woman had been raped and murdered on the spot where the establishment now stands.
(SOURCE - TUCSONCITIZEN.COM 4TH OCTOBER 2009).

ROLLER-COASTER SPOOKS: Six members of staff at the Thorpe Park theme park in Surrey have been suspended for conducting a late night séance with a Ouija board on the horror themed ride, the Saw, since then paranormal events have occurred on the ride. Staff and punters alike began reporting extreme drops in temperature, lights being turned on and off, and the special effects starting up by themselves. Even the sound of ghostly footfalls were heard when no one was present. A spokesman said: 'On the evening of Monday, October 12, an unauthorised Ouija Board session was conducted by six employees at the ride after it was closed to the public. A full investigation is under way and the six employees have been suspended pending the outcome of this enquiry. We take staff and guest feedback very seriously and for this reason we called in Rev Lionel Fanthorpe, a leading paranormal expert, to help us investigate reports that have arisen from this situation.'
(SOURCE - THE SUN: 15TH OCTOBER 2009).

GHOST UK: Paranormal group Ghost UK claim they have caught ghostly images on camera after an investigation at the Chequers Country Inn, in Leicestershire. Also a 'mysterious banging noise' can be heard.
(SOURCE - HARBOROUGH MAIL: OCTOBER 2009).

VILLAGE TERROR: Eerie screams, a murder, and a discovery of a skeleton have left villages in Kampung, Malaysia living in terror. On the 6th of October a woman was discovered murdered in her house and the body was left in a bag under the sink (her son is the chief suspect). Then a skeleton was found in a well. Since then the villagers have been suffering from the 'heebie jeebies'. Rokiah Sarumin said: 'Initially my neighbour asked me whether I heard screams at night but I just dismissed it as a joke. However, I then heard the screams. Salmah Hanim said

The Brown Lady
Raynham Hall is a 17th-century mansion in Norfolk, said to be haunted by the Brown Lady, identified as Dorothy Walpole, who became Lady Townshend and died in 1729. The ghost was known as the Brown Lady because in her portrait Lady Dorothy wore a brown dress.

In 1936 she may have been captured on film by two photographers working at the hall. They had taken a number of pictures when they came to the staircase. Then, as Indre Shira later wrote: 'Captain Provand took one photograph while I flashed the light. He was focusing for another exposure: I was standing by his side just behind the camera with the flashlight pistol in my hand, looking directly up the staircase. All at once I detected an ethereal veiled form coming slowly down the stairs. Rather excitedly I called out sharply: "Quick, quick, there's something." I pressed the trigger of the flashlight pistol. After the flash and on closing the shutter, Captain Provand removed the focusing cloth from his head, and turning to me said, "What's all the excitement about?" '

The Captain, on being told that there had been a ghost on the stair, offered to bet £5 that there would be nothing on the negative. The two men argued all the way back to London, and asked a friend to watch while the film was developed. They were adamant that the negative had not been interfered with in any way, and that they had genuinely photographed a ghost. The arguments for and against this being the case have continued ever since.

Among the flames

On 19 November 1995 the town hall in Wem, Shropshire, was destroyed by fire, an event watched from a safe distance by Tony O'Rahilly, a local amateur photographer (sadly now deceased).

Mr O'Rahilly took some photographs of the blaze, which he later developed at home, and when he printed them he was surprised to see the figure of what appears to be a young girl in one of the pictures. She is standing in the doorway of the fire escape, surrounded by smoke and flames. No living person could have been standing there, because it was too dangerous, and the fire-fighters were keeping people away. She appears to have long hair, and to be wearing an old-fashioned bonnet.

One suggestion is that she was the ghost of a young girl who accidentally started a fire in Wem in 1677. She knocked over a lighted candle in the thatched cottage where she lived, and the fire spread rapidly through the town. Another suggestion is that the burning timbers just happened to look like a girl's face – but it is interesting that workmen who were working in the town hall after the fire claimed to have seen a ghost there.

So the story has run for the last 15 years... In 2010 the mystery was said to have been solved, when someone noted that a photograph taken in Wem in 1922 showed a girl looking very similar to the 'ghost' in the 1995 photograph. Did Tony O'Rahilly create his 'ghost' photograph by inserting the 1922 girl into his photograph of the Wem blaze? Sadly we cannot ask him, but before his death he did deny faking the image. It is possible, of course, that his photograph does show a genuine ghost – of the girl from 1922.

Among the gravestones

In 1928 Mrs Hilda L. Wickstead was on holiday with friends in Worcestershire, and on seeing the church in the village of Holly Bush near Malvern, they decided to stop for a while. Mrs Wickstead decided to take a photograph of her friend, Mrs Laurie, and asked her to stand still while she did so. Mrs Laurie can be seen standing to the left of the tall cross by the church porch. After taking the photograph, Mrs Wickstead put her camera in the car and then went to join Mrs Laurie.

As she commented later, 'There was absolutely no one else in the churchyard at the time and she walked down the path to me. When I got inside the gate she drew my attention to the grave of a soldier who had died in service and another of a girl who had died a few months later and said, "I wonder if they were lovers." '

Six weeks later, when the film was developed, Mrs Wickstead noticed what appears to be an embracing couple among the gravestones in the trees, who would surely have been noticed by the visitors if they had been there in reality.

the eerie noise came from the well. My house is near the well where the skeletal remains were found I was terrified and told my husband but he dismissed it.' (SOURCE - THE STAR: 26TH OCTOBER 2009).

DEMONIC DOG & PHANTOM TRUCK: Bloods Point Road in Illinois is said to be haunted by a ghostly black truck and a phantom dog. A black truck suddenly appears from nowhere and chases vehicles only to disappear as quickly as it came. A school bus full of children is said to have lost control on the road with all life lost. The story is that if you stop your vehicle on the spot and put it in neutral the ghostly children will come and push you, and if you leave traces of talcum powder on your vehicle you will later find the imprints of small hands. Locals scoff at the stories, there are no records of such an accident, and local resident Russell Mothkovich claims with a twinkle in his eye that he recently bought a brand new black truck! But local paranormal researcher Mike Rutlin claims to have personally encountered the devil dog and reports: 'While I was driving down the road with a friend, we heard the sound of twisted metal dragging behind us. Just then there was a huge dog's head in the window, growling and barking. We were doing probably 40 mph. This thing came out of nowhere. I hate to make it sound like a bad horror movie, but it was a huge head, and it had the red eyes. It was in the window of my car... It seemed like forever at the time, but was probably just for 10 seconds and then it vanished.' (SOURCE - BND.COM: 17TH OCTOBER 2009).

FOLSOM PRISON BLUES: Ghosts walk the corridors and cells of the prison according to James Brown, operations manager for the prison's museum. A ghost has been seen walking around the front gate on several occasions and it is believed to be the spirit of a prison officer killed in a riot in 1927. All the usual occurrences are reported: ghostly footsteps, figures disappearing and strange unexplained noises in the night. After one such sighting all the prisoners were rounded up for a head count but none were missing.

Sightings

One guard knowingly explained that it was the ghost. A figure was seen walking around the catwalk, but when challenged to stop he ignored the requests. The guards opened fire – the figure carried on walking and then disappeared. The most haunted areas seem to be the old hospital, old death row cells and building 5.
(Source - The Folsom Telegraph: 19th October 2009).

SCARIEST PLACE IN THE WEST: Robb Canyon in Northwest Reno, near Rainbow Ridge, USA, has long had a reputation of being haunted, which comes as a bit of a surprise to the locals! According to the Haunted Robb Canyon blog people have reported 'unexplained cold spots, invisible forces that push or tug at visitors, blood curdling screams, and shadowy specters'. The screams are alleged to come from a multiple murder in the 70s, yet no trace of these murders can be found in public records. The blogs on the area even claim that the local police have given up attending calls to the area – a claim they strenuously deny. Even residents who have spent years in the region say they have no knowledge of the spooky incidents.
(Source - rgj.com: 24th October 2009).

FOLLOW ME: Justin Potts of the Indiana Paranormal Group is drawn to the now closed Central State Asylum Hospital on the outskirts of Indianapolis. He says that a strange atmosphere descends on the place after dark, and has recently experienced some strange occurrences while investigating the premises. He said sometimes 'spirits' reveal themselves in the hospital as strange shadows, mist-like clouds or tiny orbs of light. Pott has EVP recordings in which something appears to say, 'Follow me', along with, 'Can you help me?'
(Source - Indiana Daily News: 28th October 2009).

THE HANGING TREE: A French couple on holiday in the Scottish Highlands claim they have taken a photograph of a ghost at the site of an old hanging tree situated in the High Street, Fort William. Unknown to the tourists the site has had a ghostly reputation since the tree was chopped down in the 1970s. Sophie Mager, and Remy Puckey, from Jaux, just north of Paris, did not see the apparition when they took the photograph, but as usual, after they

In the cellar
This figure was photographed in the cellar of the Viaduct Inn in London, where the cells of Newgate Prison were said to have stood – but no person or ghost was seen at the time.
The photograph was taken by a trustworthy personal friend, a Dane called Lars Thomas, a zoologist by profession and not the sort of person to be so unaware of his surroundings that he failed to see a person standing in front of him when he took a photograph. He was on a guided tour of the cellar in 1988 and wanted to capture the eerie place on film – afterwards he found that he seemed to have captured a ghost.
[© Lars Thomas/Fortean Picture Library]

A ghostly dog

These two ladies and their maid, partaking of afternoon tea in the garden, are completely unaware that they have an ephemeral canine companion. The photograph was taken around 1916 at Tingewick in Buckinghamshire by Arthur Springer, a retired CID inspector from Scotland Yard. Neither he nor the ladies were aware of the dog. They did not own a dog, and when they saw it in the photograph they could not recognise it as a dog from their village.

The names of the ladies taking tea were, seated left, Mrs Kate Townsend (the mother-in-law of the person who supplied us with the photograph) and Mrs Emily Springer, whose husband took the photograph. He was using a plate camera, and a fresh pack of glass plates straight from the chemist. It is interesting that the dog is clearly standing still and therefore, if it had been a live dog, it would have appeared as solid as the people. Instead it is insubstantial and appears to be headless.

looked at the film. STV reports: 'The night-time image shows the bright lights of the houses in the town. In front, just before the camera lens, there is a white mist or smoke-like veil blocking the view.' Ms Mager said: 'It was amazing and I swear that it is not a picture with special effects. We didn't see the ghost on the spot, but discovered it when we looked at the picture. Many strange things are happening in Fort William. We showed it to the staff of the West End Hotel in Fort William, where we were staying. They too found the apparition intriguing – but scary.' The photo can be viewed via paranormalmagazine.co.uk/news (SOURCE - STV 22ND NOVEMBER 2009).

SECURITY SCARE: Security officers on a building site on the outskirts of the Ayrshire village of Dalmellington are reporting strange goings-on at the site. Guards are diverting their mobile supervisor away from his duties to complain of strange noises in their patrol room. They often hear bangs and crashes coming from the other two rooms, the kettle turning itself on and off, noises in the attic, and on one occasion a loud bang that seemed to shake the whole house which completely unnerved the guard on duty. Whereas most of the noises can be given a ready acceptable explanation, the shadowy figure seen by one experienced guard cannot be easily explained away. (SOURCE - WWW. CLAYMORESECURITY.ORG NOVEMBER 2009).

A BABY AND A BONNET: The security officer at the Roe Valley Hospital in Limavady, Northern Ireland, took a few night-time photographs of the building and the grounds on his digital camera. Later, flicking through them he was amazed to see a ghostly figure on one of the images, which he immediately showed to his manager. Investigators from the Paranormal Society Ireland held the photograph in their possession for three months before releasing it and declaring it as genuine. The picture is said to show a woman wearing

Sightings

an old-fashioned bonnet. Some say she is a nurse, holding a baby. There has been paranormal phenomena reported from the former workhouse grounds in the past; strange sounds like those of babies crying, knocks on windows, ghostly nurses, and the list goes on. The photo can be viewed via paranormalmagazine.co.uk/news (SOURCE - LONDONDERRY SENTINEL: 19TH NOVEMBER 2009).

GHOST RIDER: A man in Kennesaw Cobb County, Georgia, USA, reports: 'I've got a bad back and haven't worked in over a year so I spend a lot of time in bed. Earlier this year, late spring or early summer, I was in a half-awake state and I noticed the hazy form of what appeared to be someone in Civil War clothing on a horse standing in my bedroom. It was there for only a second and kind of dematerialized. I remember it being a kind of a yellowish colour. I am three miles from the epicentre of the Battle of Kennesaw Mountain Park and probably less than a mile from the cavalry battleground at Mud Creek.' Another man reported to the 11alive News that he and his son were driving the Kennesaw Mountain National Battlefield on the 8th of October when they saw 'something' about to cross the road in front of them. He reports: 'I quickly locked down on my brakes as the horse proceeded to come right in front of us, the rider passed straight through the fence.' Civil war buffs, the witnesses were able to identify the rider as a Union Army cavalry officer holding a sabre in his hand. (SOURCE - PHANTOMS & MONSTERS AND 11ALIVE NEWS NOVEMBER 2009).

PHANTOM FELINE: The Fairport Harbour lighthouse in Cleveland, Ohio, is said to be haunted amongst other things, by a cat. The feline once owned by a Capt Joseph Babcock who lived in the lighthouse in the late 19th century and gave many cats to his bedridden wife. His son died of smallpox at the age of five and is also said to be a spirit that lingers on at the lighthouse. Nine years ago the mummified remains of a cat was found in the brickwork when a new air-conditioning system was being installed. The ghost cat has been seen on many occasions walking the grounds, and now the paranormal group Ohio Researchers of Banded Spirits (or ORBS) will be conducting an onsite investigation to determine whether the tales are true. (SOURCE - WKYC NEWS 8TH NOVEMBER 2009).

Basilica apparition

Four friends were visiting the Basilica of Le Bois-Chenu near Domremy in France, in 1925. This church is dedicated to St Joan of Arc, who came from Domremy, and was built at the place where Joan heard her voices. The occasion for their visit was the presentation of the Union Flag to the church by Lady Palmer. Miss Townsend asked Lady Palmer to take her photograph, and she can be seen in the centre. The two other people present, Mr and Mrs W. E. Foster, were behind the camera.

These four were the only people inside the church, and none of them saw the two figures which also appeared on the photograph. Closer examination of the original print suggested to them that the figures were priests wearing archaic vestments. But if so, they are unlikely to have officiated in the basilica, which was only built in the late 19th century.

The harbour wall
George Kanigowski was on holiday in Cyprus in September 1986 and he decided to photograph the lights of Limassol harbour at night. His Olympus OM10 camera was mounted on a tripod on a 3-foot-high wall, and a time exposure of 30 seconds was used for each of the five slides. He saw nothing unusual at the time, and no one crossed his path: indeed, a person would have needed to climb on the wall in order to get into the picture. But when he got home and had the slides processed by Kodak, George found that although four were normal, one showed what may be a ghostly figure.
[© GEORGE KANIGOWSKI/FORTEAN PICTURE LIBRARY]

GHOSTS ON FILM: A photograph of what some believe are two ghosts dancing has been taken at the Tunnel Bar, Union Station Restaurant, Northampton, MA, in November. One person involved reports: 'My daughter's friend has taken successive photos in which the second photo taken a few seconds after the first shows a woman in a 50s or 60s green and aqua dress with an up-do hair style. She is floating in a tilted position with no legs. The arms and hands look oddly grey and odd looking in shape. She is near people sitting on barstools and is elevated slightly higher than they are. The person taking the photo said the woman was not there when she took the shot. No mention was made about the man behind her, however, he looks normal and could have gotten out of his seat and was heading towards the door.' The photo can be viewed via paranormalmagazine.co.uk/news (SOURCE - PHANTOMS & MONSTERS & THE TEXAS PARANORMAL RESEARCH GROUP: NOVEMBER 2009).

PHOTO PHANTOM: While at a friend's birthday party David Finch took a photograph at the Red Lion pub which is situated along Blackburn Road in Wheelton, Lancashire. He said: "I don't believe in the afterlife and all that but I can't explain the picture. It's done the rounds in the village, and everyone has come out with a story." A local senior psychology lecturer believes it may be due to double exposure or a smudged finger print, although the Paranormal team (who are usually fairly cautious about ghost photos) feel this one looks too 'good' for that explanation. But judge for yourself: the photograph can be viewed at www.paranormalmagazine.co.uk/news (SOURCE - LANCASHIRE EVENING POST 3RD DECEMBER 2009).

ANGELS AND THE DEAD: Kylie Homes from Cambridgeshire believes that her three children, Jade 11, Amber 9, and Leo 5, talk to angels and dead people. They claim to remember past lives, and even draw sketches of the beings that they converse with. While on holiday In Ireland a picture taken of them on the Giants Causeway ☞

Sightings

shows them, according to Kylie, "surrounded by a radiant white light". Kylie says: "It's just a manifestation of the energy of the three children themselves, combined with that of the place itself.' Kylie's husband is sceptical, and Chris French, head of the Anomalistic Psychology Research Unit of Goldsmiths College at the University of London says: "Most children have vivid imaginations and enjoy fantasy play and that's a perfectly healthy part of growing up."
(Source - KRGV News 4th December 2009).

THE SITWELLS: Situated in the East Yorkshire town of Scarborough and now known as the Woodend Creative Workspace, Sitwell House is said to be haunted by members of the famous literary Sitwell family who once owned it. A recent "live ghost hunt" was said to have provided proof that the establishment is haunted. Andrew Clay, centre director of Woodend, said: "They are all friendly ghosts. We have seen very strange things in the past and someone once took a picture of a face in the window. We were told some are visiting ghosts while the others are permanent."
(Source - Scarborough Evening News 18th December 2009).

HAUNTED HOTEL: First built in 1640, destroyed by the Jacobites, once owned by the man who ordered the slaying of the McDonalds in Glencoe, and set in the majestic surroundings of Loch Linnie and Loch Leven, this building has a long and troubled history. Guests and staff alike are reporting paranormal goings-on from the hotel today. Incidents include ghostly foot falls from empty corridors, the ghost of a little boy who has been photographed, an old lady in grey, piano music and even sleep paralysis. Now staff members Jim Morrison and his fiancé Heather MacLeod have started their own paranormal research group in the hope of getting to the bottom of the strange occurrences.
(Source - Lochaber News 30th December 2009).

JAILHOUSE SHOCKS: Built in the 1750s on a "busy" execution site and now owned by historian and ghost hunter Richard Felix, the jail is reported as being a "hotbed of paranormal activity." Mr Felix says he was once "confronted by a grey haze in the shape of man, who glided straight past

Two more church ghosts
This photograph was taken by Eddie Coxon in Alton church, Staffordshire, on 12 September 1993, during a flower festival. There were other people in the church, but Coxon was sure no one was in front of the camera. It was a 2-3 second exposure, with no flash used. Perhaps the flowers attracted a plant-lover from beyond the grave.

facing page A figure was caught on camera in Sefton church, Merseyside, by Paul Mason in September 1999. He was with one other person in the church. Neither of them saw the figure and the church door was locked.

him before disappearing at the end of a corridor." Doors open and close of their own accord, and many people report feelings of nausea, so much so that they have to leave the premises. People have also felt themselves being strangled and the apparitions of two men hanging from beams have been noted on several occasions. The most frightening apparition of all is a bald man who wears a leather apron.
(Source - Sunday Mercury 3rd January 2009).

FARM IN FEAR: Donna Santos, of Connecticut, called in the Northwest Connecticut Paranormal Society to help make sense of incidents on her farm. Frightened horses were often moved from one locked barn to another, the cat's bowl of milk was often moved, dogs barked at invisible beings. The whole family became very uncomfortable living there. Mrs Santos said: "I did not move the horses. My husband did not move the horses our children did not move the horses. The horses could not unlock themselves and move on their own, something had to move them." State Troopers spent the night on the farm on one occasion, they saw nothing, yet still the horses had been moved right under their noses.
(Source - The Register 6th December 2009).

COP 'FREAKED OUT': San Francisco Police officer Eric Borghesani initially set out to debunk the alleged haunting at the Hayward Mansion, but now he is a believer. He saw something out of the corner of his eye, took a photograph and caught on camera what he believes is a ghost, of what he says was a "disembodied dress-shape hovering in the right side of the photo". EVP experiments in the building have resulted in many 'spirit' recordings with phrases such as "Step ... back!" "Get ... out!" "Just let them know ... dad!" Borghesani said: "It totally freaked me out."
(Source - http://www.insidebayarea.com 13th December 2009).

ATTENTION SEEKERS: Desk clerk Kirsten Kuykendall at the Hotel Monte Vista in Flagstaff, Arizona, believes the majority of ghosts seen in the premises are just after attention. "Whatever is here is trapped and bored," Kuykendall said. "They just want to be acknowledged." Many of the occurrences take place in a room in which two prostitutes were murdered

Sightings

in back in the days when the area was the red light district.
(SOURCE - HTTP://JACKCENTRAL.COM NEWS 16TH DECEMBER 2009).

TEXAS DEMONS: A woman in Texas fled her home in terror, claiming demons forced her out. She reports seeing shadows and ghostly voices and that her daughter talked to the spirit of a girl who called herself Beth who said she was demonic. The unidentified woman brought in a ghost hunter and the Channel 5 news team to try and help with the situation. The family of four ended up sleeping in the same room, being too scared to stay alone. The owners of the leased property explained that they had never experienced anything bad in the house, suspecting that the story is made up to get out of the lease. Property manager Kay Kerr said, "a lease is a lease".
(SOURCE - KRGV NEWS 17TH DECEMBER 2009).

PARANORMAL PUB: Paul Donnor who owns the Park Gate Inn at Cannock Wood, Staffordshire, believes his premises are "a hotbed of paranormal activity." Reports of "ghostly figures, floating orbs and inexplicable temperature changes" have been reported by staff and visitors. The Park Gate Inn stands only 500 yards away from Castle Ring, the Iron Age hill fort said by some to be "one of the most mystical places in England." Strange music and ghostly entities have been reported from the area. But Mr Donnor believes the haunting at the inn could be attributed to the death of a former owner in 1969.
(SOURCE - SUNDAY MERCURY 13TH JANUARY 2010).

SUICIDE CELL: Prisoners at HMP Brinsford near Wolverhampton are "terrified of entering a possessed cell" after two "near identical suicides" in less than a year. Now hardened criminals are insisting that a priest be called in to perform an exorcism. Details of the previous suicides are not available but an inside source said that one of the former occupants of the cell was a "devil worshipper." The deaths were on the same day and at the same time. A Prison Service spokesman said there was "no truth" in suggestions that an exorcism was planned.
(SOURCE - SUNDAY MERCURY 18TH JANUARY 2010).

EXTRA GUESTS: The Boutique Hotel in Edinburgh's old town, not

Mysterious mists
Bachelors Grove Cemetery in Illinois (not far from Chicago) is an abandoned burial ground with a ghostly reputation. There have been many reported sightings of ghosts, mysterious lights, eerie mists – and strange noises have been heard (watch out if you view the website www.bachelors-grove.com – it scared me half to death!).

These photographs were taken in 1974 by Tony Vaci. He said that the mist could only be photographed in two areas of the cemetery, and that he had managed to take over 100 such photographs using Polaroid cameras. He felt that the 'thing' wanted him to capture it on film, as sometimes his camera would 'fire' by itself. He had witnesses with him when he photographed the mists, and when the camera fired by itself, including the well-known local ghost hunter Richard Crowe.

Is this Walter?
When Robert A. Ferguson was addressing a Spiritualist convention in Los Angeles, California, on 16 November 1968, several Polaroid photographs were taken during his talk. This one allegedly shows Ferguson's dead brother Walter (killed in action in France in 1944) standing next to him. According to Ferguson, however, the arm and hand held forward do not belong to either Robert or Walter.
[© Robert A. Ferguson/Fortean Picture Library]

far from Mary Kings Close has been experiencing some odd occurrences lately. The underground cellar was recently opened during renovations and now staff report feeling "an odd chill" when there. Others have reported "hearing strange bumps coming from behind the door." The hotel is only yards from the underground network of tunnels where plague victims were rumoured to have been buried alive. Mark Turner, paranormal investigator for Ghost Finders Scotland, said: "There is a huge amount of history and tales of human suffering linked to old Edinburgh."
(Source - Dead Line Scotland 1st February 2010).

22-FACED: A picture was taken at the Sammy Marks Museum in Pretoria, South Africa, which is said to show the ghost of a Scotsman who in life was a friend of the Marks family. The group of people who assembled for the photograph numbered 21, but the actual picture shows 22 people, or rather just an extra face. There is also "an extra hand" in the photograph! The Scotsman in life is said to have looked after children in the building during the 1800s; his ghost is well known and it has a tendency "to tease lady visitors."
(Source - www.southafrica.net 26th January 2010).

SLEEPLESS NIGHTS: The story goes that in the 1930s a woman with a baby in her arms jumped to her death from the Skirvin Hotel in Oklahoma. Staff and visitors have reported seeing "ghosts and hearing strange noises" throughout the years. Football team the Knicks recently blamed their recent stay at the hotel for their games loss. The players had trouble sleeping because of their fear of the "ghosts." Coach Jard Jeffries said: "I definitely believe it, the place is haunted. It's scary." The occurrences include a woman screaming, a maid's cart rolling on its own, female voices, furniture moving of its own accord, and propositions by the spirit of a female prostitute.
(Source - Daily News 12th January).

A ghostly hand

This photograph of a bureau was taken for a trade furniture dealer, probably at the very end of the 19th century or very early in the 20th century, since it was published in *The Strand Magazine* in 1903. The photographer saw nothing strange at the time. Photographic glass plates were used in those days, and an exposure time of 13 minutes was required, but no one went near the bureau while this was taking place. After he found a disembodied hand on his photograph, the photographer was at a loss to explain how it had come to be there. A similar photograph of the bureau with the lid closed did not include a ghostly hand.

Mysterious infant

A ghostly child can clearly be seen on this photograph taken in an Australian churchyard, but no one knows who it is, or can explain how it came to be on the photograph.

Mrs Andrews went to the churchyard at Gatton in Queensland some time in 1946 or 1947 intending to photograph the headstone on her daughter's grave (Joyce, who died aged 17 in 1945). Joyce's brother Cecil, who died in 1942, is also buried in the grave. Later, Mrs Andrews found that her photograph also included a young child, but she was sure it was neither Joyce nor Cecil. She also said she had not photographed any living children around that time, so if a double exposure is responsible for the 'ghost', none of the family could explain it.

When Australian paranormal investigator Tony Healy, who is related to the Andrews family, visited the graveyard in 1995, he found two graves of infant girls close by, one aged 18 months, the other 3 years. Could one of those be the ghostly intruder?

[© HARRY LESTER ANDREWS/ FORTEAN PICTURE LIBRARY]

ATTIC ANTICS: The ghost of a little girl is said to haunt the fourth-floor attic of the empty Goodale House along Sandbar Ferry Road, Augusta, Georgia. Paranormal investigators brought a doll and placed it in the room in the hope of attracting the spirit on a recent investigation. The doll was surrounded by cameras and microphones in the hope of catching any movement or sounds. The girl is often seen looking forlornly out of the window but nobody knows who she is. Mr Sims, the present owner of the house, which was built in 1799, said: "The house definitely has a supernatural presence to it; you can just feel it when you come in here. It's wonderful." Nothing was caught on the cameras.
(SOURCE - THE AUGUSTA CHRONICLE 21ST JANUARY).

FRIENDLY PHANTOMS: From the moment Martha Rixten moved into her home on Wolfe Island, Lake Ontario, 30 years ago she knew it was haunted. She said: "I felt I wasn't alone here. I felt surrounded by a loving energy." Today the friendly ghosts are still there and very active. Footsteps as though someone is wearing heavy work boots are often heard on the third floor. Other apparitions include three ladies in the bathroom (!) and a little boy. Mrs Rixten has now put the property up for sale, not because of the visitors but simply because it is time for them to move on.
(SOURCE - NATIONAL POST 24TH JANUARY).

CREEPY THEATRE: The Hippodrome in Waco, Texas, has been experiencing some odd goings-on of late. Strange figures have been seen on the catwalk, "strange mists, and eerie voices" are some of the phenomena that has been recorded. The McLennan County Paranormal Investigations (MCPI) team were called in for an investigation and certified the building as haunted. But box office manager Cristina Uptmore said: "In a theatre you hear things and it's an old building. It's creaky. I have never attributed it to paranormal activity, but it creeps you out just the same.'
(SOURCE - LARIAT NEWS JANUARY 2010).

Sightings

SEDUCTIVE HITCHER: A female ghost named by locals as Catherine has been frightening motorists in the Black Woods in Down, eastern Maine. She is dressed in a "light blue evening or ball gown" and even has the hill she haunts named after her. Catherine is said to have lost her head in a car accident and now tries to hitch a ride by standing in the road "seductively". She even talks to the drivers who dare to stop, saying: "I want to go to Bar Harbor." Of course, she disappears from the car when they reach the bottom of the hill. (SOURCE - WWW.WABI.TV 1ST FEB).

HAUNTED HOTEL: Hotel Niagara in East Java, Indonesia, is usually avoided by locals because of the frightening apparitions that haunt it. The local legend is that a Dutch woman committed suicide by throwing herself off one of the balconies, while others say she had been brutally raped and murdered by Japanese soldiers during World War 2. The fifth floor "is so riddled with malevolent ghosts" that it was closed to the public. One room in the hotel is said to fill with blood at night and it is claimed that guests may not wake up in the place where they went to sleep. But staff say they have seen nothing at the hotel. Ratti, who works in reception, said: "I've been here for seven years. I stay in the hotel 24 hours a day and I've never seen anything strange, and neither have any guests I know of." (SOURCE - THE JAKARTA GLOBE 12TH JANUARY).

RACTON FOLLY: Plans are in hand to turn this 238-year old ruin into a family home, along with its ghosts, but the present owner isn't worried as he does not believe in them. Some people describe the folly as one of the 'most frightening places in West Sussex'. Others believe the suicides, illegal raves and devil worshippers who used the Folly in the past are the ones responsible for its ghostly legends. Paranormal activity reported include the spirit of a lady in white, unseen forces throwing bricks from the top of the tower, a ghostly face looking out from one of the windows, and several accounts of people being grabbed and pushed. Oh, and not forgetting the ghostly tractor! (SOURCE - WWW.PORTSMOUTH.CO.UK 5TH FEBRUARY).

I-POD GHOSTS: Demolition worker John Fores captured what he believed was the ghost of a boy on camera while knocking down the Anlaby

Out of the earth
This photograph was taken by Matt Adams in an English cemetery in 1994, and it shows what looks like a misty face rising from an open grave.
[© MATT ADAMS/FORTEAN PICTURE LIBRARY]

Ghostly pursuers

'Ghosts' sometimes take the form of faces and nothing more. The SS Watertown was at sea in December 1924 when two of the crew, James Courtney and Michael Meehan, were suffocated by gas fumes and buried at sea off the coast of Mexico. In the days following, the crew claimed that they could see the faces of the two men in the waves, for around 10 seconds each time, before fading away.

The captain obtained a camera on arrival in New Orleans, and on the return journey he was able to photograph the faces, although nothing showed up on five of the six photographs he took. Whether this photograph really does show the ghostly faces of the two unfortunate men, or whether it is an optical illusion caused by the movement of the waves, is quite impossible to determine.

Primary School in Anlaby, near Hull. He discovered the picture later when viewing the images on his computer and he swears there was no boy present when the photograph was taken. At first glance the photograph looked to most people to have been faked and after a little internet research I found the site 'Ghost Capture,' complete with the exact same image for download. The site allows people to make their own ghostly images then download them onto their phones. Mr Fores believes fellow workers played a trick on him, sending the image to his phone via a Bluetooth application. View the photo at paranormalmagazine.co.uk/news. (SOURCE - HULL DAILY MAIL & MARK FRASER 20TH FEBRUARY).

GWRYCH CASTLE: Kevin Horkin was taking pictures at this castle in North Wales and believes he captured the 'picture of a spirit'. As usual it was not until he downloaded the pictures on his computer that he discovered the picture. Amazingly the room that the "young woman" is standing in has no floor. According to the North Wales Paranormal Group there have been "many sightings recorded at the castle." View the photo at paranormalmagazine.co.uk/news. (SOURCE - NEWSUBMIT.NET FEBRUARY).

IT'S NOT MAGGIE: The Burnett Arms Hotel in Kemnay, Aberdeenshire, described as "one of Scotland's most haunted pubs," is for sale. Former owner Maggie Duffton, who died in 1934, is said to haunt the premises, indeed her coffin is rumoured to lie in the walls of the hotel. Recently house keeper Fiona Reid, spotted a dark apparition upstairs standing in a corner. She said: "Something drew me to walk towards it then it disappeared right in front of my eyes. I can't explain it." She turned around to leave and found a 30 year old newspaper on the floor behind her, in which was a picture of her grandfather. She believes it was his apparition she saw. Mrs Reid is adamant that the newspaper was not there when she first came into the room. (SOURCE - SCOTTISH TELEVISION 25TH FEBRUARY).

Sightings

MISTY SCREEN: Two women working in the 'Simply Food & Drinks' in Durranhill Road, Botcherby, Carlyle, were stunned to see a misty figure on their CCTV which is aimed on the outside of the shop. One worker complained of suddenly becoming cold before seeing the mist, which appeared to be coming from across the road. Word soon got out and people stood in the shop looking at it; it could not be seen from outside. Assistant Miss Nolan said: "I have never believed in things like ghosts until that night but unless somebody can explain to me what it was, I believe now. I wish to God I hadn't seen it." View the footage via paranormalmagazine.co.uk/news (SOURCE - NEWS & STAR 28TH FEBRUARY).

TINY BODIES: The former brothel, Tibbals Building on Water Street, Port Angeles, USA, is said to "echo with the cries of prostitutes and their dead babies who were soon "dispatched." The premises is most famous for its 'lady in blue'. Robin Alexis of Mystic Radio and a team of investigators from Paranormal Investigations of Historic America of Monroe recently conducted an investigation on the premises. During the vigil Alexis saw the figure of a lady in Victorian dress standing by a window, and a "priest in black robes wearing a large cross," and also a Native American woman who said her name was Grouse Woman. (SOURCE - WWW.PENINSULADAILYNEWS.COM 1ST FEBRUARY).

STATION 3: Firefighters in Chicago's Station 3, situated in the Green Garden Township, are convinced their fire station is haunted. Lt. Todd Hamm said: "I used to see things going in and out of the ambulance – shadowy things. One was a dark-clothed, blackish figure that walked right in front of me." Among the ghosts are an "angry cowboy", a figure in blue and apparitions somewhat akin to the 'shadow people.' Firefighter Tom Warszalek said: "They're freaking me out.' (SOURCE - SUBURBAN CHICAGO NEWS 4TH FEBRUARY).

THE KING'S TAVERN: Witnesses describe "chills to the bone," the ghost of a baby girl which has allegedly been caught on camera, the sounds of a baby crying, as well as a host of other paranormal phenomena in this building built in 1729 and located in

Floating face
This photograph was taken in Iona church in May 1928 by Donald G. Mackenzie, a chemist from Glasgow, who commented later that 'I am candidly a disbeliever in Ghosts...' However, his photograph shows clearly what appears to be a disembodied face in front of the stone wall in the centre of the photograph.

Old Nanna

In 1991, when he was two years old, Greg Sheldon Maxwell started saying 'Old Nanna's here!', while pointing up into the air. He was referring to his late great-grandmother, who used to say to her daughter that she wanted her to see her when she was dead. When this photograph was taken, nobody saw anything unusual, but Greg certainly seems to be looking at something. Was he seeing Old Nanna in what appears to us to be a column of mist?

Two years later, when Greg and his mother were in England for a few months (the family normally lived in Abu Dhabi), and visiting his grandmother, he was asked if he still saw Old Nanna. He said, 'No, but I can show you what she looks like', and took his mother and grandmother into the hall where he pointed to a photograph on the wall and said, 'That's how she looked when I saw her.' He had never mentioned the photograph before and presumably hadn't been told who it was.

Natchez, Mississippi. Three skeletons, two male and one female, were found bricked up during renovations. The female is thought to be Madeline, a mistress of a former owner; it is her spirit who is believed to be the main cause of the haunting. There is a haunted mirror, doors open and close of their own accord, objects are thrown off shelves, to name but a few of the recent manifestations. (SOURCE - WWW.TIME.COM 5TH FEBRUARY).

FORT HAYES: The now abandoned fort in downtown Columbus, Ohio, is haunted by former recruits, according to present day custodians. "An angry ghost" throws clothes around, marching soldiers, ghastly screams have been heard, footsteps, bangs, doors opening and closing of their own accord and whispering are a few of the incidents that have been reported. The most common feeling is that of being followed. (SOURCE - WWW.DISPATCH.COM 14TH FEBRUARY).

WHISPERS: Situated on Warren Street in Mitchell, Indiana, this B&B has five graves in the back gardens and is said to harbour a host of ghosts, according to one recent investigation by the Louisville Ghost Hunters Society. Disembodied voices which sound like two men talking have been recorded and noises such as "thuds and tinkering sounds" were also heard. Present owner Jarrett Marshal has experienced many odd occurrences on the premises, but believes that among the several ghosts the most active is that of a little girl called Rachael. (www.michigansotherside.com 19th February).

CURSED CAMPUS: Frightened students at the Northern Illinois University, believe that their building and the grounds are either cursed, or haunted. They have reported "eerie sounds in the campus hallway, and shooting sounds in the night." Rumours are that it is the ghost of the gunman who shot dead five people and wounded 19 before shooting himself. One student said: "This was bound to happen. The shooting may be because the ghost of the 2008 killer wants the whole incident repeated again. It's really creepy." (merinews.com 19th February).

Experiences

Readers' letters taken from the pages of *Paranormal Magazine*

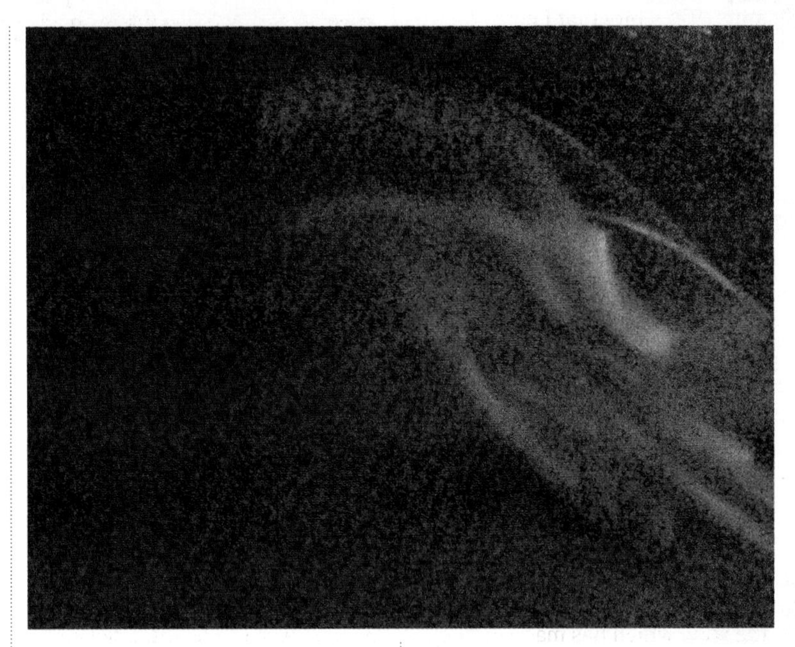

Glastonbury Ghouly

I have just finished reading the 'Unidentified Floating Organisms' article in Issue 33 of *Paranormal Magazine*. I was very interested indeed in the words that appeared in the write-up regarding the 1913 short story by Arthur Conan Doyle entitled 'The Horror of the Heights', the reason being that on the 6 March 2007 at 22.56 I took this photograph with my Finepix 4.1 mega Pixel camera which I had pointed up into the sky not far from Glastonbury Town Hall, Somerset.

I had previously taken some other shots and on these the flash went off – but for this one, my 'Glastonbury Ghouly' as I call the picture, the flash did not.

The picture has been shown to many people, none of whom seem to have any real suggestions as to what it was. My thoughts are that although the picture is not very clear, it appears to me to look like a very large jellyfish with tentacles hanging downward – just as described in the article. It also looks as though it has teeth.

Joan Saunders, Somerset

The Sky Slug

Your article by Dr Shuker last issue about 'Unidentified Floating Organisms' reminded me of a strange experience I had in my teens. I am at a loss to explain it.

I was on top of a double-decker which at the time was travelling along Hall Road, Hull. It was sometime during the late 70's, on a bright summer evening, but the exact date now escapes me. I saw a funny bright 'egg' in the sky, over the fields out towards the Dunswell area; or rather it was pear shaped. I cannot judge the size or the speed, but it seemed to be very large as it ambled across the sky. The colour was a blend of pale red and orange.

The strangest thing of all is that it would continually change its shape. It was like a large floating light bulb: it certainly was not a cloud, nor did it seem to be a solid structure. It put me in mind more of some gigantic life form, like a kind of giant slug that lived in the sky, rather than a more 'conventional' type of UFO.

Funnily enough, after watching it for a few minutes I lost interest and turned my mind to other matters. The next day the *Hull Daily Mail* ran an article on the 'object'. A number of people had seen it around the same time; some rang the police while others informed the local radio and papers. One particular chap

"The strangest thing of all is that it would continually change its shape. It was like a large floating light bulb: it certainly was not a cloud..."

saw it at close quarters. He lived somewhere on the outskirts of Hull and had been working in the garage when he turned round to be confronted by this thing in the sky, which I have dubbed the 'Sky Slug'. It is a pity that I never kept the newspaper clippings.

Several years later I happened to be talking to a colleague at work when we began chatting about UFO's, and it turned out he also saw this object and happened to be on the top deck of a bus on Noddle Hill Way at the time. He also describes it as being an orangey-red colour and with the same ability to change shape. But he adds that all at once it accelerated to an incredible speed and disappeared from his view in seconds.

Mark Fraser, Kilmarnock

Our invisible lodger

Since we first moved in our home, I have felt a presence there. I have felt a gentle hand placed on my back as though to move me out of the way, which has made me step to one side to let them past. I had been shocked at this at first, as I would turn thinking it was my hubby to find nothing there. I also see a shape on the stairs and look – to see nothing.

My husband and I had an argument, something really silly, and he couldn't sleep. He went downstairs and was sitting at the table having a cup of tea when he felt a swipe at his face, a kind of wafting wind past it, as though something went quickly past his face. He thought he had imagined it but it happened again a minute or so later.

On another occasion we were both lying in bed just nodding off when he jumped up in alarm, and said a hand had moved over his tummy and then come to rest on him. I was half asleep and told him he was dreaming but as we settled back down, I felt someone sit on the end of my side of the bed – I even moved my feet away so they could sit down. Realising what I was doing, I quickly sat up – to see nobody there once again. I don't know if it's related but a few nights before the bed incident, I apparently had a fight with 'nobody' while in my sleep and had to be restrained by my husband. I don't recall any of it.

Kim, Whitby

"I felt someone sit on the end of my side of the bed – I even moved my feet away so they could sit down. Realising what I was doing, I quickly sat up – to see nobody there once again."

Ghost light encounters

I have been a paranormal researcher and field investigator (primarily of UFOs and Bigfoot) in Northern California since 1968. Back in the early 1990s, when I was considerably more public and active (I have since trimmed back on my activities), I had some personal experiences of ghost lights/orbs that might add to your knowledge base.

I have had several occasions when these little critters have been observed sometimes very close with the naked eye. Once, a group of six was observing the night lights and during the night we observed small faint red lights flickering around on the hillside below us. These moved quite rapidly and only occasionally 'flared' to the point that they were visible. They appeared to be interested in us and were moving quite rapidly up the side of the hill to our position on a road.

Several of us had them come up around the ground level quite near and once I turned just in time to see one 'bloom' (becoming rapidly brighter and becoming white like a quick but faint flash bulb). This phenomenon was repeated on several subsequent night watches, and they always appeared the same. We found that one thing affected our ability to observe them and that was the degree of moonlight. If it was too light, we could not see them. This is why we surmised that they were in the infared range. Subsequent events would bear this out.

On several occasions we had reports of locals seeing translucent orbs. Once I spoke to a man and his teenage son who had seen 1-meter in diameter translucent orbs 'floating' along a riverbed. Once, while on a night stand just behind Beale Air Force Base (the home of the Blackbird here in Northern California), my close associate and I had two translucent orbs 'float up' to within about 20 feet from us. These were very similar to the ones observed by researchers in the Pine Bush area of New York state, including the late Ellen Crystall (who successfully photographed them). It should be noted that recent research has found a very strong magnetic area very close by. I feel that this is a clue.

It should be noted that none of these occurrences involved the use of cameras, either old style or digital. In the early 1990s I

did come across an interesting video that was made right after one of the early Rachael Nevada conferences. It did involve both digital and night vision equipment, but the results indicate that the observed orbs were not reflections or residual effects from the camera or the night vision gear.

These are the circumstances: The people who were present had set up a night watch stand as is normal at the mailbox at the entrance to the Groom Road. It was about 11 in the evening. The camera was set up on a tripod and aimed at the Jumbled Hills beyond which is the Groom Base. It was an early model VHS camcorder which had attached to the front of it a first generation night vision scope (the kind which shows a circular opening and the normal green image). The time and date counter was running in real time and the image was dead steady. You could occasionally hear the people watching in the back of this set-up.

In my observation, the events that were about to unfold were not seen by the people in their cars and standing behind the camera. At about 12:11, from the lower right zoomed what appeared to be a fuzzy plasma ball about .25 meters in diameter. It zoomed between the sagebrush bushes at about .5 meters off the ground, weaving around the individual bushes. This critter was moving very fast. I estimate the speed at about 50 meters per second. This object moved out into the field in front of the camera, about 100 meters away and was joined by another one which came from the left. They rapidly moved back and forth for about 10 seconds and then one came right up in front of the camera and stopped. It then split into two parts momentarily then recombined and then zoomed off to the left. The length of the event was less then about 2 minutes, and there was absolutely no reaction from the people behind the camera. The event was observed after the video was analyzed later. It was also enhanced to get a closer view of the 'split'.

It is my opinion these are naturally occurring effects. They exhibit intelligence, based on their actions. They also appear to be occurring very close to where UFO craft have been observed. Large magnetic fields are also observed in relation to their appearance, being very close by. Some of these are very strong magnetic fields, some of which have attracted official attention.

Steven Jones, Sacramento, California

'Evil' church cast its eerie spell

I was interested to read Damien O'Dell's article 'Unquiet Beds' and especially his comment that Clophill church is 'the most evil place in the county', because I experienced the full force of its malevolence way back in 1972.

Intrigued by its reputation for black magic, my husband and co-author Colin and I decided to take a look for ourselves, and see if there was anything worth photographing. I admit it was a gloomy January day, and the church's reputation was well known to me, so I was probably already in a heightened state of tension as we stepped through the lych gate. But I was not prepared for the feelings that overwhelmed me. Over the last 40 years I have visited more ruined churches and graveyards than most people, but I can safely say that this was the spookiest place I have ever been to.

SPOOKIEST PLACE: Janet Bord's picture of Clophill church, showing the white patches which only showed up on that one negative. © Fortean Picture Library

As I walked round as fast as I could, looking for good camera angles, I constantly had the feeling I should look over my shoulder, and there was a powerful sense of oppression overwhelming me. I felt very panicky and only managed to grab one quick shot of the church before I had to retreat. Going through the lychgate, I

"The church's reputation was well known to me, so I was probably already in a heightened state of tension as we stepped through the lych gate. But I was not prepared for the feelings that overwhelmed me."

turned and quickly took a second photograph. It was a great relief to jump in the car and drive away from that evil place.

Needless to say, I have never been back. I recall the visit clearly, 37 years later, and Colin can recall it, too, though he did not experience the evil sensation as strongly as I did. A final puzzle arose when he developed the black and white film and found that the negative taken through the lychgate was streaked with brown stains which cause white patches when the negative is printed. It may simply be something that happened in the process of development, but none of the other negatives on the film was affected in any way, and Colin, who is an expert photographer with more than 60 years' experience, still can't explain it.

Janet Bord, Denbighshire

The thing in the woods

Back in the early 1990s I was a student at Saint David's University College, Lampeter (now University of Wales, Lampeter) in mid Wales. I often used to go for very late night walks (as you do when you're a student) up past the Falcondale Hotel along an access road that ran past Falcondale Farm and through a patch of woodland to reach a crossroads then onto the Falcondale Lake, a mile or two from the town. I often heard crunching sounds in the woodland, as if someone or something very large was walking along slowly and carefully, breaking twigs as it went.

This stretch of woodland was very dense, many of the trees growing closely together and lining the side of the road to the point that the trees sometimes formed a dense canopy overhead blocking out the moonlight. At times it was difficult to see my hand in front of my face and I often used a cigarette lighter or match to light the way. It would have been nigh on impossible for a person to have picked his way through the woods without the aid of a torch and certainly not to have walked in a straight line. The sounds were usually to my left, sometimes on my right but only for a certain distance.

"It seemed that the steps matched my own – it was a slow, deliberate, heavy tread – and I often nervously stopped to listen. Once or twice I heard a footfall after I had stopped."

It seemed that the steps matched my own – it was a slow, deliberate, heavy tread – and I often nervously stopped to listen. Once or twice I heard a footfall after I had stopped. There was no chance that this was an echo, or that it was my over-active imagination. I am quite level-headed by nature and would not jump to conclusions that easily, so I found it exceedingly odd. I never thought that a person was moving about and I never felt fear, just a general feeling of unease. It felt like I was being 'stalked'. I often used to call out to it: 'Hello ghoul, hello goblin. How are you doing?'

It was an odd patch of woodland, alas felled long ago. I remember the burning tree stumps and the depressing sight of the cleared land. A lot of people were angered by this. It used to be a lovely walk in the summer. I knew pagans who thought that this patch of woodland was spiritually significant and I occasionally saw pagan types there or thereabouts.

It is a quite curious spot – in order to enter the wood you have to cross a small bridge over running stream water and to leave the wood you have to cross another small bridge over another stream. The road was also quite low down, situated between two hills and woods – Ty Hên Wood and Hen-feddau Wood. I know there is a long standing historical connection between bridges, water and the supernatural (think of Celtic mythology, black dogs, vampires, etc) so perhaps this is significant? Perhaps natural 'earth energies' are concentrated between these two points, forming a gateway between this world and another? The hills and woods on either side may magnify this. I certainly think it is a very ancient 

place with an interesting past.

Interestingly, there are parallels with US and AUS encounters with bigfoot. Hearing footfalls, the feeling of being watching or stalked and in the AUS experience between water and the Yowie – Yowie's are often associated with streams, creeks and rivers – is suggestive. Healy and Cropper's book on the Yowie provides a number of interesting eye-witness reports. I'm not suggesting for one moment that a real life 'hairy man' exists in mid Wales, but there's a possibility that it may be something more supernatural or paranormal in origin. Nick Redfern's book *Man Monkey* is an interesting study of this kind of phenomenon. As I say, all I heard were heavy footfalls – I never saw eyes shine or a fleeting figure disappearing in the woods. But I found it very odd all the same.

Mr S. Buckinghamshire
(full name and address supplied)

EDITOR'S NOTE: It is interesting to note that 'Hen-feddau' is Welsh for 'old burials', which implies that prehistoric burial mounds might once have been visible in the area. The location of this experience can be viewed on online maps at grid reference SA48 7ED.

Great balls of fire

I have just been reading the UFO sightings in the back of this month's mag and there are 2 concerning balls of fire. I too have seen these recently.

The first time was at 6pm on Saturday 14th February, 2009. I live in a town called Fareham on the south coast of England. It was in the west about the height of a plane that has either taken off or is going in to land at Southampton airport. It looked like a ball of flames.

I commented on it to my mum who was with me and she saw it too and at the time we both thought a plane tragedy had happened and we were witnessing a plane on fire but it didn't move. It never dropped, it never traveled and stayed in the same spot for a good five minutes before it just vanished. There was no cloud in the sky and as soon as I got home I checked the news to see if there had been a plane accident but there was nothing reported.

The second time was Tuesday 24th February, 2009, at 8.10pm. I saw exactly the same thing in a similar part of the sky to before, but this time it was slowly moving from west to east. I was alone this time round but it was exactly the same thing I had seen before. Had I not seen it with my own eyes I wouldn't have believed it and would never have said anything or told anyone if I had not read the two reports in your mag.

Sarah, via email

Robots or angels?

After reading your editorial in Issue 33 on the strange activities of floating down the stairs, I can confirm that I also had this weird and wonderful experience in 1963-64. I was only 4 or 5 years old and it was a really harsh winter. I can remember the event so clearly, like a film running in your head.

I can remember in vivid colour floating down the stairs in our council house on the Norton Estate in Stourbridge, West Midlands. As I floated down the stairs, I can remember the front door of the house opening and I could see the front garden covered in glittering and sparkling pale blue snow just like it looks when moonlight shines on it. The oddest thing was that at the bottom of the stairs were two or three little robotic looking humanoid forms and their arms tried to either catch me or maybe they were helping me to levitate above their heads.

I can't remember anything else after that until I woke up in the early hours of the morning on a park bench at least a mile away from home. The only thing that woke me was the milk bottles rattling in a passing milk float. I was freezing cold and frightened and ran all the way home. So what does this mean and how can so many people seem to have the same thing happen to them?

There could be many reasons for this strange phenomenon. I am a level-headed man of 50 years this year and I still wonder to this day why this happened and what it means. Perhaps it was a dream and I sleepwalked down to the park in the worst weather we have ever had but if this is the case, why did I not die of hypothermia and also why did I see robotic humanoids when I had never seen anything like this in any sort of film?

Another thought is one of my own that may be controversial. What if – and this is if you believe in God

"The oddest thing was that at the bottom of the stairs were two or three little robotic looking humanoid forms and their arms tried to either catch me or maybe they were helping me to levitate above their heads."

"Twenty to thirty people came outside to have a look at the UFO, which looked like a giant railway carriage and was just missing the chimney pots."

and angels – we have a connection to those angels? What if we are the offspring genetically to what we call angels, otherwise why would human children have dreams of flying? Were we abducted by an outside influence?

I had epilepsy from the age of 13 till I was 22 years old. Now I have severe migraines which doctors can't find out anything to help. It would be interesting to find out how many children had this experience, what age they were and in what timeline in our history. There has to be a pattern to what happened to children like Mark Salmon and myself. Could there be a clue to the areas, ages and dates that they have occurred in? This is a big mystery that needs to be researched. Who knows where it will end?

C. Armfield, via email

The roads round Borley

Following on from Janet Bord's letter about Clophill church, I recall visiting Borley church in about the year 1966. Supposedly there are 'fireflies' on the pews and a banging door which resembles no other door in the building. Not much happened when I was there and I saw nothing unusual. But a friend who used to cycle past there everyday said there was usually a mist hanging around the area of the church and it would suddenly appear behind him even though he hadn't passed through it. Sadly he died in the 70s.

Another friend was on his motor scooter near the church when he noticed a man on his left side going at 45 mph beside him. As he called to his girlfriend on the pillion, the man just pulled in front and disappeared into the hedge on the right. They both saw this. They said that the man wasn't running or anything, he was just 'there'. There are other tales/rumours of a coach with a headless driver and even headless horses galloping around the area. Perhaps it's time I made another visit.

Another incident: A couple were crossing the railway line in their car one late evening at Melbourn, Cambridgeshire, when they saw a UFO. Somewhat shaken they stopped at the Old English Gentleman pub to get some company and a stiff drink. Twenty to thirty people came outside to have a look at the UFO, which looked like a giant railway carriage and was just missing the chimney pots.

They all took cover inside and the landlord called the police. The local bobby rode his bike to Barrington Hill where he kept look-out for the rest of the night, but saw nothing. I think they were told that it was reflection from the clouds of the railway train, even though the nearest railway was a couple of miles away. This was in the 1970s.

Terry Dye, via email

Pandemonium in the lavatory

At the age of 19 I was living in an old house in Rock Park, Runcorn, in what was then north Cheshire and now part of the borough of Halton. Rock Park was a large gated park with huge Victorian houses around the perimeter. Once they had been ☛

EMPTY ROOM: Sandra Johnson took this photograph of this old, floor-boarded room similar to the one in the 18th century building in which she had her terrifying experience © Sandra Johnson

very desirable places to live, and were still quite beautiful when I lived there, but most of them had been turned into flats. The one I lived in was right on the banks of the River Mersey. I occupied a very small flat in one of the outbuildings; it had a slate floor and had probably been a stable block.

Every morning I walked along the cobbled lane of Rock Park, under ancient branches of Scots pine and past regal houses and a nunnery, down to Rock Ferry Railway Station where I caught the train to James Street along with other commuters to Liverpool.

It was the Swinging Sixties and I loved buying clothes and wore a wild array of coloured dresses and mini skirts, mostly in clashing colours like orange and pink and purple, usually worn with boots up to the knees or chunky high shoes. To fund my wardrobe I worked in the city. Jobs were easy to find then: you could give up one job on a Friday and find another by the following Monday.

I went to work for a firm of Chartered Accountants called Charles E. Dolby with offices in an old chambers in Dale Street. This was a decrepit building which would have been perfect for a film set of a Dickens drama. I guess nothing had changed since the 18th century. I seem to remember the date above the door was 1779.

A few other businesses occupied this building. I worked on the ground floor in a tiny office with two other girls. About six article clerks had the next office; they were paid buttons because they were training to be accountants, but actually did most of the work.

Presumably, when this building was first built it must have had some sort of water closet, but not a type we would recognise. There mustn't have been a room especially for that purpose because the office toilets were located on the top floor up four flights of stairs and were inside a very large room. This was definitely not originally designed for toilet facilities – such a waste of space, especially as most of the offices were pokey little rooms. This huge room at the top of the building had about eight toilets in cubicles in a line opposite the only door. They were on a higher level and you had to climb up a step. The whole area was floored with old wooden boards, not polished but in a dry, dusty, untreated condition.

All the offices had their own key to this room and the door was a very heavy old-fashioned one of solid oak, with a new Yale lock fitted so that when you closed it, it locked behind you. Outside, the steps leading up to this door were made of concrete, obviously a later addition to this building, with no wood in sight. I suspect there were original back stairs somewhere.

Now, I've been in many haunted places, including pubs and stately homes, and I have never felt a thing. Not the slightest vibe. I would stay the night in them, no problem. I even went on a ghost walk once when one of the group was totally spooked because she felt a little invisible hand hold her hand. The rest of the group were frightened. I didn't feel a thing. So it is really amazing that whenever I entered this room at the top of the offices, I could feel an atmosphere immediately – so much so that I would only use those toilets if I was absolutely desperate.

The minute I entered there was a total quietness, it was freezing and I could feel I was being watched. It was terrifying. I never mentioned this to anyone. I don't know why, perhaps because I thought they would think me odd. No-one else seemed to be bothered about it and all the staff used the toilets whenever they needed to with no comment about them.

One morning I decided to get in early because I had stacks of work to do: all the end of year accounts had to be typed. I wanted to get a head start, so I caught an earlier train from Rock Ferry to James Street Station. I picked up the mail on the way into the building but then, instead of opening up our office, I found I needed the loo, so without thinking I got the key off the hook in the outer office and ran up all the flights of stairs, opened the big old door and dropped the mail onto a sink before going into the loo.

As soon as I locked the door, the whole room erupted into bedlam. The room outside my cubicle was filled with the sound of wooden clogs running and jumping on the bare boarded floor. Outside the room, the floor and stairs were concrete, so I knew this was all happening inside on the wooden floorboards. Voices raised and high

"Voices raised and high pitched were making sounds so terrible I felt that if I opened the door I would be faced with mad lunatics all in an uncontrollable frenzy."

"The minute I entered there was a total quietness, it was freezing and I could feel I was being watched. It was terrifying. I never mentioned this to anyone. I don't know why, perhaps because I thought they would think me odd."

pitched were making sounds so terrible I felt that if I opened the door I would be faced with mad lunatics all in an uncontrollable frenzy.

This went on for ages – and I really mean ages. I stood behind that door unable to move for 15 to 20 minutes, and all the while pandemonium was on the other side of a thin wooden door with gaps above and below. I went into a state of total shock, so petrified that I couldn't move a muscle. Even writing this now my heart is racing – I have never known fear like it.

Somehow I managed to get my brain to work. I realised I had to get out of there, I had to make a run for it, through a crowd of crazed ghosts. How do you get up the courage to do that? I was all too aware that whatever was making all that noise was not of this earth. They were spirits of some sort and definitely not friendly. After a few false starts and shaking with fear, I opened the door.

Silence hit me, total and absolute silence. I was faced with an empty room, freezing cold, and almost humming with silence. It was as if someone had just flicked a switch and turned off a blaring radio. I ran for the door, forgetting the post and in a fumbling panic got out of there.

I was shaking, almost hysterical when I got back to my office. So much time had passed that everyone were at their desks working.

I never went into that room again, nothing would induce me to enter it. If ever I needed the loo, I would leave the office and use the facilities of Exchange Station. Soon afterwards I left that company and went to live in Portugal.

Years later I found myself in Liverpool and discovered that the old chambers had gone – been pulled down to make way for a new building. I wonder if the ghosts went with it, or have they somehow found their way into the new building?

Sandra Johnson, Mouldsworth, Cheshire

Gliding down stairs

In common with other readers, I too have a vivid memory of floating down the stairs as a child. I must have been 6-8 years old. I remember standing at the top of the stairs before gently gliding down.

C Armfield's point of view that it may be due to sleepwalking is interesting, as I do sleepwalk, but this was in daylight. I remember being slightly bemused afterwards, but just carried on with what I was doing. I didn't see anything unusual, although, many years later, I and a sibling heard 'ghostly' footsteps on the stairs.

I wonder whether I was daydreaming or had 'switched off' and imagined it. About ten years ago I crossed a very busy main road with no recollection of doing so. One minute I was on one side, the next I was on the other. I even checked to see whether I'd been knocked down by looking for bruises or cuts but found none. I do have a tendency to 'switch off' if I am bored, and have many a time spent a bus journey in this state only to have no recollection of passing through areas even though I've been looking through the window the entire time.

My episode of floating down the stairs would have occurred in about 1980-82 and in North Wales. I am not epileptic and can't explain the incident in any other way than overactive imagination – that's if I have to explain it. I'd like to think it happened but have no witnesses. I don't remember it was unusual at all, just 'funny'. It certainly didn't warrant telling anyone.

Wouldn't it be fabulous if we all had this ability? It'd certainly make living in a flat easier. Out of interest, does anyone remember floating upstairs?

(Name and address supplied), Manchester

The column of smoke

I had a very weird experience that only happened once shortly after I moved into the house I've been living in now for the past eight years or so.

I'd just put my little one to bed – she'd have been only about a year old then – and was getting my shoes, which were on the floor. My dog Bobby kept snarling and making a fuss for some reason I couldn't understand. He kept pushing himself between my legs and being generally irritating, so I picked him up and took him downstairs. I realise now he was aware of something strange going on.

Soon afterwards I was in the 

kitchen doing the washing up when I suddenly felt this cold breeze on the back of my neck. It was just as if someone had walked behind me with an electric fan blowing. I went into the living room expecting to find a window had blown open or something but didn't find anything, so I went back into the kitchen. And there I saw this weird thing.

"It was tall, about as tall as me, and really thin, no more than three inches wide. It was a rectangle of fog or smoke, and I mean a perfect rectangle like it was held in a glass box."

It was tall, about as tall as me, and really thin, no more than three inches wide. It was a rectangle of fog or smoke, and I mean a perfect rectangle like it was held in a glass box. It was floating about 2ft off the ground. I stood there, stock still, and watched it as it went through the back door and out into the back garden. It went to the back of the garden and disappeared. It was daylight, so I could see it clearly.

Then I sort of came to myself and realised my baby was screaming her head off upstairs. I rushed to her but she was hysterical, it took me ages to get her to sleep, and even then she was making these kind of scared sobbing noises while she slept. I'm sure she saw something I couldn't, being a grown-up, and maybe the dog did, too. If someone had told me that morning that I was going to see that thing, I'd have picked up the baby and the dog and everything and got out of there, but at the time I wasn't scared. Only afterwards – I didn't get to sleep till 4am!

There was one other weird thing. Just after I saw the fog and for several hours afterwards, the house was all echoey – the way an empty house sounds when it doesn't have any furniture in it. I could hear it when I spoke or when the baby was crying. It was very strange. Anyway, I've never seen it again and nothing weird has happened here since.

Talking to my mum about ghost stories, it turns out my great-grandfather saw one of those big, black dog things. He was rabbiting in the field near Milford Street one night when him and his mates saw this huge black dog. Its eyes were bulging out of its head, it was drooling and snarling and it had great big teeth. It jumped on them, and they all dropped to the ground. It jumped right over them – and disappeared!

My mum's best friend, Collette, saw it as well some years later. It walked along beside her but when she reached out to pat it, it vanished. Apparently, a big black carriage has been seen rattling down that street, too.

Leanne Mitchell, Mold, Flintshire

Strolling round the church

Myself and three friends from school (about 30 years ago now) decided to take a week's camping one summer holiday in the village of Pluckley in Kent. Having already heard of its supposed ghostly reputation as Britain's most haunted village, we decided to do a bit of ghost hunting ourselves.

After a couple of nights and days in the 'screaming woods' and the site of the old brickworks (well-known Pluckley haunts) with nothing at all, it was decided we would investigate the church the next day. We got to the church at about 12.30pm on a beautiful summer's day. After having a good look around the church to make sure we were the only people about, we left a tape recorder about 10 feet away from the front door (a typically thick church door) on the last pew and set it to record. We then waited outside the church door, leaving it open about a foot.

After about 10 minutes the great door slammed closed – and without wind this took some doing. Two minutes later the automated church clock chimed the hour at one o'clock, and five minutes later we re-entered the building, immediately turning off the tape recorder.

Upon leaving the church, we listened to our tape and what we heard amazed us all. Firstly we heard ourselves leave the church, then after five minutes we heard heavy footsteps (possibly wearing clogs) walking down a stone-clad aisle, although the aisle was carpeted. They reached our recorder, which sent loud static for a couple of seconds, and then the door slammed shut. The steps then moved away and we heard the belfry door open and then the bell rang. The belfry door then closed and the heavy footsteps continued back up the now carpeted but once stone aisle, this time not bothering our recorder. The next sound was us entering the church and switching it off.

This phenomenon was recorded three more times on the hour.

OUT OF TIME: Youthful ghost hunters recorded the sounds of ghostly footsteps in Pluckley Church, Kent, three times, bang on the hour. © Heart of Kent

to the ravages of time, I often wonder, was it the old parson or church warden, not realising the bells are now automated and continuing on his ghostly duty?

Mick Crispin, via email

Only half a man

My dad used to work for Ford's motor company in Dagenham, manufacturing moulds for engine parts, and building various bits and pieces for the casting processes in the foundry. He often worked a night-shift, and so as I would be getting up for school, he was already having his breakfast, having just arrived home.

One Tuesday morning – about 8 o'clock – I came down the stairs half-asleep, but could see that my dad was visibly agitated. He told me and my mum that while he and his workmates were cleaning up in preparation for the 3am lunch break, they had heard terrible screams coming from the canteen, which was just around the corner. Running around to see what was wrong, they were shocked to find one of the canteen women unconscious on the floor, and the other one backed into a corner screaming her head off, her hands held in front of her, as if being attacked by something invisible.

One of the men ran off to get the doctor, while my dad and another chap tried to revive the unconscious woman who, according to my dad, was 'out like a light'. When the doctor arrived, the woman had to be taken out on a stretcher, while the other lady, who was still screaming uncontrollably, had to be sedated.

The doctor managed to calm her down, and when she had regained her composure somewhat, she said that while she and the other lady had been getting the meals ready for the 3 o'clock lunch hour, a man had walked into the canteen. Initially, they had only seen him in their peripheral vision, but as they turned to speak to him, they realised, to their horror, that he was invisible from the waist down, as though he had been chopped in half. There was no sign of blood or torn clothing, it was just as if he only existed above the waistline.

He seemed to float towards them, and as he did so, one of the women – understandably perhaps – fainted dead away, and the other became hysterical. The woman who had passed out did not regain full consciousness for about 15 minutes, but when she recovered, she reported exactly the same details of the legless ghost.

Of course, my dad saw none of this, but he felt something in the atmosphere, something cold and sinister. The other blokes said that they felt the same thing, and my dad was completely sure in his mind that the ladies had really seen something terrifying.

This would have happened in the mid-1970's, and I can remember the details as clearly today as when my dad first told them to me. As far as my dad knew, there was no record of anyone being killed in that horrible way, although there were plenty of other terrible accidents that had happened through the years.

When I first heard this story, the incident was only about five hours old, and it scared the absolute crap out of me, mainly because my dad, who was fairly unflappable, was obviously affected by the experience. My dad passed away a few years ago, and so I have no real proof of what happened. I don't know anyone else involved in the incident, but I have a clear memory – as does my mum – of the story my dad told, and I have no doubt whatsoever that it actually happened.

Alan Friswell, Dagenham

"About three nights into the stay I became restless during my sleep. When I woke and raised my head I could clearly see the silhouette of a lady standing at the window in our room looking out into the garden."

Experiences are continued on page 66

In the last three decades of the nineteenth century and the early years of the twentieth, so-called 'spirit photography' was all the rage. A living sitter would go to the studio of a medium with a gift for spirit photography and sit for a photograph; if he/she was lucky, there would also be another figure on the print, allegedly someone who was dead, possibly a family member. It was sometimes said that the image of the dead person did not resemble any known photograph.

Of course trickery was often suspected and sometimes proved. The usual procedure was for the photographer to use a glass plate (which was used instead of flexible film in those days) onto which the spirit image had already been exposed. For this reason, sceptical sitters would take their own plates and try to ensure that the photographer did not switch them for ones he had prepared earlier.

Spirit Photography

A glimpse of the future?
One wonders why Edward Volpi, a captain in the Italian army, was photographed sitting beside an empty chair in December 1879. Maybe he hoped that a spirit would be found to be sitting there? The spirit apparently leaning on the back of the chair was called Rena, or so Captain Volpi's dead wife told him through a medium. She also said that he had known Rena in a previous existence, and she was connected with his future.

Two years later he married a woman called Irene, and later realised that the spirit looked like her. When told the story, she said that she used to be known as Rena. If all this is true, then it is clear that the 'spirits' which appeared on these photographs were not necessarily all dead people, but included living people too!

Sightings

Taken from the pages of **Paranormal Magazine**

SPOOKY & FREAKY: The Supreme and District Court building in Brisbane, Australia, has been described as "spooky and freaky" by security guards patrolling the premises, and they all now believe in ghosts. Incidents include "unexplained whooshes of air rushing down corridors, a seemingly-possessed elevator and a judge's chair that mysteriously spins in the night." Although no actual ghosts have been seen, local historian Jack Sim believes the premises are haunted by the ghosts of the prisoners who died in the cells in the late 1800s. (SOURCE - BRISBANE TIMES 23RD FEBRUARY).

TOOLED UP GHOULS: Workers restoring a church in Rutland Place, in the city of Edinburgh, are convinced ghosts are stealing their tools. They have now refused to work night shifts. Apart from the missing tools, the workforce have seen vague shadows flittering around and heard footsteps from empty parts of the building. Foreman Ross McMillan said: "People were really troubled about being here at night. On some occasions some of the guys said they wouldn't come in. It's been really quite scary. We've been seeing things, particularly in the morning when shadows just move for no reason. On night shifts, when there were just a few of us, we would hear walking noises from the upper floors – even though we knew nobody was up there." (SOURCE - EDINBURGH EVENING NEWS: 5TH MARCH).

ELECTRIC BRAE: Monks are said to haunt the road around Ayrshire's natural magnetic phenomenon, the Brae, as well as the nearby Crossraguel Abbey at Maybole. It has been a long time since any reports came from the area, but I heard from a friend that a motorist in early March had a terrifying encounter after passing the Brae, heading for Denure. He braked in terror as three figures crossed the A179. The description he gave was of monks in black robes, floating off the ground, their heads covered and bowed by their hoods. They never looked up, but floated eerily away to his left. They floated in single file with the lead figure holding something to his chest in cupped hands. The incident lasted a matter of seconds, but was enough

Stead's final proof?
William T. Stead was a newspaper editor and champion of spiritualism, who died in the Titanic sinking in 1912. This photograph of his daughter Estelle, taken by medium Mrs Ada Deane in Crewe in October 1915, includes the face of Stead – and Estelle said she had never seen a photograph of him like this one.

Dr G. Geley

S. De Brath

I certify that this photograph was taken at Crewe by Wm Hope, Nov. 1919, on plates bought in London same day, opened by me and signed, not lost sight of during the whole process. Recognised by the lady's brother (non-spiritualist) and by three intimate friends. She "died" Aug. 1913. There is no similar portrait extant. S. De Brath. M.Inst.C.E.

His sister's spirit?
This photograph shows parapsychologist Dr Gustave Geley (seated on the left) with S. De Porath, and the hand-written certification by De Porath states that they had supplied their own plates, bought in London on that same day, opened by De Porath, signed, and not lost sight of during the whole process. In the same certificate he adds that the spirit image in the photograph was 'recognised by the lady's brother (non-spiritualist) and by three intimate friends. She "died" Aug. 1913. There is no similar portrait extant.' The photographer was William Hope, who was operating at Crewe, and he took this photograph in November 1919.

for the witness to state that he would never travel alone on that stretch of road in the dark again. (Source - Personal communication).

IRISH EXORCISM: A family fled their house in terror after their son was hurled from his bed by an invisible force. Now a local priest plans to hold an exorcism on the premises. Laura Burke, her partner Ritchie and her son Kyle are too terrified to stay in the house in Hollyhill, Cork. The family have seen "glowing orbs" hovering in rooms, and religious pictures have been knocked off the walls. Laura said: "It's an evil spirit. I don't believe it means us well. We tried saying prayers in the house and the next thing all you hear is banging furniture upstairs or clothes being fired out of wardrobes." Locals said that no previous residents have reported unusual activity in the house. (Source - Belfast Telegraph: 20th March).

GHOST LAGS: Now that the Victoria Road Prison, Douglas, on the Isle of Man has closed, tales of its ghostly residents are emerging. Ex-prison officer Norman Douglas Quilliam said: "There were three cells in this prison which were extremely haunted and I speak from personal experience. One night when I was sleeping in the officers' room upstairs I had the bed clothes pulled off me by, what I can only describe as, an entity. So I can say with conviction that the haunted stories from Victoria Road were true." Prisoners took to putting bibles under their bed as the phantoms banged and crashed around their cells on a night. (Source - BBC: 10th March).

14 GHOSTS: Joy Hanson never believed in the ghosts that she was told haunted the Mason House Inn in Bentonsport, Iowa, at first. But after buying the property her mind has now been changed. "A little old lady" haunts one particular bedroom, and Joy reports that they have had "fourteen full bodied apparition sightings" over the years. All the usual phenomena occur at the Inn, including footsteps, door-knobs rattling, bangs and crashes, lights being turned on and off etc. Joy said: "Personally, I and my husband and daughters have seen an old man with white hair and wearing a black suit, a middle-aged man with a reddish beard and longish hair, a teen aged girl named Amanda, a boy with dark hair, the little old lady on the third floor, and the cat." (Source - travelparanormal.com 9th March).

Sightings

HAUNTED HOTEL: The oldest hotel in Denver USA, the Oxford, not surprisingly is the most haunted. The room with the most activity is number 320. A male ghost often frequents the downstairs ladies toilets, and there is a ghost of a little girl searching for her canary in the attic! Guests tell of strange events and visitations while they sleep. Mediums, the curious and professional investigators are all queuing up to spend a night at the hotel. (SOURCE - DENVER.YOURHUB.COM 12TH MARCH).

CREEPY COOPERS: Members of The Atlantic Paranormal Society have recently conducted an investigation at the Otesaga Lake resort in Cooperstown, NY, as part of a television documentary. Tech manager Britt Griffith said: "Everybody has a ghost story in this town." The local cemetery on River Street has an eerie reputation among locals for being haunted by deceased members of the local Cooper family. A wall near Cooper Park had the strange habit of buckling. The skeleton of a Native American, who was said to be a "great Mohawk Chief", was discovered along with pipes, weapons and other artefacts. After the skeleton was found in the 1960s the wall never buckled again, according to some. (SOURCE - THE DAILY STAR, 24TH MARCH).

MORE TAPS: The Atlantic Paranormal Society is also investigating reports of paranormal activity from the Southern Mansion in Cape May, New Jersey. Reports indicate that some people believe that a former resident, Ester Mercur, still haunts the building. Strange things began happening after a restoration, "a soldier dressed in civil war clothing" has been seen on several occasions, and a dark haired woman has also been spotted. The TAPS team had some degree of success with male voices caught on tape, and an invisible something grabbed hold of one of the investigators arms. (SOURCE - SHORE NEWS TODAY: 8TH APRIL).

PREDATOR: On April 2 a couple were on their way to Abilene in Texas at 07.30hrs along the 180 west bound near the bridge over Hubbard Lake, when they saw something strange run across the road. One witness reports: "It was like seeing small feet and partial legs in a fast trot across the road. It was almost like something mirroring the road surface, but visible above the road by about 10 inches or

A lost boy (1)
Spirit photographs were normally taken indoors, but this is a rare open-air photograph, made in 1924 by psychic photographer William Hope at Exmouth. It shows the Buxton family, and careful examination will reveal Mrs Buxton's dead son above her head, and to the right of the spirit is the head of his dead white pony Tommy.

Mrs Buxton was thinking of her son while the photograph was being taken, 'wishing that he could have been one of the group'. There also appears to be a face on the front of Mr Buxton's waistcoat, said to be his brother who had died the previous year.

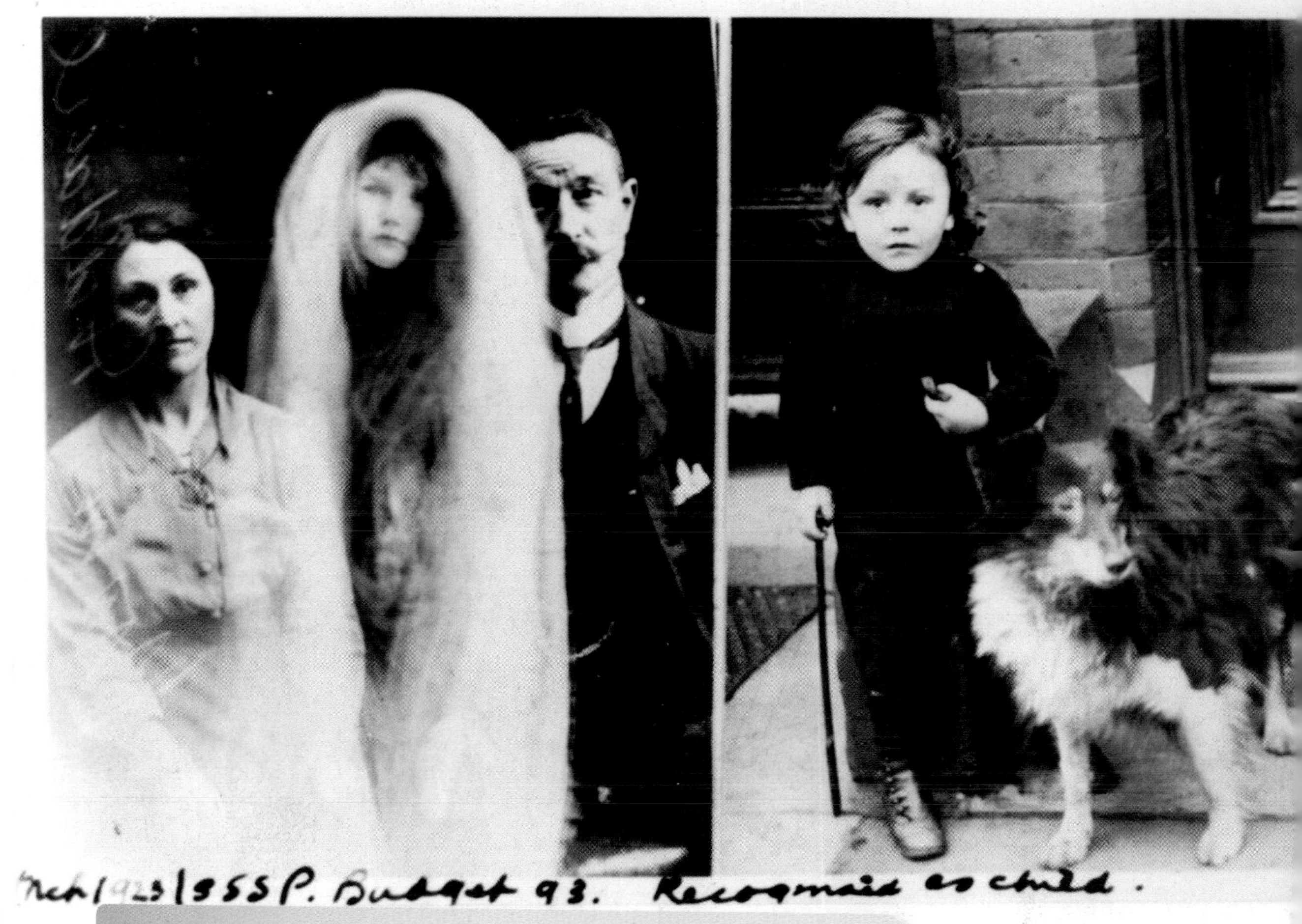

A lost boy (2)
This spirit photograph was taken in Crewe around 1922, by a member of the same circle of mediums to which William Hope belonged. It shows a Liverpool couple with the spirit image of their dead son; to the right is a photograph of the boy as he was around 1916. The likeness is undeniable, but of course this does not prove the authenticity of the spirit photograph.

so. It reminded me of the Predator in the Arnold Schwarzenegger movie. I could not see above the calf area of the legs, except the rippled, distorted sky behind the object, about the size of a body." Only one witness saw the apparition. (SOURCE - PHANTOMS & MONSTERS, APRIL).

SECRET ROOM: The Farla family from Telford in Shropshire discovered a secret basement in their Victorian home after checking out a three metre metal grid which had always puzzled them. Behind the grate they found a hole just big enough to crawl through which led to a large room underneath the house. On the floor was a large wooden cross and stairs that led back to the back of a cupboard in their house. The family now believe they have released a "ghost" as strange events now occur, including floating orbs which they have captured on camera. (SOURCE - DAILY MAIL 11TH APRIL).

ORBS: Paul Cliff, publican of the New Inn along Midland Road in Rotherham, could not, apparently, believe his eyes when he checked his CCTV footage and saw "a mysterious orb of light" float across the bar. He said: "I've never seen anything like it. I just can't explain it. The whole episode is just extraordinary. We've been here for 12 years and this is the first time we have experienced anything like this." (SOURCE - ROTHERHAM ADVERTISER 25TH APRIL).

CLEOPATRA HILL: The Jerome Hotel on Cleopatra Hill in Los Angeles has several spectres that keep the guests awake on a night. Staff and visitors alike have reported being kept awake by the spirits, who are said to be a caretaker who hanged himself in the boiler room, a handicapped man who wheeled himself off the balcony, and an executive who shot himself in Room 32. The nosiest ghost is said to be Harvey the caretaker, who was killed in a lift accident in 1935 when it came down on his head. Desk clerk Debra Altherr said: "He plays with the lights too." Other manifestations include noises akin to "moans and groans" and a lady in white. (SOURCE - LOS ANGELES TIMES 12TH APRIL).

Ectoplasm

Ectoplasm is a mysterious substance which was exuded by mediums during seances in the late nineteenth and early twentieth centuries. It could come from any bodily orifice, and often took human form. Sceptics believed it to be a gauze, or cheesecloth, or something similar that had been swallowed by the medium and then regurgitated – though that does not explain the ectoplasm which emerged from other orifices than the mouth.

There were always other people present when ectoplasm formed, and we often see the hands of the observers holding the medium's hands. Either they too are in on the hoax, and know full well that the ectoplasm is faked, or else the medium is so skilful she is able to fool them even though they are close enough to touch her. The other possibility of course is that sometimes the ectoplasm may be genuine...

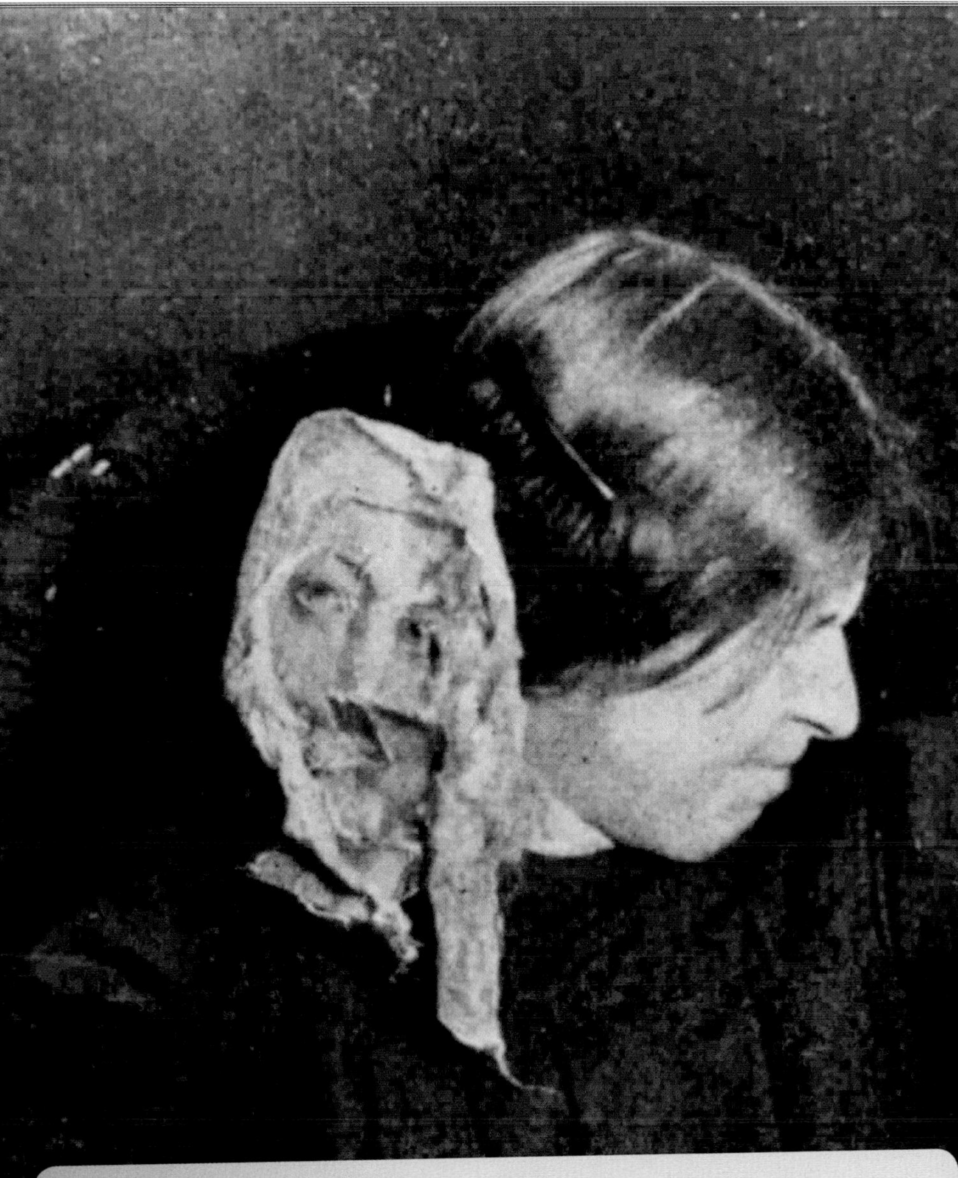

The case of Eva C

Hundreds of experiments were performed with the French medium known as Eva C, who was able to produce ectoplasm and full spirit materialisations. Professor Richet described how, in one 1912 seance, 'White substance appeared on the neck of the medium: then a head was formed which moved from left to right and placed itself on the medium's head. A photograph was taken. After the flashlight the head reappeared by the side of Eva's head... connected by a long bunch of white substance. It looked like the head of a man and made movements like bows....'

Certainly the head looks artificial, so were the scientists being fooled in some way? They did take steps to ensure that no trickery was taking place, and specifically to find out if the production of ectoplasm was faked, they administered a strong emetic on one occasion in 1913 after the flow of ectoplasm had been reabsorbed into Eva C's mouth but after ten minutes she had still not vomited, and so they were satisfied she had not swallowed anything that could have been used to fake the ectoplasm.

Sightings

Taken from the pages of
Paranormal Magazine

SEDUCTIVE HITCHER: A female ghost named by locals as Catherine has been frightening motorists in the Black Woods in Down, eastern Maine. She is dressed in a "light blue evening or ball gown" and even has the hill she haunts named after her. Catherine is said to have lost her head in a car accident and now tries to hitch a ride by standing in the road "seductively". She even talks to the drivers who dare to stop, saying: "I want to go to Bar Harbor." Of course, she disappears from the car when they reach the bottom of the hill. (SOURCE - WWW.WABI.TV 1ST FEBRUARY).

HAUNTED HOTEL: Hotel Niagara in East Java, Indonesia, is usually avoided by locals because of the frightening apparitions that haunt it. The local legend is that a Dutch woman committed suicide by throwing herself off one of the balconies, while others say she had been brutally raped and murdered by Japanese soldiers during World War 2. The fifth floor "is so riddled with malevolent ghosts" that it was closed to the public. One room in the hotel is said to fill with blood at night and it is claimed that guests may not wake up in the place where they went to sleep. But staff say they have seen nothing at the hotel. Ratti, who works in reception, said: "I've been here for seven years. I stay in the hotel 24 hours a day and I've never seen anything strange, and neither have any guests I know of." (SOURCE - THE JAKARTA GLOBE 12TH JANUARY).

RACTON FOLLY: Plans are in hand to turn this 238-year old ruin into a family home, along with its ghosts, but the present owner isn't worried as he does not believe in them. Some people describe the folly as one of the 'most frightening places in West Sussex'. Others believe the suicides, illegal raves and devil worshippers who used the Folly in the past are the ones responsible for its ghostly legends. Paranormal activity reported include the spirit of a lady in white, unseen forces throwing bricks from the top of the tower, a ghostly face looking out from one of the windows, and several accounts of people being grabbed and pushed. Oh, and not forgetting the ghostly tractor! (SOURCE - WWW.PORTSMOUTH.CO.UK 5TH FEBRUARY).

Sightings

I-POD GHOSTS: Demolition worker John Fores captured what he believed was the ghost of a boy on camera while knocking down the Anlaby Primary School in Anlaby, near Hull. He discovered the picture later when viewing the images on his computer and he swears there was no boy present when the photograph was taken. At first glance the photograph looked to most people to have been faked and after a little internet research I found the site 'Ghost Capture,' complete with the exact same image for download. The site allows people to make their own ghostly images then download them onto their phones. Mr Fores believes fellow workers played a trick on him, sending the image to his phone via a Bluetooth application. View the photo at paranormalmagazine.co.uk/news. (SOURCE - HULL DAILY MAIL & MARK FRASER 20TH FEBRUARY).

GWRYCH CASTLE: Kevin Horkin was taking pictures at this castle in North Wales and believes he captured the 'picture of a spirit'. As usual it was not until he downloaded the pictures on his computer that he discovered the picture. Amazingly the room that the "young woman" is standing in has no floor. According to the North Wales Paranormal Group there have been "many sightings recorded at the castle." View the photo at paranormalmagazine.co.uk/news. (NEWSUBMIT.NET FEBRUARY).

MISTY SCREEN: Two women working in the 'Simply Food & Drinks' in Durranhill Road, Botcherby, Carlyle, were stunned to see a misty figure on their CCTV which is aimed on the outside of the shop. One worker complained of suddenly becoming cold before seeing the mist, which appeared to be coming from across the road. Word soon got out and people stood in the shop looking at it; it could not be seen from outside. Assistant Miss Nolan said: "I have never believed in things like ghosts until that night but unless somebody can explain to me what it was, I believe now. I wish to God I hadn't seen it." View the footage via paranormalmagazine.co.uk/news (NEWS & STAR 28TH FEBRUARY).

IT'S NOT MAGGIE: The Burnett Arms Hotel in Kemnay, Aberdeenshire, described as "one of Scotland's most haunted pubs," is for sale. Former owner Maggie Duffton, who died in

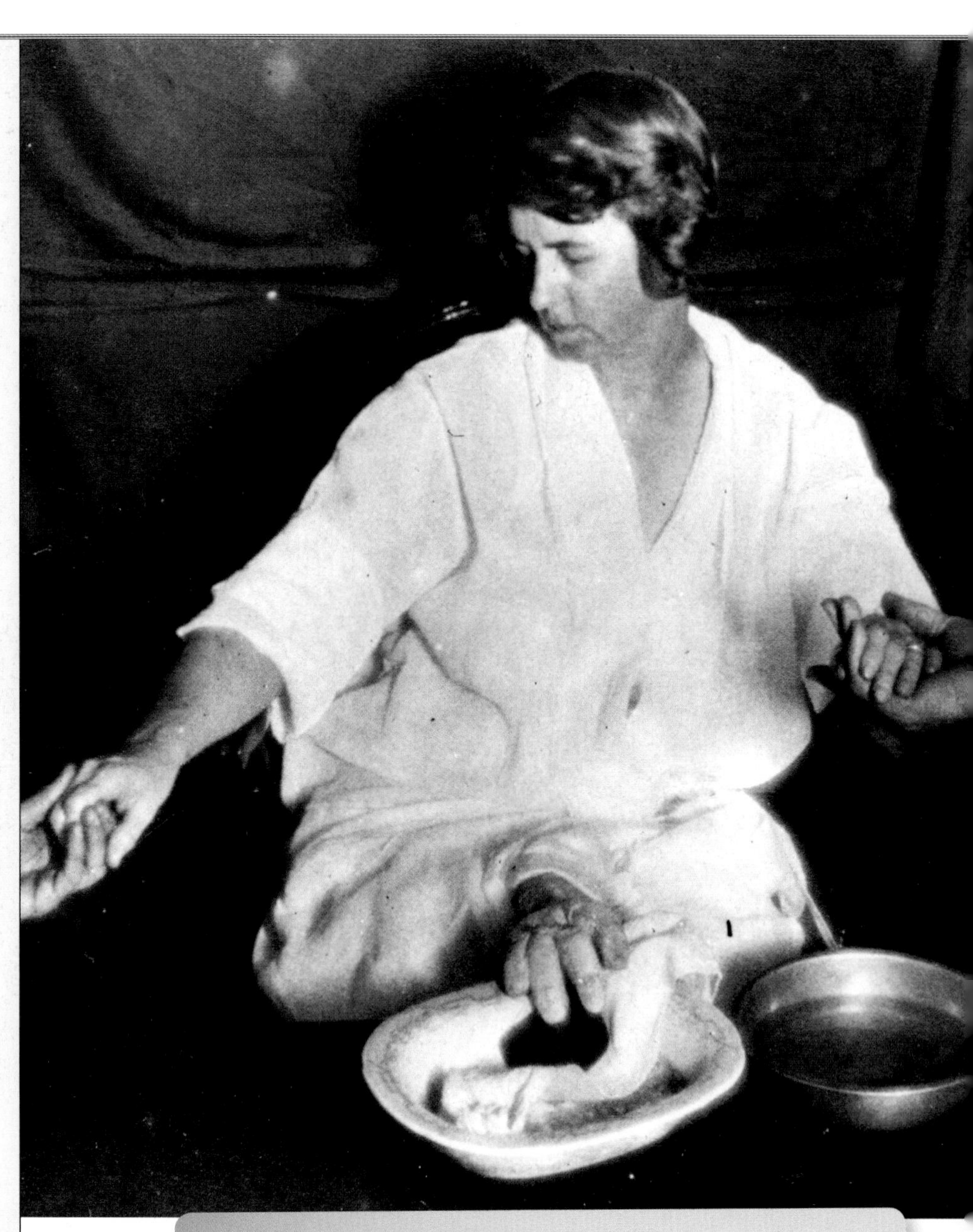

Margery Crandon's manifestations
One of the most famous mediums of the early twentieth century was Mrs Margery Crandon, wife of a Professor of Surgery at Harvard Medical School. She underwent detailed scientific investigation and the experts were divided as to the genuineness of her abilities. Dr Hereward Carrington, an experienced English psychic investigator, pronounced it 'one of the most baffling and extraordinary cases in history'.

One photograph shows Margery with ectoplasm apparently issuing from her ear, while her hands are held by two puzzled observers. In the other, she has produced an ectoplasmic hand, apparently from her vagina, while being controlled by two witnesses.

1934, is said to haunt the premises, indeed her coffin is rumoured to lie in the walls of the hotel. Recently house keeper Fiona Reid, spotted a dark apparition upstairs standing in a corner. She said: "Something drew me to walk towards it then it disappeared right in front of my eyes. I can't explain it." She turned around to leave and found a 30 year old newspaper on the floor behind her, in which was a picture of her grandfather. She believes it was his apparition she saw. Mrs Reid is adamant that the newspaper was not there when she first came into the room. (SCOTTISH TELEVISION 25TH FEBRUARY).

TINY BODIES: The former brothel, Tibbals Building on Water Street, Port Angeles, USA, is said to "echo with the cries of prostitutes and their dead babies who were soon "dispatched." The premises is most famous for its 'lady in blue'. Robin Alexis of Mystic Radio and a team of investigators from Paranormal Investigations of Historic America of Monroe recently conducted an investigation on the premises. During the vigil Alexis saw the figure of a lady in Victorian dress standing by a window, and a "priest in black robes wearing a large cross," and also a Native American woman who said her name was Grouse Woman. (WWW.PENINSULADAILYNEWS.COM 1ST FEBRUARY).

14 GHOSTS: Joy Hanson never believed in the ghosts that she was told haunted the Mason House Inn in Bentonsport, Iowa, at first. But after buying the property her mind has now been changed. "A little old lady" haunts one particular bedroom, and Joy reports that they have had "fourteen full bodied apparition sightings" over the years. All the usual phenomena occur at the Inn, including footsteps, door-knobs rattling, bangs and crashes, lights being turned on and off etc. Joy said: "Personally, I and my husband and daughters have seen an old man with white hair and wearing a black suit, a middle-aged man with a reddish beard and longish hair, a teen aged girl named Amanda, a boy with dark hair, the little old lady on the third floor, and the cat." (SOURCE - TRAVELPARANORMAL.COM 9TH MARCH).

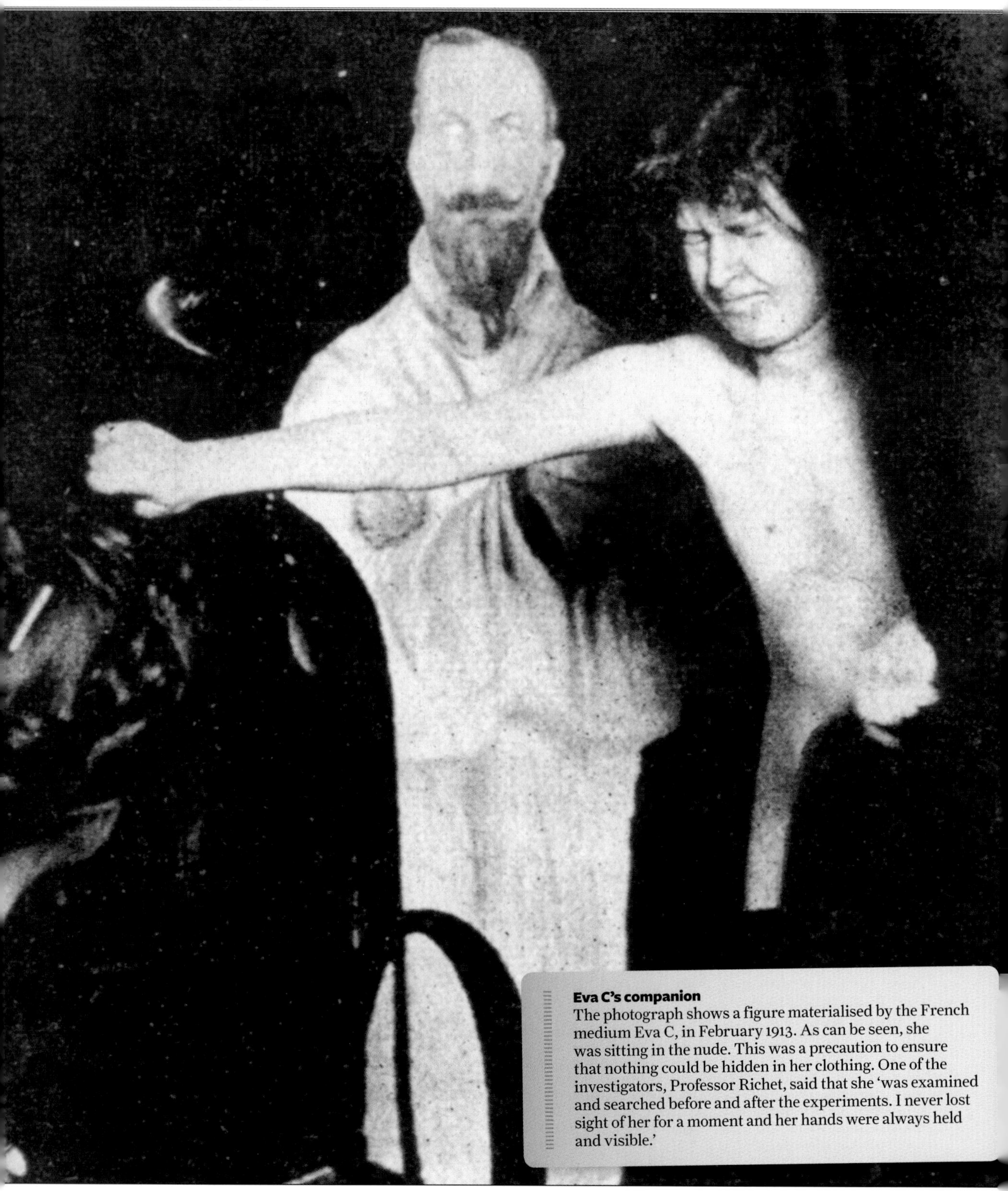

Eva C's companion
The photograph shows a figure materialised by the French medium Eva C, in February 1913. As can be seen, she was sitting in the nude. This was a precaution to ensure that nothing could be hidden in her clothing. One of the investigators, Professor Richet, said that she 'was examined and searched before and after the experiments. I never lost sight of her for a moment and her hands were always held and visible.'

Seance materialisations

As if the production of ectoplasm were not sufficient to convince the world of their powers, many mediums also claimed to be able to materialise complete figures of spirits, often using ectoplasm to form the bodies. Undoubtedly there were many cases of fraud, but the investigators were on the lookout for this, and sometimes used strange methods to prevent it.

Captain Olcott fastened the medium Miss Compton by passing threads through the bored holes in her ears and tieing them to her chair. She was concealed in a small cabinet, and when a phantom appeared outside, Olcott asked it to stand on a weighing machine. He did this three times, obtaining three different weights. At the end of the seance, the medium was found to be inside the cabinet with all the threads unbroken, and when weighed she was found to be twice as heavy as the materialised figure.

Sightings

Taken from the pages of **Paranormal Magazine**

STATION 3: Firefighters in Chicago's Station 3, situated in the Green Garden Township, are convinced their fire station is haunted. Lt. Todd Hamm said: "I used to see things going in and out of the ambulance – shadowy things. One was a dark-clothed, blackish figure that walked right in front of me." Among the ghosts are an "angry cowboy", a figure in blue and apparitions somewhat akin to the 'shadow people.' Firefighter Tom Warszalek said: "They're freaking me out.' (SOURCE - SUBURBAN CHICAGO NEWS 4TH FEBRUARY).

THE KING'S TAVERN: Witnesses describe "chills to the bone," the ghost of a baby girl which has allegedly been caught on camera, the sounds of a baby crying, as well as a host of other paranormal phenomena in this building built in 1729 and located in Natchez, Mississippi. Three skeletons, two male and one female, were found bricked up during renovations. The female is thought to be Madeline, a mistress of a former owner; it is her spirit who is believed to be the main cause of the haunting. There is a haunted mirror, doors open and close of their own accord, objects are thrown off shelves, to name but a few of the recent manifestations. (SOURCE - WWW.TIME.COM 5TH FEBRUARY).

ELECTRIC BRAE: Monks are said to haunt the road around Ayrshire's natural magnetic phenomenon, the Brae, as well as the nearby Crossraguel Abbey at Maybole. It has been a long time since any reports came from the area, but I heard from a friend that a motorist in early March had a terrifying encounter after passing the Brae, heading for Denure. He braked in terror as three figures crossed the A179. The description he gave was of monks in black robes, floating off the ground, their heads covered and bowed by their hoods.

Sightings

They never looked up, but floated eerily away to his left. They floated in single file with the lead figure holding something to his chest in cupped hands. The incident lasted a matter of seconds, but was enough for the witness to state that he would never travel alone on that stretch of road in the dark again. (SOURCE - PERSONAL COMMUNICATION).

FORT HAYES: The now abandoned fort in downtown Columbus, Ohio, is haunted by former recruits, according to present day custodians. "An angry ghost" throws clothes around, marching soldiers, ghastly screams have been heard, footsteps, bangs, doors opening and closing of their own accord and whispering are a few of the incidents that have been reported. The most common feeling is that of being followed. (SOURCE - WWW.DISPATCH.COM 14TH FEBRUARY).

WHISPERS: Situated on Warren Street in Mitchell, Indiana, this B&B has five graves in the back gardens and is said to harbour a host of ghosts, according to one recent investigation by the Louisville Ghost Hunters Society. Disembodied voices which sound like two men talking have been recorded and noises such as "thuds and tinkering sounds" were also heard. Present owner Jarrett Marshal has experienced many odd occurrences on the premises, but believes that among the several ghosts the most active is that of a little girl called Rachael. (SOURCE - WWW.MICHIGANSOTHERSIDE.COM 19TH FEBRUARY).

CURSED CAMPUS: Frightened students at the Northern Illinois University, believe that their building and the grounds are either cursed, or haunted. They have reported "eerie sounds in the campus hallway, and shooting sounds in the night." Rumours are that it is the ghost of the gunman who shot dead five people and wounded 19 before shooting himself. One student said: "This was bound to happen. The shooting may be because the ghost of the 2008 killer wants the whole incident repeated again. It's really creepy." (SOURCE - MERINEWS.COM 19TH FEBRUARY).

SPOOKY & FREAKY: The Supreme and District Court building in Brisbane, Australia, has been described as "spooky and freaky" by security guards patrolling the premises, and they

The charming Katie King

One of the most famous materialised spirits was Katie King, who appeared at Florence Cook's seances in London from 1872 onwards. It was reported that Katie used to appear in the Cook household frequently, walking around the house, and she even went to bed with the medium, much to her annoyance. This became even more inconvenient once the medium got married: Captain Corner used to feel as if he had married two women, and was sometimes not sure which was his wife!

Florence Cook's abilities were studied by the eminent scientist Sir William Crookes, who appears to have become infatuated by Katie. He obtained forty photographs of her, commenting that, 'Photography was inadequate to depict the perfect beauty of Katie's face, as words are powerless to describe her charm of manner.'

Two of the photographs are shown here, and one of them includes Crookes himself.

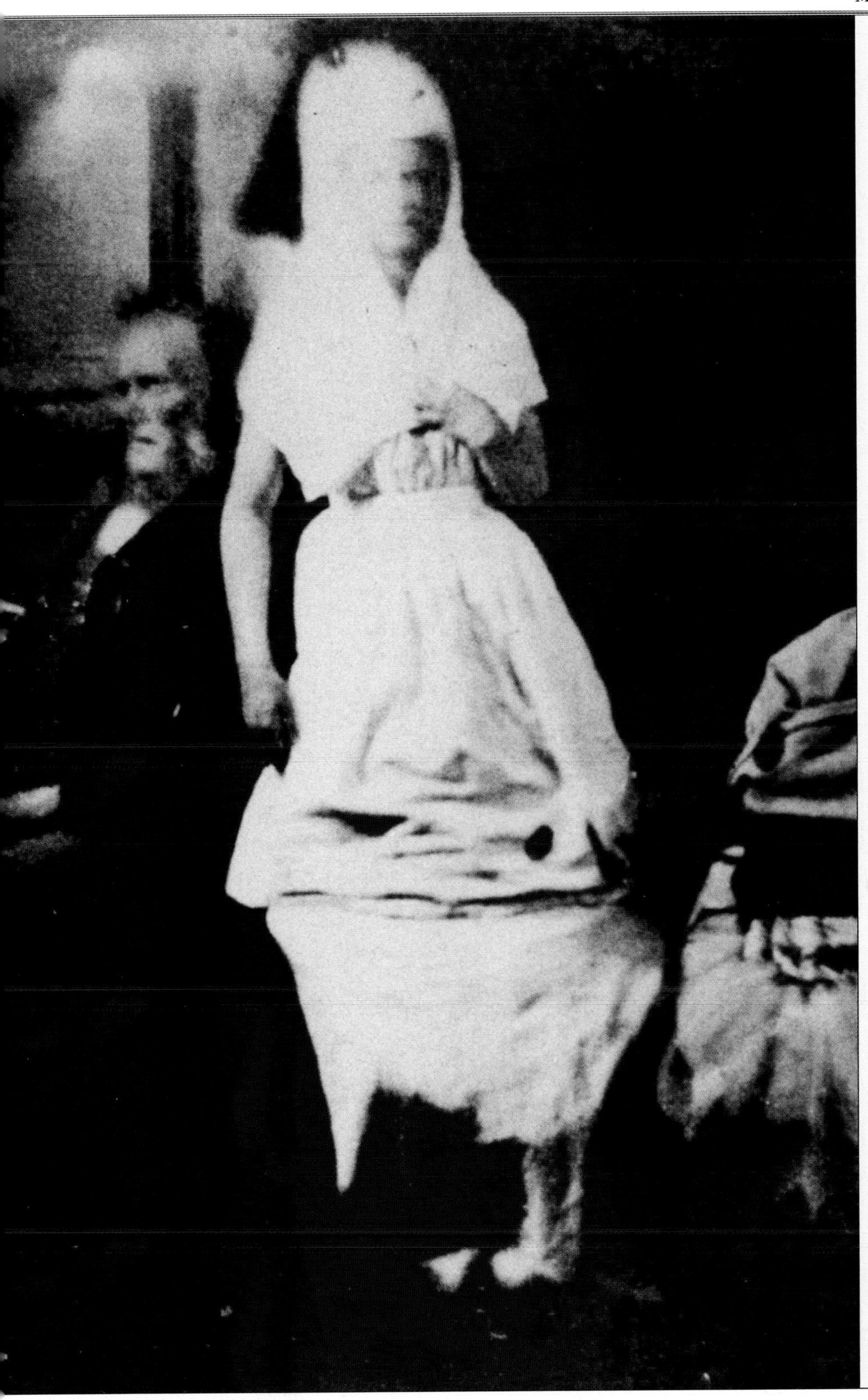

all now believe in ghosts. Incidents include "unexplained whooshes of air rushing down corridors, a seemingly-possessed elevator and a judge's chair that mysteriously spins in the night." Although no actual ghosts have been seen, local historian Jack Sim believes the premises are haunted by the ghosts of the prisoners who died in the cells in the late 1800s. (SOURCE - BRISBANE TIMES 23RD FEBRUARY).

TOOLED UP GHOULS: Workers restoring a church in Rutland Place, in the city of Edinburgh, are convinced ghosts are stealing their tools. They have now refused to work night shifts. Apart from the missing tools, the workforce have seen vague shadows flittering around and heard footsteps from empty parts of the building. Foreman Ross McMillan said: "People were really troubled about being here at night. On some occasions some of the guys said they wouldn't come in. It's been really quite scary. We've been seeing things, particularly in the morning when shadows just move for no reason. On night shifts, when there were just a few of us, we would hear walking noises from the upper floors – even though we knew nobody was up there." (SOURCE - EDINBURGH EVENING NEWS: 5TH MARCH).

IRISH EXORCISM: A family fled their house in terror after their son was hurled from his bed by an invisible force. Now a local priest plans to hold an exorcism on the premises. Laura Burke, her partner Ritchie and her son Kyle are too terrified to stay in the house in Hollyhill, Cork. The family have seen "glowing orbs" hovering in rooms, and religious pictures have been knocked off the walls. Laura said: "It's an evil spirit. I don't believe it means us well. We tried saying prayers in the house and the next thing all you hear is banging furniture upstairs or clothes being fired out of wardrobes." Locals said that no previous residents have reported unusual activity in the house. (SOURCE - BELFAST TELEGRAPH: 20TH MARCH).

GHOST LAGS: Now that the Victoria Road Prison, Douglas, on the Isle of Man has closed, tales of its ghostly residents are emerging. Ex-prison officer Norman Douglas Quilliam said: "There were three cells in this prison which were extremely haunted and I speak from personal experience. One night when I was sleeping in the officers' room upstairs I had the bed clothes pulled off me by, what I can only describe as, an entity. So I can

say with conviction that the haunted stories from Victoria Road were true." Prisoners took to putting bibles under their bed as the phantoms banged and crashed around their cells on a night. (SOURCE - BBC: 10TH MARCH).

HAUNTED HOTEL: The oldest hotel in Denver USA, the Oxford, not surprisingly is the most haunted. The room with the most activity is number 320. A male ghost often frequents the downstairs ladies toilets, and there is a ghost of a little girl searching for her canary in the attic! Guests tell of strange events and visitations while they sleep. Mediums, the curious and professional investigators are all queuing up to spend a night at the hotel. (SOURCE - DENVER.YOURHUB.COM 12TH MARCH).

MORE TAPS: The Atlantic Paranormal Society is also investigating reports of paranormal activity from the Southern Mansion in Cape May, New Jersey. Reports indicate that some people believe that a former resident, Ester Mercur, still haunts the building. Strange things began happening after a restoration, "a soldier dressed in civil war clothing" has been seen on several occasions, and a dark haired woman has also been spotted. The TAPS team had some degree of success with male voices caught on tape, and an invisible something grabbed hold of one of the investigators arms. (SOURCE - SHORE NEWS TODAY: 8TH APRIL).

SECRET ROOM: The Farla family from Telford in Shropshire discovered a secret basement in their Victorian home after checking out a three metre metal grid which had always puzzled them. Behind the grate they found a hole just big enough to crawl through which led to a large room underneath the house. On the floor was a large wooden cross and stairs that led back to the back of a cupboard in their house. The family now believe they have released a "ghost" as strange events now occur, including floating orbs which they have captured on camera. (SOURCE - SOURCE - DAILY MAIL 11TH APRIL).

ORBS: Paul Cliff, publican of the New Inn along Midland Road in Rotherham, could not, apparently, believe his eyes

Kluski's birds and beasts

Franek Kluski was a Polish poet and writer who also had psychic powers. Strange creatures materialised during his seances in 1919, including a large bird of prey (see photograph), said to be a hawk or buzzard, which 'flew around, beating his wings against the walls and ceiling' before settling on the medium's shoulder.

A large animal like a lion without a mane sometimes appeared, with a mouth full of large teeth, and eyes which glowed in the darkness. It liked to lick the sitters with a moist and prickly tongue, and left everyone smelling of an acrid wild-beast scent.

Kluski also materialised an ape-like creature with a shaggy head and the smell of a wet dog. It was so strong it could lift full bookcases, carry a sofa over the sitters' heads, and also lift heavy people in their chairs right up into the air.

when he checked his CCTV footage and saw "a mysterious orb of light" float across the bar. He said: "I've never seen anything like it. I just can't explain it. The whole episode is just extraordinary. We've been here for 12 years and this is the first time we have experienced anything like this." (SOURCE - ROTHERHAM ADVERTISER 25TH APRIL).

PREDATOR: On April 2 a couple were on their way to Abilene in Texas at 07.30hrs along the 180 west bound near the bridge over Hubbard Lake, when they saw something strange run across the road. One witness reports: "It was like seeing small feet and partial legs in a fast trot across the road. It was almost like something mirroring the road surface, but visible above the road by about 10 inches or so. It reminded me of the Predator in the Arnold Schwarzenegger movie. I could not see above the calf area of the legs, except the rippled, distorted sky behind the object, about the size of a body." Only one witness saw the apparition. (SOURCE - PHANTOMS & MONSTERS, APRIL).

Experiences

Laughed at – but not for long

About twelve years ago my girlfriend's family and I spent a week in Dorset. We stayed in an old converted brewery. It had been converted into about six terraced cottages. The group consisted of myself and my then girlfriend in one room; her mother and father in another; and their friend was in a room on the lower floor.

About three nights into the stay I became restless during my sleep. When I woke and raised my head I could clearly see the silhouette of a lady standing at the window in our room looking out into the garden.

I thought it was my girlfriend, so I turned to see her lying in the bed fast asleep. I knew it couldn't be anybody else, as the doors in the cottage had the latch on the inside only and not the outside, and the door was closed shut. Thinking nothing of it, I went back to sleep.

The following morning I went to breakfast and described what I had seen. Laughter was what followed. I told them it had to have been some sort of spirit (I firmly believe) but the reply came that there was no such thing as ghosts.

The day went by with a few jokes aimed in my direction but the following morning I got an apology off my girlfriend's mother. Due to a bad hip, she had to sleep in a separate bed and that night she had an experience.

She explained she felt someone sitting on her bed beside her and felt a depression on the blanket. At first she thought it was her husband so she told him to get off the bed and go back to sleep, which to her surprise it did. She then realised that all through her experience she could hear her husband still snoring.

It felt good the following morning when I got a handful of apologies.

Wayne Seadon, via email

Weird gifts from beyond

I am retired after spending most of my life in the radio, TV broadcast engineering field. I have always had an avid interest in science and electrical engineering and never thought much about life and death until my wife died eight years ago. I became interested in a possible life after life. I did spend some time reading and researching the internet, but never became convinced.

About a year after my wife died, strange things started happening to me here. Articles disappear for days then sometimes reappear in plain sight, sometimes never appear. Articles found in plain sight I had never seen before. I live alone, my only visitors are my grown-up grandson and my daughter-in-law. A few could be connected to my wife and religion, but many had no apparent connection to her.

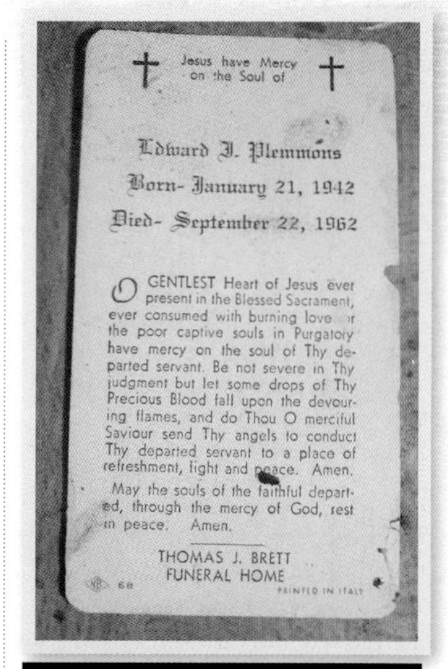

Jesus have Mercy on the Soul of

Edward J. Plemmons

Born- January 21, 1942

Died- September 22, 1962

O GENTLEST Heart of Jesus ever present in the Blessed Sacrament, ever consumed with burning love r the poor captive souls in Purgatory have mercy on the soul of Thy departed servant. Be not severe in Thy judgment but let some drops of Thy Precious Blood fall upon the devouring flames, and do Thou O merciful Saviour send Thy angels to conduct Thy departed servant to a place of refreshment, light and peace. Amen.

May the souls of the faithful departed, through the mercy of God, rest in peace. Amen.

THOMAS J. BRETT
FUNERAL HOME

68

PRINTED IN ITALY

EERIE: A 46-year-old funeral card that suddenly turned up on the floor in Mr Mangold's home. © William Mangold

This activity is still going on I have spent seven years and hundreds of hours documenting them and I have kept many of the objects. For example, when I got up one morning, I noticed something on the floor by my bed. When I picked it up I found it was a small, clear plastic packet. It had powder in it and some printing on it:

'Lot 04 Exp. 10-07 / Phenocopline HTV / Do not use if strip pack is broken.'

I showed it to my neighbor, who is a pharmacist, and he said it was a drug prescribed to treat urinary infections, and it usually comes in tablet form. I showed it to my own pharmacist and he said he had never seen one like it. How could this current prescription drug with

"About a year after my wife died, strange things started happening to me here. Articles disappear for days then sometimes reappear in plain sight, sometimes never appear. Articles found in plain sight I had never seen before."

unusual packaging get placed on the floor of my bedroom overnight? Anyway, no one I asked had had any urinary infection lately.

No less than 83 light bubs have failed here during the last four years. The line voltage has never checked over 121 volts. They don't blow, just fail to come on and the filaments, and sometimes their leads, are missing.

Last month I noticed a card on the floor of my spare bedroom. When I picked it up, I found it was a card from a Funeral Home, the type they give out at funerals. It apparently was one given at a funeral for Edward Plemmons, a friend of my son. My son had mentioned him but neither my wife nor I had ever met him. It was dated September 1962, 46 years ago. Our son was at the Coast Guard Boot Camp at that time and he told us later Ed had killed himself at Florida State University. Neither my wife and I, nor my son, went to his funeral or even knew where it was held. How would a poltergeist get hold of a funeral card?

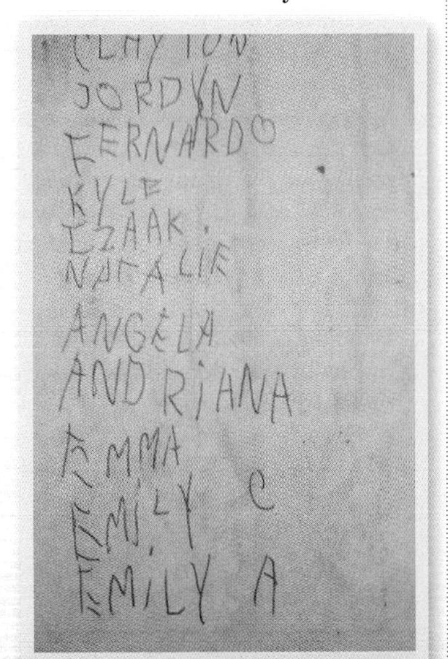

ANOTHER MYSTERY: Another gift from the spook was this piece of paper in a handwriting Mr Mangold didn't recognise carrying names he didn't know. © William Mangold

"When I got home, I just lay on my bed cuddling her shawl, and crying a lot, when out of nowhere, I heard her loud and clear, calling me, and sounding extremely happy and surprised."

This 'Something' can also operate my cameras and can make thing happen to my computer, which no person could have done, and make recorders do things impossible for a human to have done.

William Mangold, St Petersburg, Florida

The phantom jaywalker

One afternoon at about 3pm I was driving on the A628 near the Stocksbridge Steelworks when I saw a dark silhouette of a figure step on to the road. I swerved to avoid it but when I stopped and checked the roadside, I could see no trace of anyone.

The steelworks are at Sheffield near the Ladybower Reservoir. The road splits into a dual carriageway just before the steelworks because of a steep hill. I had moved over to let a car past when I caught sight of the figure. I couldn't honestly tell you whether the figure was male or female because there were no features: whatever it was, it was like a dark blank canvas. With it being August, I thought some kids from a village nearby might have been playing pranks, throwing stuff in the road, but when I stopped to check but there was no trace of anything.

I was using the road to get to the Woodhead Pass for North Wales to visit relatives but I haven't used the same road since because it scared the hell out of me. I've never forgotten it.

Gareth Evans, via email

A comforting visit

On the 14th September 2006 I was in my bedroom relaxing after being to a hospital 20 miles away to visit my mum who had just been transferred from my local hospital.

The lights in my bedroom kept flickering. I didn't think much of it, then my daughter phoned me and said someone was knocking on her friend's bedroom window, then the door (she was having sleepover at her friend's home). I told her it was maybe her friend's brother or sister playing tricks, but apparently they were asleep. The flickering in my bedroom was still going on and I asked my hubby if something was wrong with our lights, which there wasn't.

At about 1am on the 15th September, the hospital rang to tell us to get there quick as my mum was dying, so I rushed to the hospital praying I'd get there in time. When I did get there, it was too late, and my lovely mummy had gone. I was totally devastated, confused and angry: why had she died when she was getting better!?

When I got home, I just lay on my bed cuddling her shawl, and crying a lot, when out of nowhere, I heard her loud and clear, calling me, and sounding extremely happy and surprised. Then I heard my uncle

who had passed away five years previously. He called my name.

All I can think of is that she knew I went to the hospital and saw me there. Maybe she waited for me in spirit and came to let me know she was ok, and very excited about being out of her body and her spirit was flying around saying bye to everyone. My mum was housebound for 13 years, and spent a lot of her life in agony, so even though it broke my heart losing her, I know now that she is no longer in pain, and is free from her poorly old self. As for me hearing my uncle, I think that he came to help her on her way to the other side, and wanted me to know he was there, too.

I still cry a lot when I talk about my mum, as we had a very special relationship. I still miss her lots, and I still say goodnight, love you and blow her kisses. Even writing this I am crying and the screen is blurry, but I am extremely grateful for her to come to me and call me, and to know that there is life after death.

Nina White, via email

We've snapped three UFOs

This event happened on the 17th March at about 8.30pm. I can see the sky from my living room window in Pym Street, Heywood, north of Manchester. The window is south facing. Whilst watching TV I noticed an unusual light. I saw a second one and then a third one.

I jumped up and ran out shouting my partner to get her camera. She took the attached photograph. My partner has lightened the photo so that the lights show up more clearly. This is the only modification she has made.

We watched the lights for a good three minutes. They were heading north west across the front of our view. They were travelling at an equal pace, each at the same speed, as they retained the same distance in separation. The weather was clear and still with very little wind.

At 45 degrees WSW the lights 'went out' one by one, the first one in line disappeared first. I had a visual fix on this light and when it went out there remained a dark mass with no definable shape.

The following day I contacted the MOD and received what seems to be a standard letter from the RAF Business Secretariat 13 stating that there were no other reported sightings.

Three days after the sighting I also saw what appeared to be an orange meteor tail in the same area in the sky.

Bill Grayson, Heywood

"We watched the lights for a good three minutes. They were heading north west across the front of our view. They were travelling at an equal pace, each at the same speed, as they retained the same distance in separation."

Pain from the past?

Morton Corbett Castle in Shropshire is the ruins of a medieval castle and a Tudor manor house of the Corbetts, which was devastated during the Civil War.

I have recently done an investigation at Morton Corbett.

If I am honest, I was not entirely comfortable at this location and had a bad experience.

My experience started as I was going into a section of the ruins to do some glass divination. We started to do the glass divination and I started to feel very unwell and strange and felt that I needed to sit down. I had been sat down for a few minutes and I still was not feeling any better, in fact the feeling was getting worse, I was feeling so light headed and also as if I was actually still standing.

Then the strangest thing happened. I felt a sharp blow to the back of my head as if something had been thrown at me, it really hurt. It felt like I had blood running down the back of my neck but when I checked and kept feeling there was nothing there. I then started to feel really sick again.

After a short while of sitting down, the feeling had passed and I started to feel better again and it was as if nothing had happened and I managed to carry on with the rest of the investigation with no problems.

This was a very strange experience for me and I can't explain at all what was happening but I found it very interesting.

Richard Woolley, via email

MYSTERIOUS: Lauren Merry took these photos of her friend Andrew in the Hellfire Caves – is there a ghost standing behind him?

"Then the strangest thing happened. I felt a sharp blow to the back of my head as if something had been thrown at me, it really hurt."

Is this Sukie?

I have recently been to The Hell Fire Caves in West Wycombe. My friend Andrew and I were taking photos of each other when we noticed in one of them that there was a figure standing behind one of us.

The funny thing about the photo is that Andrew is standing next to a sign which is talking about a girl called Sukie who supposedly still haunts the caves. The story is she went to the caves after being told her lover was waiting for her. She was then pelted to death with stones by the lads who played the cruel prank on her. Before taking the photo I said out loud: 'We've got you a new husband. His name is Andrew.'

You can see a figure standing to the left of him. After I showed him the photo I took another one, to see what would happen, and a flash of light showed up next to Andrew.

Lauren Merry, via email

'George! Put the kettle on.'

As a child I lived at Tyn y Morfa Farm, near Gwespyr, in Flintshire. It's a very old house, parts of it dating back to the 15th century. It had been divided into two homes some time before we moved in in 1982 and me, mum and my dad lived in one half of it. We ran it as a farm, as had my taid [grandfather] before that.

I was only about three years old when we moved in. I used to have these vivid dreams that I was playing with a young boy. He'd sit on my bed and wake me up. I'd then dream that we'd go into my parents' bedroom and through a door – which didn't exist – and then down a few steps into the bathroom. The significance of this is that the bathroom had originally been a nursery. This went on until I was six, when one night I woke up crying because my little friend had died and gone away. My mum comforted me by telling me that I'd just grown up too much and didn't need him anymore.

However, a few years later, my parents decided to decorate their room. Under layers and layers of wallpaper they found a door – my door. When they opened it, they found the few steps me and my imaginary friend used to go down. Only one of the steps had been visible: it was being used as a shelf in the bathroom.

I can only just remember my little playmate; I remember his funny clumpy boots. I also remember that he sometimes had a maidservant with him. She was dressed in black with a white pinny and her hair swept back.

Later on, the main ghost we were aware of in the house was a character we called 'George'. We never saw him – just the results of his pranks – but we all felt that he was male and that he was, shall we say, a lot more interested in women than men. Most days he'd come and join us in our sitting room. The house had very old and heavy doors that could sometimes be a bit of a struggle to open. But the door to the sitting room

HAUNTED HOME: Tyn y Morfa and, above, Dawn with her Nain outside the house during the years when she was visited by a little boy in 'clumpy boots'. The 'apparition' in the upstairs window is actually just a big pink teddy!

would frequently open of its own accord. We'd just call out 'Come in, George!' Sometimes you'd feel a cold chill down your side as if he'd sat down next to you – at least girls would. Once it felt like he'd sat down between me and my friend – we each felt the chill on either side of us.

Other than that, he'd often turn the TV on when no one was in the room. Once, a light-bulb unscrewed itself from its fitting and fell down a flight of stone steps without smashing. The weirdest experience was when my mum and I thought we'd heard my dad come back from market. We heard someone in one of the back rooms and my mum called out: 'Emlyn, can you put the kettle on?' Sure enough, we soon heard the kettle boiling. But it didn't stop boiling – it was whistling away – so I went in to switch it off, even though it should have clicked off automatically. There was no one in the kitchen but it was full of steam. I flicked the switch up, assuming that it must have stuck, although it didn't feel stuck. Slowly it grew on my mum and me that we were alone in the house: my dad hadn't come back at all. He didn't come back for a couple of hours. Our ghost had put the kettle on!

"You could hear his tread come from the empty part of the house next door, through the more modern partition and the boarded-up door onto our landing, then back again, over and over. The footsteps were accompanied by a strong smell of pipe smoke."

That became a bit of a gag between us all. On a later occasion, my mum and dad were arguing about who should leave the cosy sitting room and go to the cold kitchen to make a cup of tea. Finally, my dad called out as a joke: 'Put the kettle on, George!' And he did. The same thing happened as before. It happened a few more times – it became like our party piece.

I felt fond of George. He was a friendly presence. I used to talk to him up until I was about 16 (not that I ever got a reply!). Unfortunately, we also had another ghost who wasn't so friendly, in fact, he used to scare me, though I couldn't tell you why, there was just a hostile feeling about him. We used to hear him pacing about on the landing at night. You could hear his tread come from the empty part of the house next door, through the more modern partition and the boarded-up door onto our landing, then back again, over and over. The footsteps were accompanied by a strong smell of pipe smoke.

We'd hear him about every six weeks or so. If I woke up in the night and heard him wandering about, I wouldn't dare get up and go to the loo, unless I really needed to – then I'd wait for him to go back through the partition and make a frightened dash for it!

One other very strange thing happened when we were due to leave the house. The farm had been sold from under us – we were only tenants – and we were very sad to go. One evening I went to make a cup of tea and found I needed sugar or something. The long passage to the pantry was in darkness, so jokingly, the way the family did, I called out: 'I need the light on, please.' And it came on. This sort of thing didn't faze me now, so I just said 'thank you' and went to the pantry. Once there the light went off again. 'Come on, stop mucking about,' I said, 'I need the light on to get back to the kitchen.' It came back on again. In the kitchen the light in the passage started flashing on and off, on and off – and it was operated by a pull cord, so it wasn't down to a wonky switch. I called out something like 'There's no point being angry with us, we don't want to go either.' I then burst into tears, because we were all very fed up about having to leave. Then some instinct made me say: 'Don't worry. You'll be all right.'

That was the end of it. After I said that, it felt like the presence went away. We didn't experience any more ghostly activity. The atmosphere had changed.

Dawn Lloyd-Williams, Great Sutton, Wirral

As I press the button on the remote, a black 'shape', for want of better words, goes from above my TV and 'flies' over my head and into the wall behind me. Then my TV turned back on.

Storm fairy

It was mid evening and the air was humid and the rain was pouring from the sky like a monsoon. Even so, I had the patio door open, firstly because it was very humid and secondly to watch the spectacular lightning displays in the sky. As I sat watching, a strange creature flew in the door and hovered directly in front of me.

At first I thought it was an insect but on closer observation I saw tiny arms and legs. The 'being' hovered in front of me for about 30 seconds then just vanished. It did not fly out the door but disappeared in front of me. My husband says I am mad but I am sure I had a visit from the Faerie World that night.

Elaine McCall, via email

A not-so quiet night in

One Saturday night back in 2007 I was sitting watching TV, having a few beers and a boring 'quiet night in' when a series of events really freaked me out.

Firstly I had just leaned forward to grab a can of beer when I felt as though someone was standing right next to me (and by that I mean imagine if you are sitting in a car and someone presses against the side window by you... that feeling of closeness), then within a few seconds my TV turned itself off. So I'm now sitting in a dark room...

I reach for the TV remote to turn the TV back on. As I press the button on the remote, a black 'shape', for want of better words, goes from above my TV and 'flies' over my head and into the wall behind me. Then my TV turned back on.

Suffice to say I'm a tad freaked out and scared at this moment and to make matters worse as I've leaped up to turn the light on and I've grabbed my mobile phone to text my friend to tell him about what had just occurred when I realise that my mobile phone has been turned off as well!

Now is this just a series of coincidences or do you guys think its something else as I'd never really experienced anything ghostly or spooky in my flat before that Saturday night but since I've had a few more strange occurrences, noises, feelings of being watched etc.

Russ Browning, via email

What on Earth – or off it – was it?

On July 4, I spotted a very strange object in the sky, grabbed my phone and photographed it. My phone tells me the picture was taken at 9.09pm. It was still bright, the sky blue with some high, patchy cloud. Sunlight was coming from the right of the picture, and I was facing north where the object could be seen above Hope Mountain in Flintshire. The grey structure you can see bottom right of the frame is a squat radio mast on top of the mountain.

The UFO appeared to the naked eye as a big, black blob. It was stationary but pulsating, kind

of throbbing round the edges. I suppose it was in my view (from an upstairs window) for about 20 seconds including taking and checking the photo. Then I went downstairs and told my girlfriend Heidi about it, but by the time we'd got to a window it had gone.

I must admit the photo, even more than the object itself, really freaked me out – it looks like a black hole in the sky. The camera isn't great quality, 3.2 mp, mind you, but the fact that police helicopters have been buzzing about on the mountain ever since has done nothing to help my paranoia!

I'd love it if anyone could let me know what they think it might have been. A practical, down to earth explanation would be very welcome.

Robin Bell, Hope, Flintshire

Time slips in the trees

I live in Snettisham, Norfolk, and walk my dog regularly in the nearby woods, known as Ken Hill Estate. I have had a few 'time slip' experiences up there as well as an awful feeling of foreboding, panic and general unpleasantness.

The first time slip I experienced was as I stood looking out toward the sea and I suddenly felt as if my feet were wet. I could see the sea coming in across what is now a field, and lapping round my feet.

On another occasion, I heard sounds like a battle and turned to see just that: a battle going on, with clashing of swords and yells etc. It was such a brief snapshot that I couldn't really make out who the men were, but I feel they may have been Roman, as I got the impression of leather armour.

The third time slip experience was as I walked along I was suddenly aware that I was a man, much taller and strongly built, with cloth trousers bound round with leather straps. I was carrying two dead rabbits in one hand and a sling-shot in the other. I actually said to my husband walking alongside me: 'I've shape-shifted, I'm a man and I've been hunting. I've got two rabbits for the pot.' This was a tall Anglo Saxon man, I believe, from the style of clothing I was wearing.

The unpleasant experience happened one August day when I was again walking with my husband and our dog. As we approached a row of beech trees I felt very, very uneasy, almost to the point of being frightened (I'm not easily frightened by spirits or the paranormal). I just didn't like the energy and felt there was someone there. Hubby looked

'I've shape-shifted, I'm a man and I've been hunting. I've got two rabbits for the pot.' This was a tall Anglo Saxon man, I believe, from the style of clothing I was wearing.

around and said there was no-one about, but he trusts my instincts on this sort of thing and asked, do we need to get out of here? I said I felt it wasn't intending harm but was just very unpleasant and let's just walk faster. Once we were further away from the trees the feeling passed.

A couple of years later, I was walking the same area with a friend and happened to mention my experience and she said that a man had hanged himself from the branches of one of the beech trees. Earlier this year, another friend who is a paranormal investigator mentioned that in talking to another friend of his, he learned that a man had hanged himself in Snettisham woods on the 13th of August some years ago! Spooky or what?

Julie Gillott (Whitefeather), Norfolk

Was it our baby?

Eleven years ago, tragedy struck our family: our 21-month-old son died in house fire. We were absolutely devastated and beside ourselves with grief, and guilt that we couldn't save him. It was horrendous. I can't begin to describe the pain and suffering we went through, and still do.

Two months later, with only three months left in my pregnancy, we moved away from the area with our two daughters and started a new life, in a new house. This one, unlike the last, had a good feeling about it. I knew as soon as I walked in. I gave birth in October 1998 to our fourth child, our second son.

I found it difficult to sleep at night because of what had happened. Most nights I would just lie awake in bed until my eyes got so heavy I could no longer fight going to sleep.

I felt so at ease. They were so beautiful. I didn't want them to leave. I wanted to watch them all night, but after five minutes they went.

One night was much the same as any other. My husband slept and I spent it wide awake looking through the window at the orange glow from the street light outside. I glanced around the room. In the corner of the room was our TV, which was switched off, but surrounding it were several balls of light, in different sizes. They were flashing on and off like disco lights when they flash to the music's beat. I was fascinated and mesmerised by them. I didn't know what they were or what they could possibly be. I wasn't scared, just calm and relaxed. It lasted for five minutes before they went one by one.

I wanted to tell my husband the next day of what I had seen, but thought better of it in case he thought I'd gone round the twist!

The following night it happened again, in the same place. I felt so at ease. They were so beautiful. I didn't want them to leave. I wanted to watch them all night, but after five minutes they went. They left me with an inner peace I couldn't explain.

On the third consecutive night it happened again. This time my husband was awake! I watched, but didn't say a word to him. When it was over, he said to me, 'Did you see that?'

I wasn't sure if he'd seen the same as me so I said, 'Did I see what?'

'The lights by the TV,' he replied.

'You saw it, too?' I said, surprised. He nodded and smiled. I was thrilled because I thought maybe I had been seeing things.

It was the last time we saw them in that house. We moved again several months later to the house that we occupy to this day. Two months after we moved in I saw them for the last time, on my landing. I wondered if it was our son who had passed over, coming to let us know that he was all right, his own way of trying to ease our grief. If so, for those few minutes he did.

Lisa Plowman, via email

I was followed from the shower

I am a fan of the Paranormal Magazine and love reading about the various paranormal experiences detailed in the magazine.

In issue 38 you asked for readers to tell you about their own paranormal experiences so I thought it would be the perfect opportunity to tell you of one of mine. This is an experience that dates back to when I was just 13 years old, I am now 37 and I shall never forget the day I am about to tell you about.

In 1985 I went on a week-long school trip to the Conway Centre in Menai, North Wales, this was a trip that was offered to all the third year seniors each year.

Every year claims would be made by the pupils who attended the centre that the third dormitory was haunted, and that footsteps could be heard walking the length of the dormitory, doors would open and shut yet no one was seen doing this and lights would switch on and off by themselves. ☞

I would often say it was just imagination but when I went on this school trip I was soon to learn it was no one's imagination at all. Indeed all the above continued to happen and the taps in the shower room would come on by themselves, too. One day all the pupils where carrying out a canoeing activity, I asked if I could be excused from doing that as I was afraid of going under water.

I then decided to take the opportunity to head back to the dormitory alone and take a shower before everyone settled for the day. What happened once I got into the shower is something I shall never forget. As I was in the shower I felt a rather chilling coldness down my left hand side, it was an unusual coldness not like any kind of breeze coming through a window for example, however I did look to see if there was a window open and it appeared there was not.

I then heard the taps being turned on and off, I called out the names of some of the girls who shared that dormitory (getting no response) as I first thought maybe someone was playing a trick as most teenagers do in school. I then got out of the shower and proceeded to walk out back into the dormitory towards my bed. As I walked I heard what sounded like someone walking behind me, however what I found unusual was whoever it was seemed to be dragging one foot along the floor.

I walked into the dormitory and was still being followed, not only could I hear this I could feel the coldness on my back. I stopped and looked behind me but could not see anything. I continued to walk towards my bed and whoever it was continued to follow me. When I reached my bed I felt a hand touch my shoulder. I again turned round and no one could be seen.

For all these years I had been intrigued and wanted to know who it was, so I recently carried out some research and this is what I found out.

On the ground of the Conway Centre is the home of the Earl Of Uxbridge, Henry William Paget, 1st Marquess of Anglesey, who fought in the Battle of Waterloo and was shot in his right leg by a cannon, necessitating its amputation. Henry had an artificial leg, presumably of wood, which might have caused him to drag it when he walked.

Could it of been the Earl of Uxbridge who followed me out of the shower room that time?

Janet Finn, via email

I continued to walk towards my bed and whoever it was continued to follow me. When I reached my bed I felt a hand touch my shoulder. I again turned round and no one could be seen.

Caught on camera – but what is it?

I was visiting the old slate mines in North Wales in early September and took lots of photos. In one of them is a bright white object which looks to be moving very fast. I have no idea what it is.

Based on what I was taking a photo of and my proximity, the object was about 8m away from me and about the size of a softball. Photo was taken on a digital camera at 14.7 Mega Pixels, so the image is quite good. It was broad daylight, too, and I'm certain no flash went off.

At the time of taking the photo I think I saw movement but can't be 100% certain as I did not discover

I was studying for a science exam when the dresser mirror began shaking and twisting as if something was gripping it and twisting it.

the strange glowing object until the following evening. I have all the camera setting recorded with the image as well. It certainly is strange!

Nick West, via email

Tales from the Bronx

I had two experiences in my life that I would say were paranormal. The first occurred many years ago while living in the Bronx, just a block away from the zoo. It was shortly after 1am and I was studying for a science exam when the dresser mirror began shaking and twisting as if something was gripping it and twisting it. My room temperature got very cold which was odd because the radiator was hissing. This lasted about 10-15 seconds and it never happened again.

My second experience occurred several weeks after my brother died of cancer. Before Mike died I asked him if it was at all possible if he could visit me or let me know how he was on the other side. He said he would try. On 9/2/94 at about 2am I heard a knock on my table the way the Three Stooges would knock. That's the way my brother always knocked on my door when visiting. I knew it was him. Although I could not see him I wished him a safe and happy journey and his wife who also died of cancer several months before he did.

Aaron, via email

Wandering healer

Back in 2004 I was working in Lunn Poly Travel Agents in Littlehampton, West Sussex, it was a spring day and business was slow that day. So I was quite glad to see a lady open the door and approach my desk towards the front of the shop. She sat down and requested some info on flights, but I got the direct impression she was not really interested about the flights but more myself as she started to ask me questions. As we chatted I studied the woman: she had an open friendly face hard to place an age against, but I would say she was in her late 50's to 60's, with bright inquisitive eyes.

What happened next really spooked me out. She said I had suffered some major emotional damage and it involved my family. This was true as my parents were going through a rocky patch in their marriage and it had upset me badly. She then said it was not my fault and I needed healing and that something called the Star of Bethlehem would help. At that point she left the shop.

This left me a little bewildered as I had never mentioned my parents to her and she had seemed to look straight into my soul and see how much my family were hurting me. Anyway, I managed to pull my senses back together and get on with some work and maybe think she was just a strange old lady.

So I was very surprised to see her again about half an hour later. She leant over my desk and gave me a small carrier bag containing a bottle of 'Rescue Remedy'; she said this would help me calm my mind. She then quickly left the shop.

One of the major ingredients of this natural remedy is the Star of Bethlehem, an extract from the Flower of Bethlehem, thought to have healing powers of the mind. I have always wanted to thank this mysterious lady for her kindness but I never saw her again and left Lunn Poly later that year.

Mark Barnes, Worthing

Night visitors

In 1965 when I was 4 years old my older brother and sister and I were woken up by the bedroom light being switched on and by the time the dazzle of the light had faded my brother and sister were both standing at the foot of the beds and so I joined them.

Standing in front of us were a blond man and woman. The women was on the right hand side of the man and behind them was an airing cupboard door, so I would say they were just under 6ft tall, both slim and dressed the same (I don't recall the clothes now). To the man's left was the bedroom door that was ajar and led to a small hallway with another bedroom off and a bathroom. My brother asked them if they were my dad's friends as he often came home from work late at night with people he worked with. The man said yes but I never saw his mouth move and the women looked down at me and smiled. Then the man looked at the bedroom door and as he did so I heard another man in my head say 'It's OK'.

Thinking back now, my dad may have stirred, anyways just after this my brother pushed me back towards the bed, so I got back in and went to sleep. The next morning we were up early and went into mum and dad's bedroom and told them about dad's friends. My dad shot out of the bed and ran around the whole place, checking all the doors 

TIME SLIP?: A quiet corner of Fountains Abbey in Yorkshire may have belonged to a different century.

and windows from the night before but they were still locked.

My dad said it was a dream but I know it wasn't and could all three of us have had the same dream? This was the start of many things in the paranormal world to happen over the last 44 years of my life and I have been an investigator for many years.

Clive Hodge, Hunstanton, Norfolk

Did we visit the past?

When I was in my early teens (more years ago than I care to remember) my friend and I were taken on an outing to Fountains Abbey in North Yorkshire. It was a lovely day and we were enjoying exploring the beautiful ruins when we came upon a little room. It was equipped as a kitchen, complete with scrubbed wooden table and lots of wooden cooking utensils, pottery bowls etc. There were also bunches of dried herbs hanging from the ceiling. The atmosphere was so calm and relaxing that we stayed in there for quite a while. We could hear no sounds whatsoever from outside and no-one else came into the room.

After a while we decided to go and fetch my friend's parents so they could see this lovely place, but when we returned with them we could find no trace of the room at all, despite searching the entire ruins more than once. My friend's parents enquired of the person on gate duty but they were told there was no room, much less a kitchen, so we were left to conclude that we had somehow experienced something from the past – I have always wondered since what would have happened to my friend and me if we had still been in the room when it 'disappeared'?

Yvonne Stimpson, via email

When we returned with them we could find no trace of the room at all, despite searching the entire ruins more than once.

Are you awake?

I was having a well-earned break with my brother at a B&B in Shipdham Norfolk, after putting mum in a rest home for 10 days. I had been in my bedroom for a few nights before anything really happened. Suddenly I awoke quickly at 1.17 in the morning by a voice shouting down my ear, saying 'ARE YOU AWAKE, PAMELA?'

When I woke nothing else happened. My brother had not knocked on the door to tell me we had had a call about mum. But that shout was in my room and it was no one with a Norfolk accent. In fact, it sounded like my deceased father! He had died in 2002. We were taking our hols in 2005.

As nothing more happened I went back to sleep, I did not ask to be put in another room and nothing more happened. I did try to bring the subject up with the landlord of the B&B but he ignored me! So he knew something.

Pamlea Gregson, Telford

Don't try this at home

The power of our mind is part of the quantum physics of the universe and is both miraculous and awesome, as seen in the following power flexing exercise. It brought almost immediate retaliation, which underlines its efficacy.

By virtue of the unexpected result of the appearance of a saurian – a monstrously tall reptilian – in my living room who radiated a loathsome, palpable rage and hatred, shortly after using this psychic technique,

I determined to never try this mental exercise tool again. However, a skilled TEAM might bring marvelous results.

With your eyes closed, visualize an alien craft, a large UFO, above our planet or within our skies, many miles overhead. This large craft, full of reptilians and subservient greys all busy at machinery should be seen in full detail for a full half minute. Jar the craft violently and throw it in space, like a football, end over end. See it hurled across a distance in space at a tilted, pitched angle and imagine all on board, startled and frightened. I used a quick head tilt to accentuate the mental suggestion of the craft's jump. (Imagination is a word that should be eliminated from our language.)

A Mothman-like, tall reptilian materialized and radiated a palpable loathing and rage, all of which instantly amazed and frightened me. It vanished after ten seconds or more.

Later, days and weeks later, that saurian vendetta manifested through a series of horrid and painful accidents which seemed to underline the smouldering, tangible hatred and rage that it radiated towards me. To my mind, in retrospect, all those agonies and sudden misfortunes more than suggested that our minds can be a powerful weapon – tools to both rebuke and control ships that do indeed respond to powerful telepathic messages.

Paul Schroeder, via email

Paws for thought

About two years ago, I visited County Durham with my family, and decided to take a trip to the Beamish Open Air Museum. I have to say that none of us had been to the museum before, and had not looked at any information about it, or read any leaflets, so it was completely unknown territory.

The night before our visit, I had the most vivid dream. I dreamt myself to be petting a very small brown dog. It was ridiculously small – it sat almost in the palm of my hand! – and in my dream its name was Sooty. I was playing happily with it, when something went wrong in the dream, and the next thing was, I had lost the dog, and then suddenly became terribly upset. In my dream, I was calling for 'Sooty! Where is Sooty!' and crying bitterly.

PUPPY LOVE: A reader's dream about a small dog would seem to have been inspired by a visit to the Beamish Open Air Museum – except that the visit took place the day AFTER the dream! © Colin McLurg

I woke at that point, and felt completely devastated. I longed for 'Sooty; I had tears on my face when I woke, and the horribly sad feeling of loss stayed with me. At breakfast time, I told my parents about my dream. I still felt sad at the loss of my dog and kept saying 'But it was so small and lovely!' I could feel the dog still in my hands.

When we got to the Beamish Open Air Museum, we visited what's known, I believe, as the Piano Teacher's House, and there on the wall, just at the side of the parlour door, was a glass case and inside was – Sooty.

It was such a coincidence, that I began to tell the museum attendant about my dream, but before I could finish she said to me: 'Oh that dog belonged to the lady who lived here. It was the smallest dog in the county at that time, and she was devoted to it, but one day it got caught underneath her skirts and by a horrible accident, she stepped on it, injuring it and leading to its death. She was so overcome, she had the animal stuffed and put into that glass case.'

At that point, my blood ran cold, and I think I was almost relieved to find that the name of that dog was Rose. But why did I dream that? Whatever name the attendant gave it, I'm convinced that 'Rose' was my 'Sooty' and even as I write this, I still feel sad about how the dog died and know how much I missed it.

If anybody has any information about Rose/Sooty I would be interested to hear it. Meanwhile, it remains a complete mystery to me of WHY I should dream this?

Rebecca Lane, Alford, Lincolnshire

Experiences are continued on page 106

Poltergeists

Poltergeists have always been with us. There are recorded cases as far back as AD 530, and from all parts of the world. The sheer quantity of cases on record, and the time-span, indicate that this is a genuinely mysterious phenomenon – one that remains inexplicable despite much investigation.

The German word Poltergeist means literally 'noisy spirit', and that describes its behaviour very well. Among its manifestations are banging noises, things being thrown around, furniture being piled up, and also more destructive behaviour such as attacking people and lighting fires. It can express itself in other quieter ways, such as hiding things or writing messages. The poltergeist is seen as a mischievous spirit because that is what the behaviour suggests: a disembodied spirit that enjoys upsetting people.

Just as there is no real evidence that ghosts are the spirits of the dead, so too it cannot be proved that poltergeists are discarnate entities. It is clear that many poltergeist activities do not follow the rules laid down by science. Objects move without being touched, sometimes they move slowly through the air, and solid objects have apparently passed through other solid objects. Spontaneous fires occur, water appears from nowhere, and so on. It is possible that these paranormal events are triggered by powers and energies we have not yet recognised, but which everyone has the potential to use.

The Runcorn poltergeist
The Glynn family living in Runcorn (Cheshire) suffered a poltergeist outbreak in 1952. Their invisible intruder was fond of moving furniture about, and even when the police set traps and kept watch, the disturbances continued. Here John Glynn surveys his wrecked bedroom.

Sightings

Taken from the pages of
Paranormal Magazine

SECRET ROOM: The Farla family from Telford in Shropshire discovered a secret basement in their Victorian home after checking out a three metre metal grid which had always puzzled them. Behind the grate they found a hole just big enough to crawl through which led to a large room underneath the house. On the floor was a large wooden cross and stairs that led back to the back of a cupboard in their house. The family now believe they have released a "ghost" as strange events now occur, including floating orbs which they have captured on camera. (SOURCE - DAILY MAIL 11TH APRIL).

ORBS: Paul Cliff, publican of the New Inn along Midland Road in Rotherham, could not, apparently, believe his eyes when he checked his CCTV footage and saw "a mysterious orb of light" float across the bar. He said: "I've never seen anything like it. I just can't explain it. The whole episode is just extraordinary. We've been here for 12 years and this is the first time we have experienced anything like this." (SOURCE - ROTHERHAM ADVERTISER 25TH APRIL).

HINKY PUNK: Construction workers on a 15th century church in Anglesey which is currently undergoing renovation have reported seeing unidentified "balls of light" on several occasions, which they described as "a wispy ball of light that moves around slowly and seen to grow smaller and dissipate." Steve Mera from the UPIA group visited the scene and discovered the church was surrounded by marshland, he reports: "A closer inspection of the area revealed rotting plants baking in the afternoon sun and a slight scent of methane. It would be no surprise to me if under such conditions that marsh gasses could manifest themselves as Ignis Fatuus which is Latin for Foolish Fire, and also known as will-o-wisp, jack-o-lantern, friar's lantern and hinkypunk. (SOURCE - PHENOMENA MAGAZINE UPIA & MAPIT MAY).

CLEOPATRA HILL: The Jerome Hotel on Cleopatra Hill in Los Angeles has several spectres that keep the guests awake on a night. Staff and visitors alike have reported being kept awake by the spirits, who are said to be a caretaker who hanged himself in

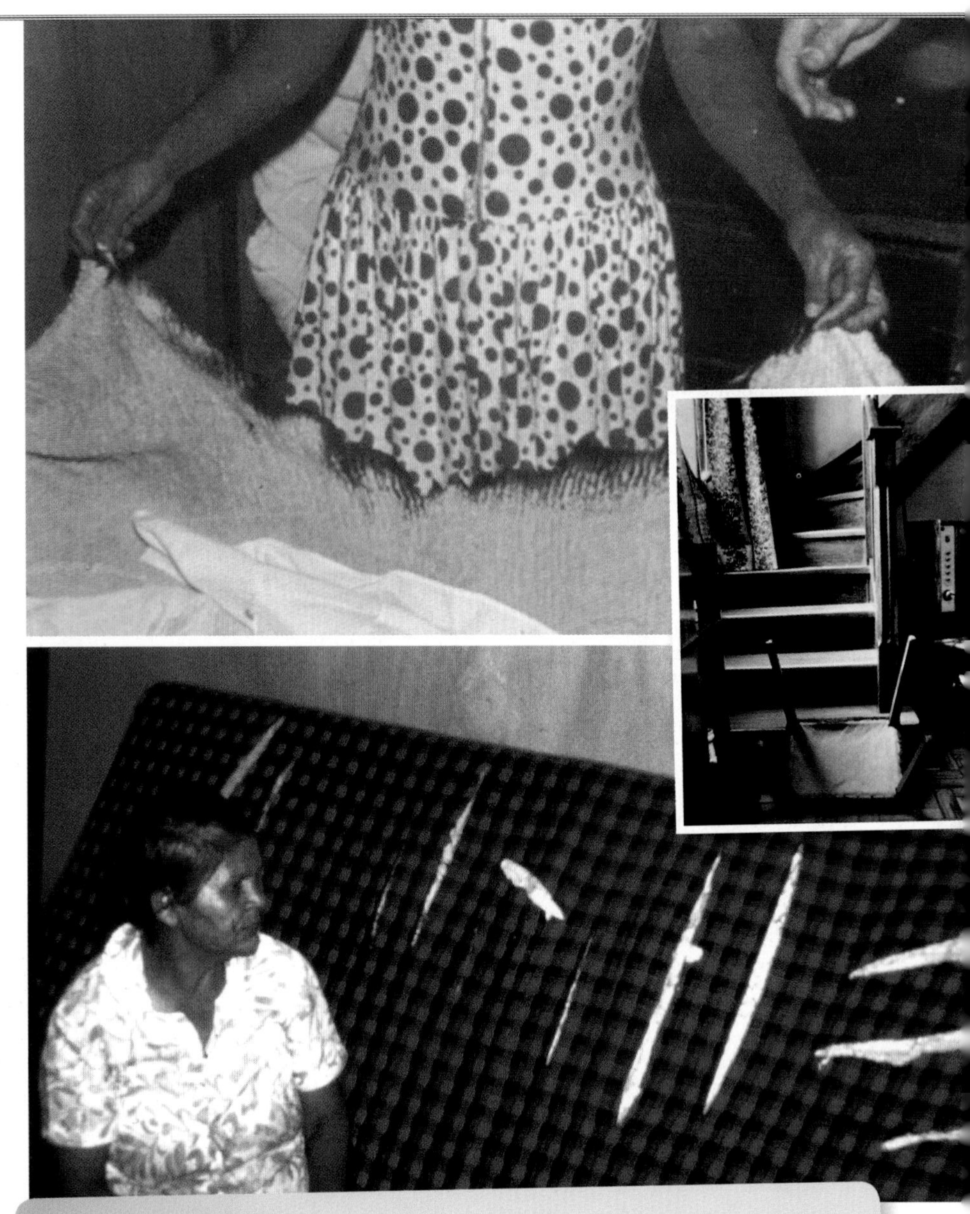

Poltergeists in Brazil
During the early 1970s, paranormal investigator Guy Lyon Playfair was living in Brazil, where he investigated numerous poltergeist outbreaks around the city of São Paulo. At Suzano in 1970, spontaneous fires were breaking out, and one witness told Guy she saw a calendar on the wall go up in flames. She even burned herself when she checked if the fire was real! The photograph shows a blanket that was burned.

Furniture was damaged by an invisible slasher at Guarulhos in 1973 (see photograph); and also in 1973, when he was sleeping in a house haunted by a poltergeist at Ipiranga, Guy photographed a stool which fell downstairs into his room. It had been stored on top of a wardrobe in the room above, and had apparently come through a closed door. There was no one in the room: less than a minute later, a drawer of clothes was thrown from the window.

The Rosenheim poltergeist
For a few months beginning in November 1967, inexplicable events took place in a solicitor's office in Rosenheim in Bavaria, Germany. Light bulbs exploded, neon lights would go out and were found to have been unscrewed, fuses blew, bangs were heard, and the telephones went haywire with large bills being received. Technical investigations of the power supply and telephone failed to solve the mystery.

Professor of Parapsychology Dr Hans Bender was called in, and he noted that the phenomena happened when a new girl, Anne-Marie Schneider, was present. As she walked down the corridor, electric lights hanging from the ceiling would begin to swing, an event which was captured on video (see photograph); and glass from exploding bulbs flew towards her. In her presence paintings on the walls would swing, filing cabinets would move and their drawers would shoot out – but all activity ceased when she was away from the office.

the boiler room, a handicapped man who wheeled himself off the balcony, and an executive who shot himself in Room 32. The nosiest ghost is said to be Harvey the caretaker, who was killed in a lift accident in 1935 when it came down on his head. Desk clerk Debra Altherr said: "He plays with the lights too." Other manifestations include noises akin to "moans and groans" and a lady in white. (Source - Los Angeles Times 12th April).

HAUNTED LIBRARY: Pam Ziobran was working late at the Deep River Public Library in Connecticut, recently, when she sensed she was not alone. She said: "It was just a feeling. It was just so light and airy, like a female coming down the stairs. It was very, very real." Susan Oehl was the only person in the area when she heard a sound coming from the next room, and reports: "I heard distinctly a woman clearing her throat, but when I checked there was nobody there." The ghost is said to be a man, but no more details of him are known. (Source - Connecticut Courant 20th April).

COLD SPOTS: The Oakdale Leader newspaper claims that its premises in Oakdale, California, is haunted. In April the Western Region Paranormal Research (WRPR) group conducted an investigation on the premises. Editor Marg Jackson reports: "One evening, working late, I had my daughter at the office with me and saw her go past my door, out of the corner of my eye. I went back to check on her, because I assumed she went to the break room but when I got there, the lights were out and she wasn't there. In fact, she was still seated at the desk up front when I went there. So she wasn't who I saw go past my door. And no one else was in the building." (Source - Oakdale Leader 21st Apr).

COWBOY: Brent Aspinall who owns the Emerado bar in Gilby, North Dakota, believes a ghost called Cowboy tugged his shirt while he was working behind the bar, and the incident has even been captured on CCTV, although the ghost was not seen. On another occasion customer, Penny Sorteberg, reports: "I saw a figure by the dart board. It was quick

Sightings

and fast. It was an older man with dark rimmed glasses and a hat that snapped in front." Brock McAdam, another customer said: "All of a sudden I heard a tap on the bar, and I got chills and my hair stood up on my arms and just got cold all of a sudden." (SOURCE - WOAI.COMNEWS 1ST MAY).

SOPHEA: What is said to be the ghost of a dead actress called Sophea is still making curtain calls today at the Schonell Theatre, University of Queensland, in Australia. Several members of staff, including cleaners and supervisors have been frightened by the ghost who wears "an old fashioned long dress and appears as a real 'flesh-and-blood' human." She has been seen to enter a particular dressing room but never leave. When checked no one is inside even though there is no other way out. Sophea also plays games with the cleaners, discarding rubbish in a previously cleaned area. Vera, one of the cleaners says she just tells the spirit to "stop it" and that "usually does the trick." (SOURCE - ABC.NET 15TH APRIL).

AFTER THE DISASTER: Survivors of the Chilean earthquake claim they can hear the screams and moans of those that died in the tragedy. The Elmercurio News reports: "Ghostly shadows cross the Cardenal Raul Silva Henriquez Bridge in Constitucion; cell phone screens light up suddenly, as if trying to receive phone calls. The moans and tears of children and their mothers resonate throughout the wooded Curanipe camping grounds, where thirty people lost their lives on February 27th." Ricardo Figueroa, a psychiatrist specializing in disasters at the Catholic University Hospital, explains: "When unexpected deaths or states of grief exist, it is normal for people to report experiences that may catalogued, in quotation marks, as supernatural. But this is a normal occurrence that increases during catastrophes." (SOURCE - ELMERCURIO NEWS 5TH MAY).

DJINN: A series of fires in Deir al-Balah in the Gaza strip are being blamed, by locals, on the Djinn (genies). Two unexplained house fires in March and late April caused such an uproar with the local population that the police had to issue a statement denying that Djinn were responsible. The police also threatened legal action to anyone who said that Spirits were responsible for the fires. (SOURCE - TRUESLANT.COM 24TH APRIL).

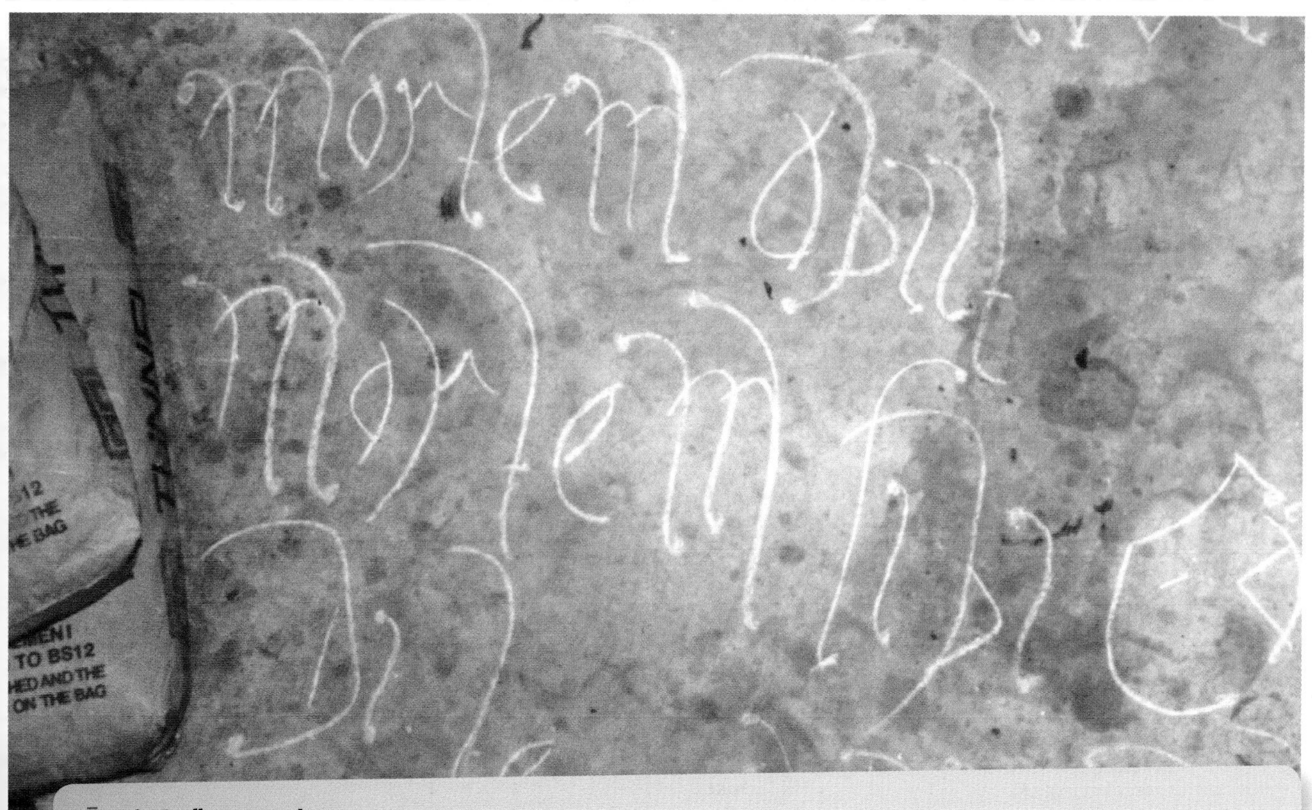

The Dodleston mystery
The strange events at Dodleston near Chester began in late 1984 and lasted for a couple of years. A small cottage which was home to a young couple, Ken and Debbie, became the focus of a poltergeist outbreak, with furniture being thrown around and small items, such as cat-food tins, being stacked up. The photograph shows their wrecked kitchen.

The mystery deepened when strange messages were found on their computer. This was many years before most people started to have computers at home, and long before email was invented. Ken and Debbie learned that their correspondent, named Tomas Harden, had lived in a cottage on the same site as theirs, but in the 16th century. He seemed to be still alive, and he also started to write messages in chalk on the cottage floor (see photograph). Between 1984 and 1987 about 300 computer messages were received – some of them were dated 2109! When Tomas had to leave his cottage, in his 16th-century world, all communications ceased.

Because the story was so incredible, many people suspected it was all an elaborate hoax, but this was denied by Ken and Debbie – and often there would be no one in the cottage when the computer messages arrived. The still-unexplained events were described in Ken Webster's book The Vertical Plane. [© Ken Webster/Fortean Picture Library]

MIRROR IMAGE: A couple claimed they took a photograph of "a weeping girl" in the mirror of their hotel room in Watford, Hertfordshire, and then fled from the building in terror. They said: "The girl had curly locks and a check dress, and was crying." After the hotel owners saw the picture they locked the room so that nobody else could stay in there. A guest said: "The couple went to reception and were hysterical. The man said he wanted to get out of the room ASAP. They were upset and said the image of the child was crying and it was moving in the mirror." Investigations by UPIA revealed that the photograph was a hoax manipulated by the iPhone application 'Ghost Capture'. (Source - The Sun 6th May).

PARK AFTERLIFE: Paul Reed was walking his dog Harry through Kelsey Park in Beckenham, Kent, when he saw a ghost behind a park bench. He said: "Harry wasn't his usual self. He was cowering back towards me and I must admit I was shocked when I saw the ghost appear before my eyes. Another walker said the ghost could belong to a woman who was buried in the park in the late 19th century." He describes the apparition as being a "woman dressed in Victorian clothing." Harry the dog would not move from the spot while the phantom was present. A local said a woman who used to walk in the park loved it so much, she was buried there, and could be the phantom that Mr Reed and Harry saw. You can see the pictures at http://hauntedbritain.blogspot.com (Source - The Telegraph: 14th May).

STAGE FRIGHT: According to recent investigations by the Everything Paranormal of New England group, the Hackmatack Playhouse in Maine, is haunted by a "singing woman, and a very angry Native American." The group's founder, Renee Alling, assured staff and customers that the spirits were not there to harm anyone. Photographs of orbs have been taken and alleged contact with the Native American has taken place via rapping and tapping. (Source - fosters.com 10th May).

Science has always denied the possibility of paranormal powers, as they do not follow the rules. Like ghosts and poltergeists, strange powers are inconvenient: they just will not go away.

Telepathy and clairvoyance both involve the power of the mind to obtain and convey information. Precognition is the perception of events that are still in the future. Some people claim psychic powers, being able to communicate with the dead, or to produce psychic art, psychic music or automatic writing. Psychic healing is just one of the ways in which gifted people use their powers for the good of others.

Psychokinesis (PK) is the power to affect objects using the power of the mind, and some people can harness PK to perform metal-bending, levitation, and thoughtography.

If all these abilities one day become scientifically respectable, humanity will truly enter a new age, and the scientific developments of the 20th century will seem very primitive by comparison.

Strange powers

Self-healing dervishes

Scientists at the Paramann Programme Laboratories in Jordan have been testing dervishes from the Sufi School of Tariqa Casnazaniyyah ('the way that is known to no one') because of their ability to injure themselves and heal the wounds within seconds.

Their brainwaves were monitored as they stabbed themselves, pierced themselves with skewers, swallowed glass and razor blades, burned themselves for 5 to 15 seconds, were bitten by poisonous snakes and scorpions, and more. A few drops of blood would appear on the wound but in all cases the wounds would heal within seconds and there were no infections, even though the implements they used were not sterilised. However, if a dervish should be accidentally injured, he suffered the same pain, bleeding, infection and so on as any other person.

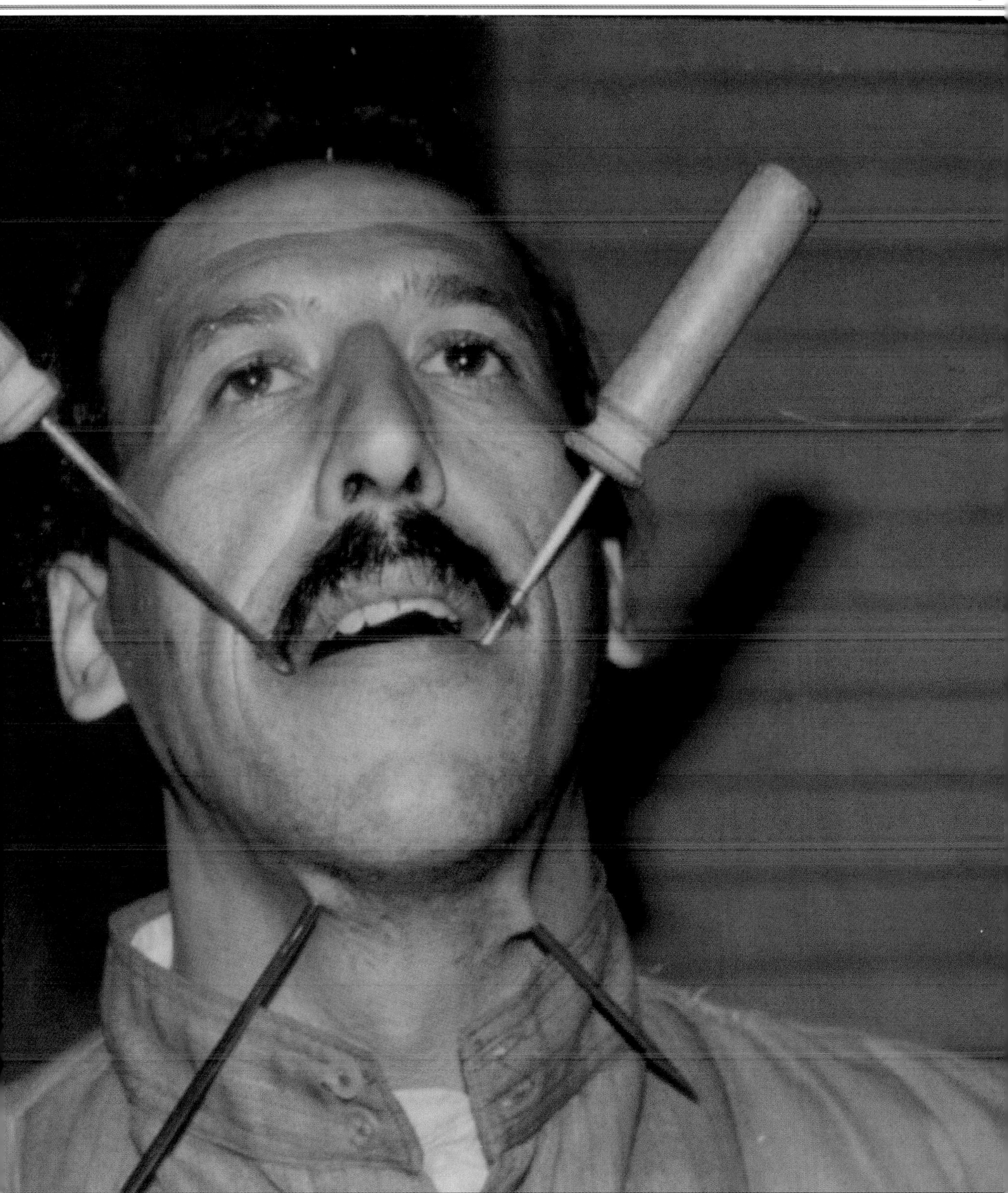

Sightings

Taken from the pages of
Paranormal Magazine

NESSIE CAUGHT ON CAMERA?: Ian Monckton and Tracey Gordon pulled into a layby near Invermoriston at 11pm, with the window down, and heard a commotion in the loch. Using the car headlights, they snapped a picture of what the believe to be Nessie. Mr Monckton said: 'There is clearly a very large shape in the water that looks aquatic a few metres out from where I was standing and you just see the tips of the trees lower down the slope to the loch in the photo.' He has passed the picture to naturalist Adrian Shine of the Loch Ness Project to get his expert opinion. (SOURCE - DONALD WILSON, HIGHLAND NEWS).

YORKSHIRE PANTHER: A witness relates: 'I was sat on the front seat above the driver of the Classic Coach Tours Bus, and we had left York City at 4.15pm to avoid heavy traffic. We travelled along the A1M which is three lanes of traffic, travelling north, and a car on our left overtook the bus; we were in the middle lane, and there was a car or vehicle on our right, which was just about to overtake us. As I watched out of the front window, I saw what I thought to be a feral cat (small), but as we drew closer, the cat was not small, but very large. The cat had nowhere to go, and turned into our lights, snarled and drew close to the ground, and then bounded towards us on the left side of the bus. Its large thighs and the huge thickness of the base of its tail (about 7-8 inches wide), flew past the window into the blackness. The cat had leapt into the road and the middle lane, but because of two other vehicles coming ahead of the coach, it could not attempt to reach the sides of the road at either side, and had no choice to try and escape anyway it could. I hoped it had not been hit by anything behind us.' (SOURCE - BIG CATS IN BRITAIN).

WINGED THINGS: A motorist on the outskirts of Harrisburg, Pennsylvania, spotted 'a huge bird-like creature drop from the trees', and approach his vehicle. The witness got out for a better look. He said the creature 'seemed to soar or glide without flapping its wings – it looked prehistoric'. In Washington County a 'huge dark-coloured flying creature' which resembled a giant bat was spotted circling cars. One

Psychic Joe Nuzum
There is evidence to suggest that some people have the ability to raise themselves off the ground by paranormal means, or to similarly cause objects to levitate. Joe Nuzum is an American whose alleged psychic abilities were studied for more than 15 years in the 1980s-90s by psychiatrist and psychic researcher Dr Berthold E. Schwarz, of Florida. Dr Schwarz found that Nuzum was 'in a trance state maybe 90 percent of the time', adding, 'He's in his own world. He makes reality conform to his own standards of vivid fantasy.'

Dr Schwarz became convinced that Nuzum is no illusionist but a man with genuine psychic powers, including the ability to materialise water or blood, dematerialise crystals, bend laser beams – and levitate. This picture of him levitating is one of a sequence that shows that his unsupported position remained unchanged. There is no blurring caused by movement, and a photo-technician who independently studied the negatives could find no strings or attachments.

A medium's power
Stanislawa Tomczyk was a Polish medium who took part in psychic experiments under strict test conditions with leading researchers in the early 20th century, including some conducted by the Society for Psychical Research and others at the Physical Laboratory in Warsaw. The photograph shows her levitating a spoon, and as well as levitating objects for researchers, she was able to influence a roulette wheel and stop a clock in a glass case.

of the drivers was spotted taking a photograph of the creature but no one has come forward with a photograph yet. (SOURCE - HTTP://STANGORDONUFO.COM).

BIGFOOT: The Pennsylvania Bigfoot Society (PBS) received a report of a large hair-covered man-like beast climbing up a house lattice onto decking. The witness watched it from her patio door in Warren County. (PBS)

QUEENSLAND TIGER: Colin Rossow, who lives in Glynwood, Gympie, Australia, believes there is a giant cat stalking the area. He said: 'I grew up in the bush and I know when big cats are around. I've heard this cat before. It's not a kangaroo or a dog... it's a caterwauling and sometimes it sort of grunts and chuffs.' A recent find of a print in the area is all the confirmation Mr Rossow needed to assume that he has been correct all along, despite protestations from witnesses. (SOURCE - THE COURIER, AUSTRALIA).

YAMAPOIKARYA: A large mystery cat has been spotted on Japan's Iriomote Island. Known as the Yamapikarya, reports first surfaced from hunters chasing wild boar. They described it as being similar to a leopard or jaguar, 1 to 1.3 metres in length and stoutly built, with a dark yellow or orange coat. This is most definitely not to be confused with the Iriomote wildcat. (SOURCE - BRENT SWANCER, CRYPTOMUNDO.COM)

GUARD MONKEY: A monkey in India's southern Karnataka is attacking officials who are attempting to knock down a shrine dedicated to the monkey god Hanuman. The usually calm monkey is placing itself between the shrine and the officials. Video footage of the monkey keeping them at bay has been taken. The temple was built around 20 years ago and a dead monkey was buried beneath the idol. (SOURCE - DPA - ANI - EARTHTIMES.ORG).

SCOTTISH WOLVES: A witness claims she came across two unusual creatures near Moffat, and reports: 'We were driving from Moffat and a few miles past the Devil's Beeftub we came onto a long stretch of road with the forest on either side. Ahead on the road we saw what looked like a large black dog but as we came closer we saw that it was more wolf-like. It was then we saw another one on top of the embankment. We slowed down a

Sightings

bit and they just leapt over the ditch and ran into the forest. Me and my daughter were stunned.' (SOURCE - PEEBLESHIRE NEWS, JAN 23).

ON TWO LEGS: Sam Bradbury spotted a strange creature on Falmouth beach, Swanpool, Cornwall, but no one believed him. Sam reports that it was nearly dusk when he came upon the creature walking on its hind legs. It had a bushy tail and cat-like face. Mr Bradbury submitted a drawing of the animal to Newquay Zoo but a spokesman said: 'We have no clue what it is. It doesn't look like anything I have ever seen. The closest thing is a wallaby, although that does not have a cat's face.' Sam said: 'It was about two and a half feet tall, really quite a big thing. It was bigger than a dog, had the face of a cat with eyes that were glazed over and luminescent like a lion's at night. It left when it saw me.' (SOURCE - THE WEST BRITON, FEB 19).

SWANPOOL BEAST RETURNS: After the initial sighting by Sam Bradbury two more people have come forward claiming to have spotted the two-legged animal. Rita Shelton, on Pendennis headland, and local historian Sheila Bird, who spotted it animal back in 2006. She says: 'It was about 10.15am and I was walking across the cliff path from Gyllyngvase to Swanpool and around the pool when I noticed a large black form up in the branches. I looked closer to see a large cat-like animal with its ears pointing up. It was high up in the trees so in order for the creature to get up in the branches it must have been quite agile. It was curled in a cat's cradle position and looked a bit like an enormous Kuala bear with a long bushy tail. It had long black hair with a brownish tinge.' (SOURCE - THE WEST BRITON, FEB 19 / FALMOUTH PACKET, FEB 25).

HOUSEWIFE'S NIGHTMARE: A giant rat, with teeth over one-inch-long has been caught in the Chinese province of Fujian. The rodent weighed six pounds and had a tail 12 inches long, and was caught by a local rat-catcher in the city of Fuzhou. He told local reporters that he had to muster up a lot of courage before he grabbed its tail and picked it up by the scruff of its neck. 'I did it, I caught a rat the size of a cat!' he shouted. He then stuffed the animal in a bag and went home! The local forestry unit identified the rat as a bamboo rat but said they would have to examine it closely before making an official identification. (SOURCE - TELEGRAPH, FEB 18).

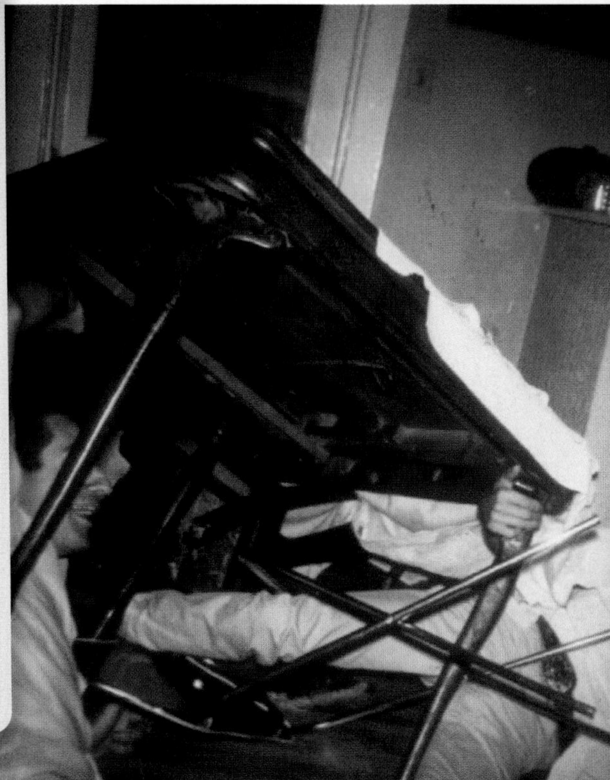

Table levitation
Countless table levitations were witnessed by the members of SORRAT (Society for Research on Rapport and Telekinesis) during their experiments in Missouri, USA, in the 1960s and later. The levitation which took place on 3 September 1976 looks peaceful enough, but ten years earlier on 7 June 1966 the participants had experienced a particularly dramatic session when an 80-pound dining table with six legs levitated to a height of 4 feet, hovered for a moment, and then crashed to the floor, breaking off two of the legs. Fortunately someone was on hand to capture the events as they occurred – and thankfully no one was hurt.

Indian Rope Trick

The classic version of the Indian rope trick has a magician throwing a rope into the air, which stands erect while a boy assistant climbs up and disappears. A more elaborate version has the magician shouting after the boy and, on getting no response, picking up a knife or sword and climbing up after him, also disappearing. An argument is heard and limbs start to fall, the magician reappears, gathers up the limbs and covers them: finally the boy reappears, restored to life and apparently unharmed.

If this sounds impossible, that's because it is: a variation of the trick was performed, but it was unintentionally elaborated by the witnesses recounting what they had seen many years later. Also, mass hypnosis, and poor viewing conditions, e.g. at dusk, may have contributed to the false memories.

However, there are early accounts of similar tricks from the Far East, so its exotic origins may be genuine. In the 1930s The Magic Circle offered 100 guineas to anyone able to perform the trick and Arthur Claud Darby, a performer going by the name of Karachi, took up the challenge. As shown in the photograph, his son climbed the rope, but did not disappear.

BORNEO DRAGON: What was said to be a snake over 100ft long was photographed along the Baleh river in Borneo. The picture was snapped by a member of a disaster team from a helicopter. Now debate rages over whether the photograph is genuine or not. According to legend, the Nabau was a terrifying snake more than 100ft in length and with a dragon's head and seven nostrils. Villagers today report sightings of the creature which is said to be a shape shifter. (SOURCE - DAILY MAIL, FEB 20).

YETI EVIDENCE: In the last four months in the Kemerovo district, in south-west Siberia, twelve 'credible' witnesses have come forward insisting that they have seen the Yeti. The 'animals' have been seen in a mountainous area known as Azzaskoy Caves, 60 km from Tashtagol town centre. The locals refer to the local Yeti as the 'Black People'. They are described as being 1.5-2 meters tall, covered in black fur 'and walking upright: like humans'. The University of Kemerovo has now organised a 'full scientific expedition to finally confirm or deny their existence'. Some academics believe that the creatures may be a relic hominid population distantly related to human beings. Meanwhile in the UK Sir David Attenborough is reported as saying that 'the evidence for the Yeti is very convincing'. He adds: 'I'm baffled by the Abominable Snowman. Very convincing footprints have been found at 19,000ft. No-one does that for a joke. I think it's unanswered." (SOURCE - ALLNEWSWEB.COM, FEB 17 / DAILY MAIL, MARCH 1).

WEREWOLF ATTACK: Kelly Martins Becker claims she was attacked by a werewolf in the São Sepé, Rio Grande do Sul, area of Brazil. She made a sketch of her attacker that she claims was half-man, half-dog. Police are considering the possibility that the attacker was a man dressed in a werewolf costume. Ms Martin was attacked on January 28 and said: 'The creature looked as big as a dog, it was standing on its back feet and walked as if it were a man.' The police confirmed the girl had scratches on her face and arm. This is not the only report of this nature that has come out of the country. In July 2008 a 'half man and half wolf" creature was reportedly stealing sheep and breaking into houses. In April of the same year residents around Santana do Livramento, Rio Grande do Sul, were attacked by a 'man in a black cape'. (SOURCE - GLOBO.COM: FEB 6).

Sightings

THUNDERBIRDS: 'We were approximately four miles west of La Pryor, Texas, when my father slowed down and crossed over into the oncoming lane to avoid hitting a deer that was feeding right on the edge of the eastbound lane on which we traveled,' reports a witness. 'As my father re-entered our lane we came upon a very large bird, gray in color, with a wingspan we estimate to be about 8-10 feet wide and had no visible feathers. We estimate the wingspan based on the width of the car in which we traveled.' The incident occurred on February 9. The previous day in Pueblo, Colorado, another witness was sitting in the study of the Rawlings Library when he saw 'a huge black bird' through the window. 'It was flying really high, about as high as a small plane flies when you can view it from the ground. I wanted someone to witness this with me, I thought about blurting out everyone look, but I couldn't disrupt, so I got my daughter's attention and she was able to witness this as well. This is really strange, I have never seen anything like it before I didn't even think anything like this could exist.' (SOURCE - PHANTOMS & MONSTERS, FEBRUARY 14 / DEVIL MONKEYSEMAIL LIST, FEB 10).

MYSTERY BODY: A body fished out of the Big Black River, Mississippi, was found not to be human. The speculation is that it is an unidentified animal, but the mystery is why it was thought to be the body of a person until they'd landed it. How human-shaped was it? Warren County Coroner Doug Huskey said he could identify nothing from the remains. (SOURCE - VICKSBURG POST, FEB 17).

ALIEN PHOTOGRAPHED: News has recently emerged of a photograph taken in 1935 of an alleged alien in Alaska. The anonymous owner of the photograph explained: 'The included picture was taken by my grandfather in the early 1930s. I scanned the image immediately after he gave it to me last week. I wish to remain anonymous since I don't want anything to do with any research or whatever on this. I know it looks like an alien or a Bigfoot and I know my grandfather was telling me the truth about him taking this picture. That's why I think it should be in the right hands. You are the only one I'm sending this to, so please respect my privacy and don't contact me about this.' (SOURCE - B J BOOTH, OF UFO CASEBOOK.)

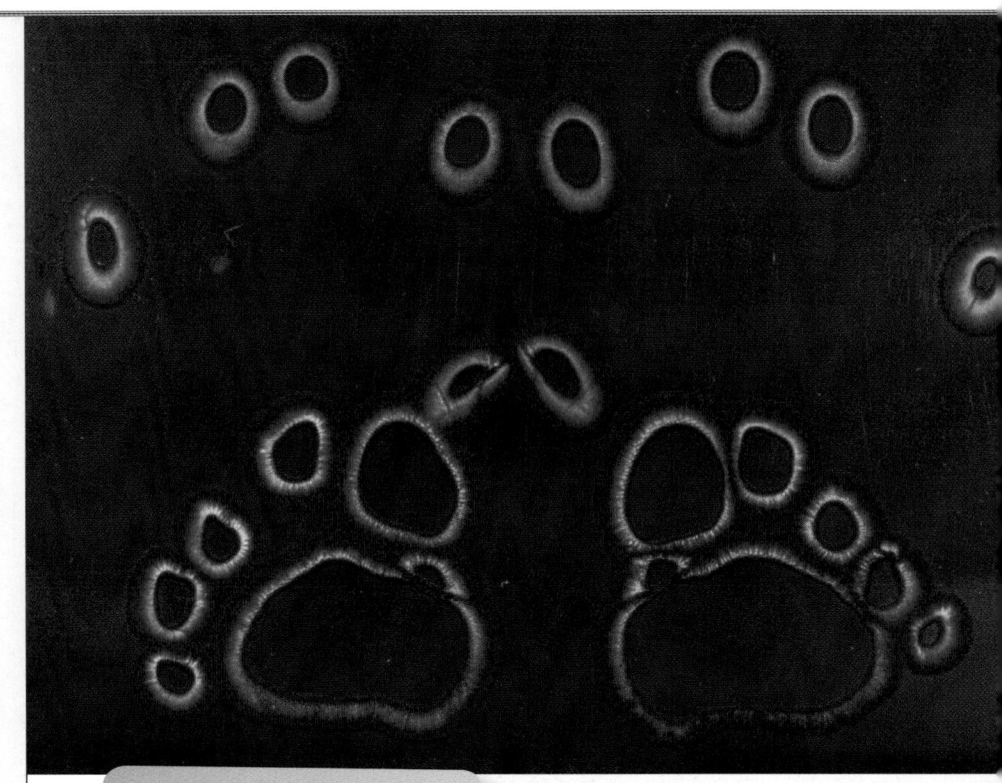

Kirlian photography

Kirlian photography is a means of taking photographs without the use of a camera: objects are placed directly on to film within a high frequency electrical field. The effect is to produce startling images showing bright splashes of colour which the inventors of the technique in 1949, Russians Semyon and Valentina Kirlian, believed showed the life-force not only of living things but also of rocks and minerals. It is also held by some that the corona of light seen around a part of a human body is evidence of the aura.

Enthusiasts of Kirlian photography have demonstrated that the vivid glow apparently emanating from a plant fades as it dies and also diminishes when a plant is cooked for food. It has also been claimed that Kirlian photography can be used to diagnose diseased tissue and even reveal whether or not certain objects have come from haunted locations.

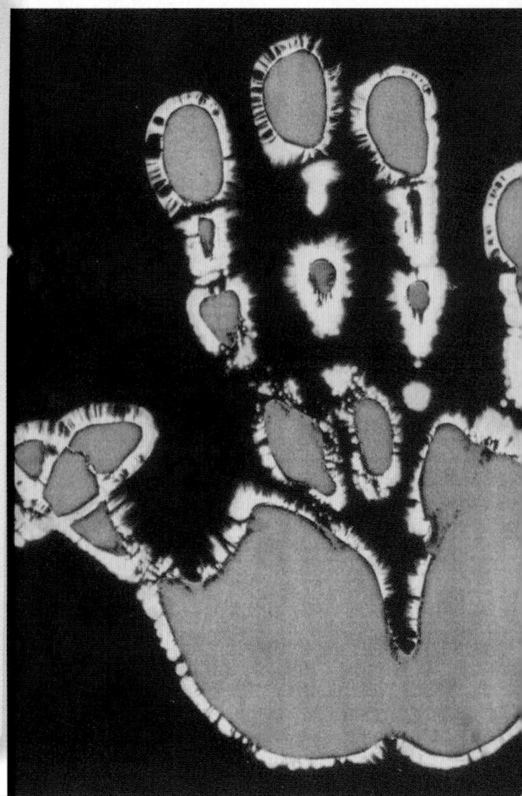

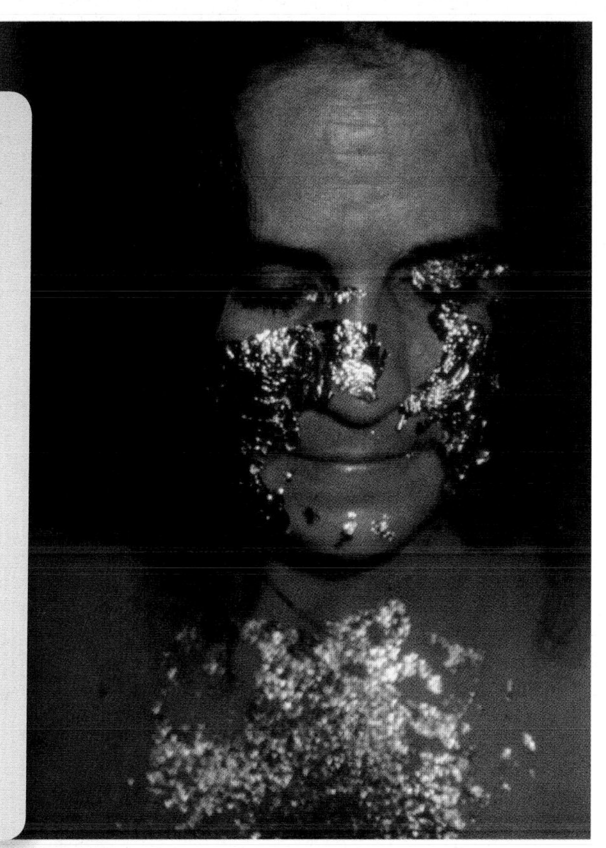

The amazing 'Katie'
During sessions in Florida in the 1980s with psychical researcher Dr Berthold Eric Schwarz, a woman identified as 'Katie' began to generate copper foil on her skin while she was in a trance state. The foil could be pulled off, just like peeling sunburnt skin away. The substance was found to be approximately 98% copper and 2% zinc. On one occasion copper foil was discovered 'growing' on the inside of a sealed bottle handled by Katie.

Dr Schwarz wondered whether the copper materialisations had any relationship with the production of ectoplasm – the strange, filmy material which often featured in seances in the past. Dr Schwarz tested Katie under laboratory conditions and was convinced that her foil production was genuinely paranormal.

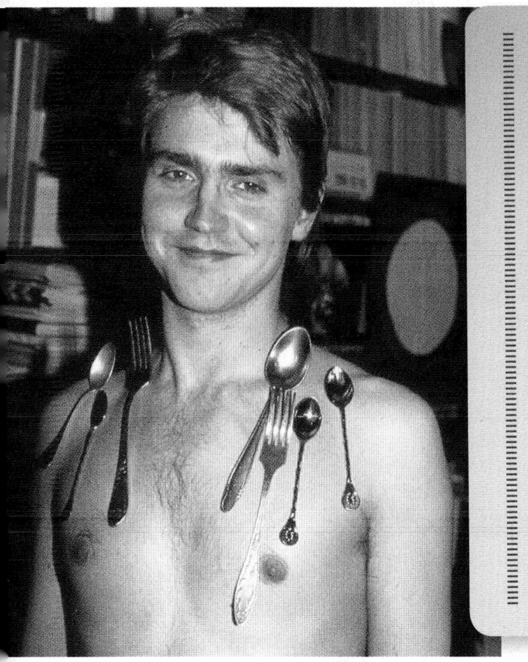

Human magnetism
Russian parapsychologist Edward Naumov with cutlery clinging to his body, apparently unsupported by any form of adhesive or artificial attachment. Mr Naumov demonstrated this ability in his Moscow apartment to Kevin P Braithwaite, who was making a documentary on Russian parapsychology in 1994.

Such 'human magnetism' has allegedly been demonstrated by a number of people, indeed during his visit Mr Braithwaite found he was able to do the same. He wrote: 'The more I seemed to concentrate the better the objects "stuck". Two other people were observers that evening and noted that the forks slightly resisted any attempt to remove them as if they were magnetic.'

However, Mr Braithwaite has since been unable to repeat the demonstration and wonders whether the presence of Mr Naumov was necessary as an 'energiser'.

UK BIG CAT FLAP: March was another bumper month for sightings of large mystery felines in the UK and here are a few. What was described as 'a panther cub' was spotted in Stoke Hammon, Leicestershire. Karen Allison of Big Cats in Britain is on the trail of the big black cat spotted near Bromyard Road, Worcester, described as 'jet-black with a long curled up tail'. Two witnesses walking their dog in Howard Park, Kilmarnock, saw a large 'striped unusual cat'. Their dogs became frightened and the witnesses headed off in the opposite direction. BCIB received video footage from a couple in Measham, Derbyshire, of a black feline, but with no scale to the photograph it could be a large domestic. On March 23, Tony Young saw what he believes was a dead big cat in Preston Dock, Lancashire. He said: 'I was walking on the dock at about 8.15am and I saw it. The face of it looks like a big cat, like a puma or a panther. It doesn't look like a soft toy because a soft toy would have a friendly face, this had a really mean face and a short snout.' The photograph can be seen at http://www.lep.co.uk/weirdnews/Riddle-of-39big-cat39-seen.5130083.jp. The Cambridgeshire Post printed a rather dubious photograph of cat in a field, obviously Photoshopped and asked if the 'Fen Tiger' had been photographed at last! Reports have also come in form Norwich, Yorkshire, Devon, Aberdeenshire, Kent, Teesside, Sussex, Surrey, Lancashire and Oxfordshire. (Source - Big Cats in Britain www.bigcatsinbritain.org; Lancashire Evening Post; Worcester Journal).

DEAD CRITTER: Tessa Barnett and her son Austin have twice seen a 'mysterious critter' near Cherry Hill, Pequea Township, Pennsylvania. They describe it as 'large, about 200 pounds, with coarse hair; (it) moved in an odd, slithery, scampering way.' Locals say it could be a lost goat called TJ. Not far away, Jo Anne Thomas found an odd looking animal dead by the roadside, she said: 'The animal had hooves and an ugly-looking face, it was not something I had ever seen before.' (Source - Lancasteronline: March 9).

ET IN BERKELEY: A blurry shape spotted on Google Maps standing in undergrowth in Berkeley Heights, New Jersey, has been claimed as an alien. Anthony Lombardo, 65, said he was responsible, although others disagree. Mark Johnson, founder

Sightings

and lead researcher of North Jersey Paranormal Research said: 'From what I saw, it is a blurry image that could be anything.' He described the shape as a blob with a bulbous top, but he admits the light beam coming down does look rather strange. Federal Aviation Administration spokesman Jim Peters also finds the beam of light interesting. 'The light looks like a Star Wars lightsaber that I bought for my two sons a year ago,' he said. (SOURCE - STAR LEDGER: MARCH 2009).

BATSQUATCH: A hiker on Mt Shasta, California, saw a large creature fly out of a crevice. The witness reports: 'This thing was huge. It was as tall as a man, as stocky as Hulk Hogan and had leathery wings. The wingspan was at least 50 feet from one end to the other. I was holding up my camera, but was paralyzed with fear as this thing flew by. I didn't get a picture, sorry. It was flying or gliding fast, it seemed to have a head of a bat or maybe more like a fox. The damn thing finally flew into a clump of trees and vanished.' (SOURCE - PAUL DALE ROBERTS, HAUNTED AND PARANORMAL INVESTIGATIONS INTERNATIONAL: MARCH 20).

CHUPACABRA SNAPPED: A family in Nuevo Laredo, Mexico, claim a camera set up at their ranch caught the critter clearly. It has now frightened the family, who say they will not stay overnight on the ranch. The family, who wish not to be identified, said they can't forget the 'eyes of the creature creeping through the night'. (SOURCE - WWW.PRO8NEWS.COM MARCH 18).

MOBILE LEPRECHAUN: Residents of Mobile, Alabama, believe there is a leprechaun in the 'hood' that has taken up residence in a tree. Scores of people are lining up bumper to bumper in order to get a glimpse of the creature, which one woman believes is just a 'crackhead up in the tree'. While most of the residents are sceptical, several claim to have seen it and were 'terrified'. (SOURCE - PHANTOMS AND MONSTERS: MARCH 2009).

UK 'ALIEN' INVASION: Dave Bennett was walking his two dogs in Keighley town centre, West Yorkshire, when the dogs ran off to chase what he thought at first was a black and white cat. He and the dogs had a bit of a shock when the cat turned out to be a skunk that sprayed the canines. Meanwhile, nurse Jackie Morgan stared in disbelief at a meerkat outside

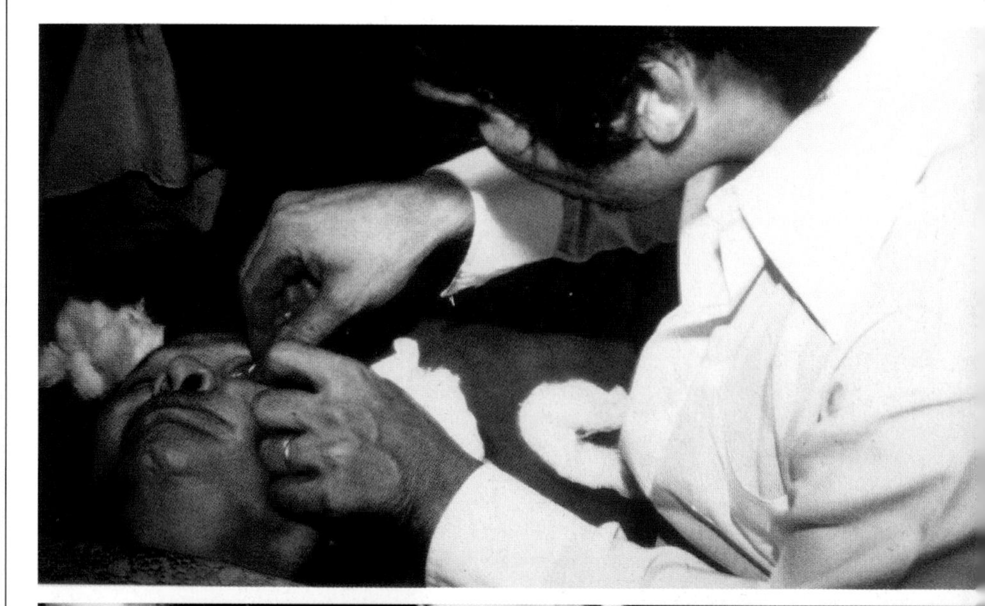

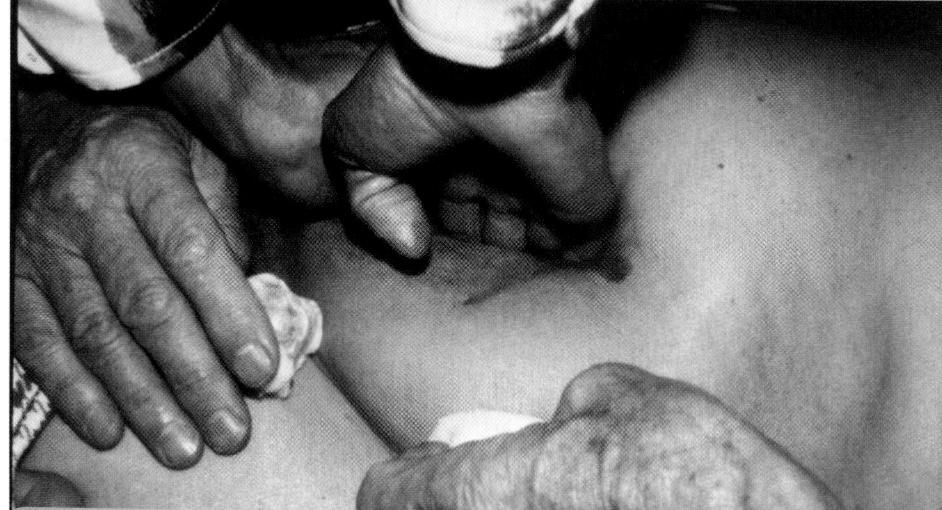

Psychic surgery

Psychic surgery first came to world-wide notice in the second half of the 20th century, when practitioners from Spiritualist communities in Brazil and the Philippines claimed to be able to perform surgical operations using only their bare hands. The surgeon would supposedly make an incision in the patient's flesh, slip his fingers in and pull out some bloody matter before wiping away the blood and leaving no scar.

Although many people have claimed to be healed, the 'surgery' has been condemned as a hoax by medical professionals, with any improvement to the patient's health being caused by the placebo effect. Stage magicians have been able to duplicate the effect, by palming small packets of animal entrails and blood, but this does not, of course, mean that all the procedures are hoaxed.

The photographs show: Ivan Trilha, a holistic healer and psychic surgeon from Paraguay, at work on a patient's eye in 1979; and Feliciano Omilles, a psychic surgeon from the Philippines, working in Mexico in the early 1970s.

Spontaneous human combustion
Mysterious fires are sometimes a feature of poltergeist outbreaks and normally they do not result in serious injury to the occupants of the house that is affected. However, some victims have experienced their clothing, and also their bedclothes, bursting into flames, and in 1975 an Indian lady, Shanti, was burned to death in such a case. Her house in Lucknow in India had been the focus of inexplicable phenomena, and one day she was set alight in her bed and died of her injuries.

A number of other sad cases are on record in which people have apparently burst into flames and either been badly injured or even burned to death, with no apparent involvement of a poltergeist. This phenomenon is known as 'spontaneous human combustion' and one strange aspect of it is that some victims have been found in their homes so badly burned that only a small part of the body was recognisable.

In 1951, elderly widow Mrs Mary Hardy Reeser was reduced to a pile of ashes in her Florida home. Only a foot in a slipper and a shrunken skull were found – but items only 5 feet away from the armchair where she died were untouched by the blaze.

The photograph shows all that remained of Dr John Irving Bentley, who died in Coudersport, Pennsylvania, USA, on 5 December 1966, presumed to be a victim of spontaneous combustion. He died in the bathroom, where a hole had burned through the floor, but all that remained of him was his lower leg and foot in a slipper.

her conservatory window in South Wales. David and Ena Webber of Walcott Avenue, Christchurch, Dorset, called the RSPCA who rescued a raccoon from a tree in their garden. Ena said: 'It had such a cute face.' Snakes have been popping up all over: Kerry Allison found two reptiles, along with crickets and a swarm of locusts, in her flat in Bournemouth. They are believed to have escaped from a nearby pet shop. The police were called in Sunderland after a woman found an 18-inch, brown and bronze-coloured snake in her kitchen. Nick Redfern reports that a witness on Staffordshire Cannock Chase spotted 'a python-sized creature ... brightly coloured with a powerful head'. African huntsman spiders turned up in boxes of bananas in Wick and Holsworthy. The corrugated crab was found in British waters in Cornwall for only the third time in a century, and a (rare) common dolphin and her calf was beached in waters near Dundee. A three-metre long oarfish came ashore near Tynemouth, and a photographer snapped a dorsal fin swimming close to bathers in Cornwall. (SOURCE - ANNOVA, DAILY POST, BBC NEWS, DAILY MAIL, SUNDAY SUN, THE METRO, THE TELEGRAPH, SUNDAY MERCURY, ALL MAY 2009)

SMALL BEAST OF BODMIN: A family in Bodmin had quite a surprise after photographing a mystery animal in their back garden; it was later identified as a palm civet, usually found in the Philippines, Himalayas and China. Stewart Muir, of Newquay Zoo, who caught the animal said: 'This is not the sort of animal you would expect to find roaming in the countryside, so it came as a big surprise to see the film footage of a civet. A small number are kept and bred in the UK as pets so I strongly suspect that it has escaped from a private collection. They are omnivorous and will eat almost anything. While they are not aggressive, they are capable of giving a nasty bite if cornered and would wreak havoc in anyone's hen house. With the mild climate in Cornwall, this chap could easily survive in the wild.' (SOURCE - THE SUN, APRIL 2009)

Religious phenomena

Over the centuries, many people have claimed to have seen a religious vision, usually of the Blessed Virgin Mary, and sometimes she has given messages to the visionaries. Such visions have rarely been photographed, despite there being thousands of witnesses.

Miracle cures have been reported at some of the shrines set up to commemorate the visions, the best-known of these shrines being at Lourdes in France where Bernadette Soubirous had a vision of the Virgin Mary in a cave in 1858. A fresh-water spring began to flow, and the water has been used for healing purposes ever since, with thousands of sick pilgrims visiting annually in hopes of a cure.

Other striking phenomena reported within the religious community include statues of saints which suddenly start to weep or bleed; devout believers producing stigmata in their hands and feet, the marks of the wounds that Christ suffered at his Crucifixion; and dead bodies that do not decay (known as incorruption).

'Striking phenomena reported within the religious community include statues of saints which suddenly start to weep or bleed; devout believers producing stigmata in their hands and feet.'

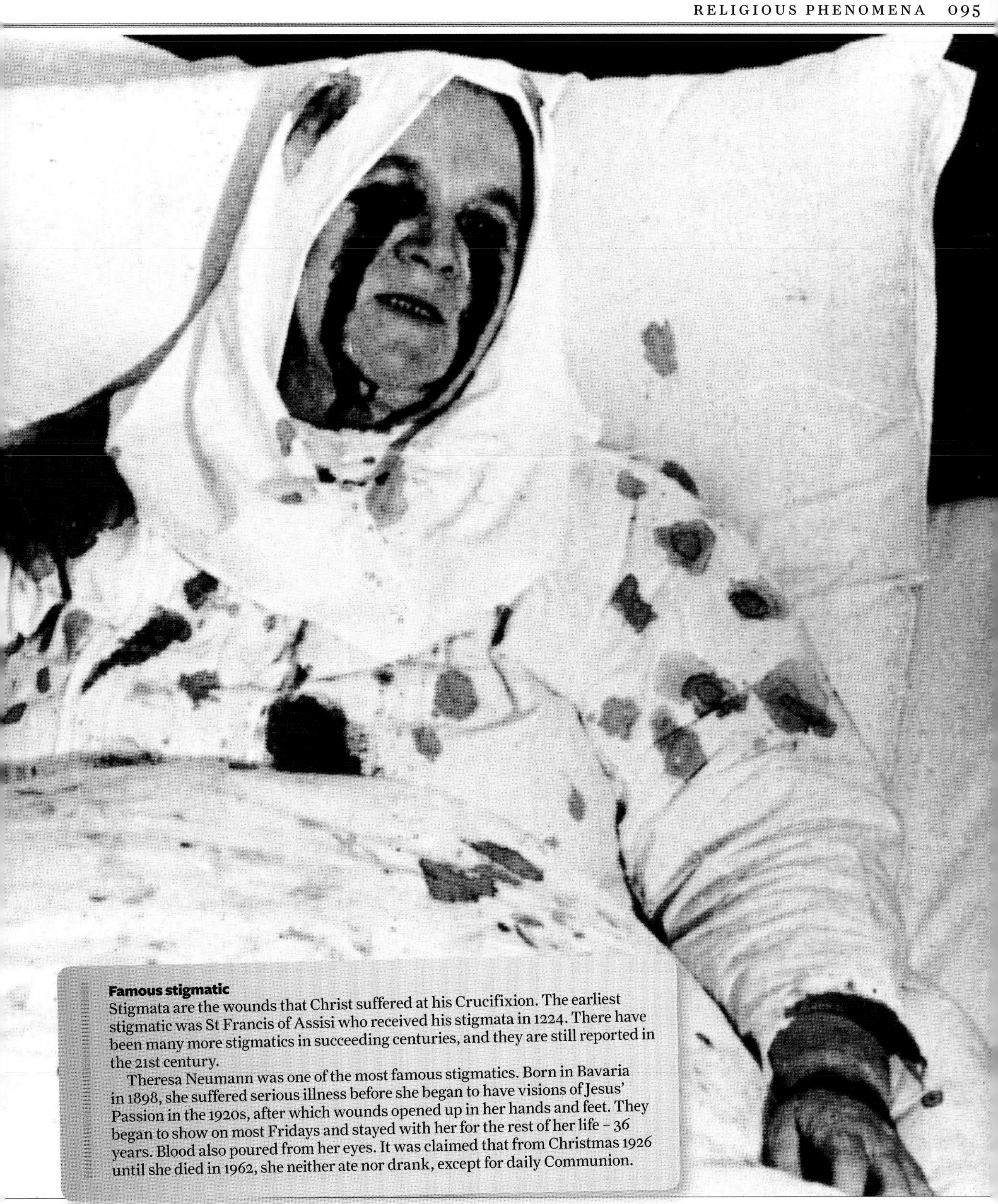

Famous stigmatic
Stigmata are the wounds that Christ suffered at his Crucifixion. The earliest stigmatic was St Francis of Assisi who received his stigmata in 1224. There have been many more stigmatics in succeeding centuries, and they are still reported in the 21st century.

Theresa Neumann was one of the most famous stigmatics. Born in Bavaria in 1898, she suffered serious illness before she began to have visions of Jesus' Passion in the 1920s, after which wounds opened up in her hands and feet. They began to show on most Fridays and stayed with her for the rest of her life – 36 years. Blood also poured from her eyes. It was claimed that from Christmas 1926 until she died in 1962, she neither ate nor drank, except for daily Communion.

Sightings

Taken from the pages of
Paranormal Magazine

UK BIG CAT FLAP: Big Cats in Britain received over 30 reports from around Britain in April, while most are just glimpses of a black feline in the night, they nevertheless leave a lasting impression on the witnesses. The organization has trigger cameras placed at three more locations. One is in a large garden in Worcestershire, where a large black cat described as a 'panther' has been taking midnight naps on the lawn. Another, in Kent on a farm where a black mystery feline has been spotted, and the other in Sightings compiler Mark Fraser's own back garden in Kilmaurs, Ayrshire, which looks out onto fields and the scene of several sightings.
(SOURCE - MARK FRASER WWW.BIGCATSINBRITAIN.ORG)

SUV RIPPED APART: A 'mystery creature' ripped apart a utility vehicle in N Carolina, USA. The authorities are stumped as to what animal could have caused such damage, remarking that they have never seen anything like it before. Even though the animal has left behind bite marks and scratches along with prints on the hood as big as tennis balls, no identification can be made. Vehicle owner Holly Gilliam, of Lincoln County, said: 'If it can do that to a vehicle what can it do to us? It scares me I never heard anything.'
(SOURCE - WCNC NEWS APRIL 6)

BIG NOISE: Locals are becoming increasingly concerned and worried about 'strange screams or animal noises' coming from the area around Lake Tahoma, Virginia. The eerie sounds are described as howls, screeching, moans and whoops. These noises have been heard near residences and by campers in their tents. Some folk think that there may be a Bigfoot in the area. (SOURCE - HTTP://WWW2.MCDOWELLNEWS.COM, APRIL 10)

BAT MAN: What was described as 'a very tall entity, standing some two metres tall, with two pairs of wings (one pair larger than the other) was seen in the state of Chihuahua, Mexico. It was also said to have a face covered with fur, and red bloodshot eyes, with 'small kangaroo-like hands'. The witness said: 'I saw a bulk on the roadway asphalt resembling a

The Hungary vision
On 3 September 1989, art-restorer Károly Ligeti was standing on scaffolding inside the church at Karácsond in Hungary, while he worked on the restoration of a painting over the altar. He asked someone to photograph him as he worked, and as he turned to face the camera, he noticed a female figure with a halo and surrounded by light, with an infant beside her. Although nobody else saw the vision, it was captured in the photograph. Ligeti thought that the figures were the Blessed Virgin Mary and the baby Jesus Christ.

People tried to find a logical explanation: perhaps it was a statue in the church that had been lit by the sun, or perhaps it was a hoax. However, the parish priest supported Ligeti, saying that there was no statue in the church that looked like the figures in the vision. Also, if Ligeti had been hoaxing, he would have chosen a familiar statue, not an unusual grouping of the figures with Jesus standing immediately in front of Mary. The vision, which remains unexplained in conventional terms, has had a profound effect on Károly Ligeti in the years since.

The Coptic Virgin
This photograph shows one of the many visions seen above the Coptic Orthodox Church of St Mary at Zeitoun, a suburb of Cairo in Egypt, in 1968. Two car mechanics were the first to see what looked like a nun dressed in white standing on the church roof. They thought she was going to jump but the figure disappeared. A week later she was seen again, and she continued to appear, with thousands of people gathering to see the visions, which lasted sometimes only for a few minutes, and sometimes for several hours. Flashing lights and clouds would gather over the church and luminous bird-like forms could be seen gliding around, before Our Lady appeared. She would move round the church roof, bowing to the crowds and moving her arms as if in blessing. The vision and church were swathed in auras of bluish-white light, which would sometimes move down the church walls to engulf the pilgrims below, and many miraculous cures were reported.

hunched-over man who seemed to be covered in a blanket. The figure suddenly stood up, taking two leaps forward and displaying a set of wings similar to those of a bat.' The witness accelerated away but the creature kept pace with the vehicle, looking in through the passenger window. Other witnesses in the area claims to have heard its screams. After a search the authorities could find no trace of the creature. (SOURCE - ING FRANCISCO PRIETO TORRES, RESIDENTS OF LA JUNTA, APRIL 6)

YOWIE FATALITY?: A seven month old puppy which had its head ripped from its shoulders is believed by Andrew McGinn to be the victim of a Yowie attack, although the dogs owners believe it was killed by dingoes. Mr McGinn said: 'The way the guy's dog was killed was typical of a Yowie. I know it sounds fanciful but over the past 100 years, dogs get killed or decapitated and people report feeling watched, having goats stolen or seeing some tall hairy thing in the days beforehand.' Large human-like prints found at the scene near Darwin, Australia, were said to have been hoaxed. Meanwhile in the Blue Mountains two back-packers near the landmark The Three Sisters, in Leura, claim to have seen a 'bigfoot' as they described it. The tourists first heard loud footsteps and the breaking of branches behind them, when they shone their torch they were shocked to see what they said was a Bigfoot, 'charge away into the distance'. (SOURCE - NORTHERN TERRITORY NEWS, APRIL 21)

MYSTERY ATTACKS: On April 9 four people in Ballia, India, were attacked by a mysterious animal: although the authorities say the culprit may be a fishing cat, others disagree. One victim was 'seriously injured' by the animal that has so far eluded not only capture but identification. (SOURCE - TIMES OF INDIA, APRIL 21)

WORMS INVADE: In China's northwest Xinjiang region, herdsmen have been forced out of the area by 'mystery worms'. They have taken 20,000 head of livestock with them. The worms, which are about 2cm

Sightings

(1 inch) in length and 'thorny green with black stripes' have not yet been identified by the authorities. Samples have been sent to Xinjiang Agricultural University. One herdsman said: 'The pasture was green a week ago. But now the worms are creeping around, and they even come into my house. I have to sweep them out several times an hour.' (REUTERS, MAY 5)

RATS AND SPIDERS: The false widow spider from the Canary Islands has established colonies in Devon, Dorset and Cornwall. The purple and black spider is about the size of a 1p coin but holds enough venom to kill a human. Its bite is not fatal, however, but it can cause pain and swelling. The spider has also been found elsewhere in Britain. In January Lyn Mitchell became critically ill after having been bitten by a false widow in her bed in Egremont, Cumbria. She said: 'I jumped out of bed, pulled the duvet and sheets back and saw a spider running over the other side. It was only tiny, black and shiny, and it ran so quickly. When I looked down I noticed two little pin marks on my chest.' The spiders began arriving over 100 years ago in banana shipments. Meanwhile, rat numbers in the UK are soaring out of control due to the fact that they are becoming resistant to poison: in fact, two towns in Berkshire have rat populations that are completely immune to any kind of poison. A British scientist warned that 'a new type of super rat with genetic mutations is infesting towns across Britain'. (SOURCE - YAHOO NEWS / THE GUARDIAN, 21ST MAY)

'ALLO NESSIE: 'Allo 'Allo actress Vickie Michelle claims she saw Nessie while on a pleasure cruise on Loch Ness. The crew picked up a signal on the sonar, and the actress rushed down to look. They saw five 'mysterious arch shapes' on the screen. The skipper of the boat said he had never seen anything like it in the 15 years he had been on the loch. Adrian Shine said: 'This has got me puzzled. It has every appearance of a genuine sonar contact. It certainly adds to the Loch Ness mystery and will be the subject of further investigation.' (SOURCE - DAILY RECORD, 28TH MAY)

MYSTERY SKULL: Plumber David Evans, working in Alvarado, Dallas, Texas, found a skull buried five feet underground beneath a school. Mr Evans said it was 'six inches from front to back and two inches wide.

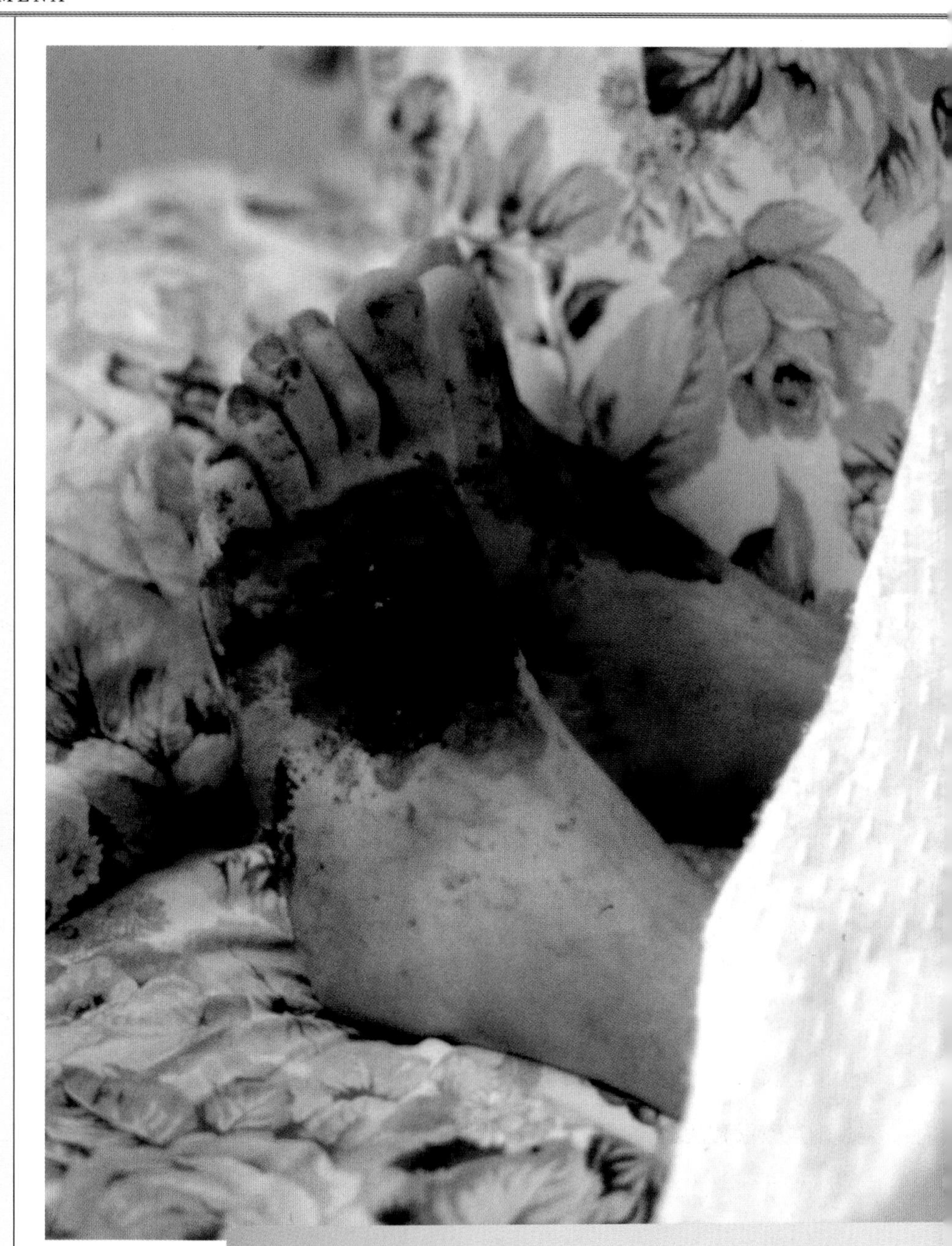

Bleeding stigmata
Italian stigmatic Giorgio Bongiovanni, born in Sicily in 1963, first received his stigmata during a visit to Fatima in Portugal, the famous pilgrim site where visions of the Virgin Mary were witnessed in 1917. The five passion marks (two in his palms, two in his feet, and one in his side) bleed almost daily – photographed here in 1993. Bongiovanni has had several visions of Jesus and Mary; the first time he saw Jesus, he was descending from a UFO and was dressed in fuchsia-coloured overalls.
© DR ELMAR R. GRUBER/FORTEAN PICTURE LIBRARY

Madonna in the sky

In 1980 Mrs Ivy Wilson photographed a rainbow at her property near Woombye, south-east Queensland, Australia. She didn't notice anything unusual in the sky, but when the picture was printed a friend noticed an image resembling the Madonna and Child. It was suggested that perhaps the photograph had been taken through a window and a small statue behind the photographer had been reflected in the glass, but Mrs Wilson was adamant that there was no glass between her and the sky.

In 1990 a seer named Susanna D'Amore moved to Woombye and claimed she saw the Virgin Mary hovering over a gum tree. She built a small chapel, found a spring of healing water, and busloads of pilgrims soon started to arrive.

Most of the teeth, including one-inch canines, are intact.' Anthropologist Dr Dana Austin from the Tarrant County Medical Examiner's Office said: 'It was definitely an old-world primate, possibly a monkey or chimp.' Other experts believe it may have belonged to a baboon. A small bone was also found nearby which could be part of a 'femur or hip'. (SOURCE - DFW NEWS, 9TH MAY)

BIGFOOT COLONY: Tom Burnett says he has seen Bigfoot-like creatures on many occasions and believes there is a colony living near Old Fort, Carolina, although he will not give the exact location. He claims the creatures are now familiar with him, and they 'have made peace' with each other, being able to live side-by-side; they even leave him gifts from time to time. He said: 'They know I'm not out to hurt them, that I'll protect them. They're used to me now. They're more aware of you than you are of them: these are very alert creatures.' Tom believes the creature's domesticate other animals. He said: 'They use bear to hunt, they hunt in groups.' He has taken photographs of the creatures and even sent a skull to the Texas Laboratory but has received no word back. He claims that a mother abandoned a baby on his a farm, but he returned it to the woods. Days later he found the creature dead. He has published a book titled Nature's Secret Agents, which is an account of his experiences and observations. (SOURCE - MCDOWELL NEWS, 9TH MAY)

BIGFOOT AGAIN: A team of up to 30 researchers scoured the Oklahoma Woods in late May to search for Bigfoot. On recent expeditions the team have seen Bigfoot several times and claim that the creatures have thrown rocks at them as they sat around their camp fire, one rock even hitting a researcher. One team member said: 'We heard whoop sounds, attempted imitations of whippoorwills and mimicking of dove and owl calls were heard.' (SOURCE - TULSA WORLD, JUNE 2).

MONTAUK MONSTER: On May 6 'a new Montauk Monster' was

Sightings

washed ashore on the coast of Long Island, New York. The 'monster' has since turned out to be a raccoon given a Viking burial by students. Video footage of the carcase can be seen at http://naturalplane.blogspot.com/2009/05/new-montauk-monster-washes-up-on-long.html (SOURCE - PHANTOMS & MONSTERS, 12TH MAY)

CHAMP: Footage taken in early June in Lake Champlain is said by some to show the legendary Lake Monster Champ. Eric Olsen who took the footage said: 'I was just filming the water when, out of the corner of my eye, I saw something move, and I turned toward it and tried to zoom in on it. You can see that it is moving horizontally, across the water, and vertically, going under the surface and coming back up. It struck me as something that was long, that it didn't have much girth.' Cryptozoologist Loren Coleman responded: 'We need to figure out what is going on here. The film needs to have a formal forensic analysis performed ... to break it down frame by frame. It needs to be looked at very seriously.' (SOURCE - BURLINGTON FREE PRESS, 3RD JUNE)

TASSIE TIGER: Richard Elliott was driving along Dry Creek Road toward Princess Margaret Rose Cave, Donavan, when he spotted a mystery animal near a pine plantation. He said: 'At first I thought it was a fox, but it was too long and gangly, it had a long tail; it definitely wasn't a fox.' The animal moved too quickly to see whether or not it had stripes, but Mr Elliott said the animal was long and skinny with exposed ribs and believes it was a Thylacine, or Tasmanian Tiger. (SOURCE - BORDERWATCH, 2ND JUNE)

DRAGON ATTACKS: Villagers who for generations have lived alongside Komodo Dragons unafraid are becoming increasingly worried at their aggressive behaviour, with an increase in outright attacks. A ranger was doing paperwork when a dragon slithered up the stairs of his wooden hut and then went for his ankles. He tried to prise its jaws open but the teeth then locked into his hand. The ranger said: 'I thought I wouldn't survive... I've spent half my life working with Komodos and have never seen anything like it.' He needed 55 stitches in his hand. (SOURCE - AOL NEWS, 26TH MAY)

STONE THROWING: In June Mark Fraser was contacted by a witness who claims that he and a friend saw 'two ape men' on Cannock Chase in Staffordshire.

Holy holes

Another Italian stigmatic is Antonio Ruffini, who has had the stigmata since 1951 when he saw an apparition of the Virgin Mary. He built a chapel at the place where this happened, south of Rome. The wounds have been examined by doctors. They go through the palms of the hands and the feet, and usually such wounds would become infected, but Mr Ruffini has had no problems and can use his hands without difficulty.

© DR ELMAR R. GRUBER/ FORTEAN PICTURE LIBRARY

Tears of blood
Weeping and bleeding statues, usually of the Virgin Mary, are a familiar phenomenon in the Catholic world. Sometimes they are proved to be hoaxes, but not always. In 1971 a lawyer in Italy awoke to find that a painting of the Madonna hanging over his bed was dripping blood from her eyes, heart, hands and feet, and the bleeding continued even after the police put the painting in a locked box at their headquarters.

This photograph shows a statue of the Virgin Mary shedding tears of blood in the home of Enzo Alocci in Porto San Stefano in Italy in October 1972. Since 1966 Alocci has also experienced the stigmata and seen visions of religious figures such as Jesus, Mary and the Archangel Gabriel.

They allegedly threw a stone at one of the witnesses who was hit on the arm, but he suffered no injuries. The witness, who wishes anonymity, said that the 'ape-men' were '5ft tall with long shaggy hair and wearing some kind of clothing.' Investigations into the witnesses' claims are on-going. (SOURCE - MARK FRASER WWW.BIGCATSINBRITAIN.ORG JUNE 2009).

BRITISH BIG CATS: Large felines are still being spotted in the country, quietly ambling through the countryside, and quietly investigated by dedicated researchers. One witness on Cannock Chase estimated the size of the black cat he saw in June to be at least three feet off the ground. Christopher Hall of Big Cats in Britain found prints belonging to a large feline on the shores of Loch Doon in Ayrshire, these are the first prints to have come from the county in several years, and the area is no stranger to sightings of large black cats. They have been spotted in Aberdeenshire, chased cyclists in Kent, killed rabbits in Northumberland and reportedly dined on sheep in Devon. (SOURCE - BIG CATS IN BRITAIN).

'NORDICS' AT SILBURY: On the 7th of July an off duty police officer was driving towards Marlborough on the A4 passing Silbury Hill near the new crop circle that had recently appeared. He saw three 'exceptionally tall beings inspecting the crop circle'. He stopped and watched them for a few minutes. They were all over 6ft tall, had blond hair and were wearing one-piece white suits, the hoods dropped back onto their backs. He shouted at them but they ignored him, he entered the field and then they 'ran at an amazing speed to the south'. The police officer said: 'I recognized that I could never catch up with them since they were exceptionally fast.' He looked momentarily away and they disappeared. The police officer became unnerved and left. (SOURCE - COLINANDREWS.NET).

GIANT SNAKES: Mike Warner and his son Greg Warner, after 23 years of research, have photographed a giant snake in the Peruvian Amazon, according to some reports reaching a length of 40 metres, and two metres in diameter. It is reportedly dark

Sightings

brown in colour and known by the locals as 'black boa' or Yucumama, meaning 'Mother of Water.' Sightings of the creature abound in the area and are even said to be responsible for recently smashing through the house of an elderly couple. On July the 1st the Maine Warden Service in the USA received two sightings of a giant snake in the Rumford canal system, near Lewiston. The local police said that two people contacted them to report seeing a snake about 17 feet long enter the canal from behind a local store. Snake expert Robbie White believes it could be a red-tail boa or a Burmese python. Sightings are still continuing in the area. (SOURCE - ULSTER STAR MAY, SUN JOURNAL (USA) JULY).

BIGFOOT: Columbia police in Mississippi are investigating a spurt of Bigfoot sightings near the Pearl River, Columbia Waterpark. Police chief Joe Van Parkman believes they are hoaxes, and said: 'An out-of-state organization had visited the area with specialized equipment for primate study and had found no evidence of anything unusual.' Detectives are following up leads and are appealing to the public for information. (SOURCE - THE RANKIN LEDGER, MISSISSIPPI JUNE 2009).

OREGON HUMANOID: On the 16th of June a man went outside for a cigarette at his Oregon home, when he saw a light in the sky: 'flickers, flashes in both crescent shapes and orbs'. The witness said: 'As I watched this very lengthy light show, I was aware of a passing car. My dog then began to get unnerved and looked in the same direction as I was looking. As the car came closer down the road, across the street I noticed a pair of eyes as if an animal's eyes were reflecting in the light, except they were a deep purple/indigo. As the car passed, I watched the spot where I had observed the eyes, and was shocked to see a whitish humanoid shape stand up and quickly walk into the neighbouring yard across the street.' His wife joined him at that point and saw the lights. The dog acted nervously throughout the experience. (SOURCE - MUFON: 16TH JUNE 2009).

MICHIGAN DOGMAN: A new film of the 'Dogman' has come to light. Researcher Linda Godfrey said the film is still under investigation, and could still be proven to be a hoax, 'but if so it's an extremely sophisticated and well done hoax'. The film was taken using an

Weeping statue
A statue of the Blessed Virgin Mary (known as the Rosa Mystica) began to weep at Maasmechelen in Belgium in late 1983.

Body on display
Some incorrupt saints' bodies have been put on permanent display, such as that of St Bernadette Soubirous (1844-79) who was the visionary of Lourdes. She was first exhumed 30 years after her death, and again in 1919, after which her face was coated with wax to preserve it and her body was placed in a glass coffin in the chapel of St Bernadette in the motherhouse of the Sisters of Nevers in France.
© Andreas Trottmann/Fortean Picture Library

8mm camera and found, allegedly, in an estate sale in the Lower Peninsula. Linda continues: 'The film is grainy, blurry, shows a lot of nondescript landscape and begins with some ordinary shots of a lady chopping a log. It appears that the filmmaker saw the creature while riding in a truck, jumped out of the truck to shoot it, then was surprised by a side ambush and ended up with a view of the creature's fangs and gaping maw – perhaps after the camera was tossed to the ground in haste as the filmer hustled back into the truck. (I think the mouth shots are the least convincing part of the film.) But the first stills that show the creature clearly indicate a canine-headed animal moving through knee-high undergrowth. It has pointed ears on top of its head and shoulders, which ordinary dogs (or bears or other quadrupeds) do not have. It turns and moves to one side, charging through the brush in a way that would be very difficult for a human to do. At one point it appears there is a long tail. (THE VIDEO CAN BE SEEN AT HTTP://NATURALPLANE.BLOGSPOT.COM).

BIG CAT ROUND-UP: MOD Police Officer Chris Swallow could not believe his eyes when he saw a giant cat on a rail track near Helensburgh, Argyll. He immediately took footage on his mobile phone while a friend took still photographs. The video was released in July, but Big Cats in Britain had the footage in their possession for two weeks before this. Initial analysis shows this to be a very large animal indeed, and definitely feline. Shaun Stevens of BCIB said: 'After size investigations, the body is at least 3.5 feet in length, which does not include the long tail. This is one of the best pieces of footage to come out of Scotland.' Meanwhile in Ayrshire the police launched a hunt for an animal, believed by them to be a big cat, that caused severe injuries to a horse near the Sundrum Holiday Park near Coylton. Photographs have also come from Aberdeenshire, Cornwall and Lincolnshire, prints from the Cannock Chase, Northampton, Aberdeenshire, and DNA samples from Wales are currently undergoing testing; in fact this has been a bumper month for reports coming into

Sightings

BCIB, far more than usual, ending with a vigil in a big cat hotspot at the end of the month in Leicestershire. (SOURCE - SHAUN STEVENS, BIG CATS IN BRITAIN, SIMON KING AND PC CHRIS SWALLOW).

BARNACLES: A strange living creature which frightened locals and holiday makers washed ashore on the Gower Peninsula in Wales. It was a writhing mass of tentacles which measured six feet from end to end. An unnamed zoology expert said it was 'like something out of Doctor Who'. People flocked to Oxwich beach to view the monster. But disappointed, they came away when scientists revealed that the fearsome tentacled creature was nothing more than 'a seething mass of goose barnacles' brought to the shore by the recent bad weather. It was once believed that geese actually hatched from the barnacles, and a Welsh monk in the 12th century claims he actually saw this happen! (SOURCE - DAILY MAIL: 5TH AUGUST 2009).

DARK SHAPE: Poachers in woods at Walkerwoods Reservoir, Cheshire, heard noises brush in front of them, then their torches suddenly stopped working. Panic set in and they ran. They stopped several hundred yards away and could still hear the noises which seemed to be pursuing them. They opened fire, they heard no sound, and then the noises began again, as though something was moving towards them, then 'from the darkness came a huge dark figure. It was about seven feet tall and was completely black in colour, they could see no features, and the thing seemed to be absorbing the darkness, as if camouflaged in some way'. The poachers fled. (SOURCE - DAVE SADLER, PHENOMENA MAGAZINE UPIA / MAPIT AUGUST 2009).

OGOPOGO: On the 16th of July Wendy Sanderson and two other witnesses were at the Okanagan Centre boat dock at 10.30hrs. Wendy wrote a letter to a local newspaper and said: 'I saw a large snake-like creature at the surface of the lake for about three minutes. It was probably 30 feet long and as it slithered across the lake, it made humps at the surface. I believe that this was a once in a lifetime opportunity that I shared with two other witnesses that I met on the dock at the Okanagan Centre boat launch. We stood there together for that moment in absolute amazement. We do not have proof of this sighting, but

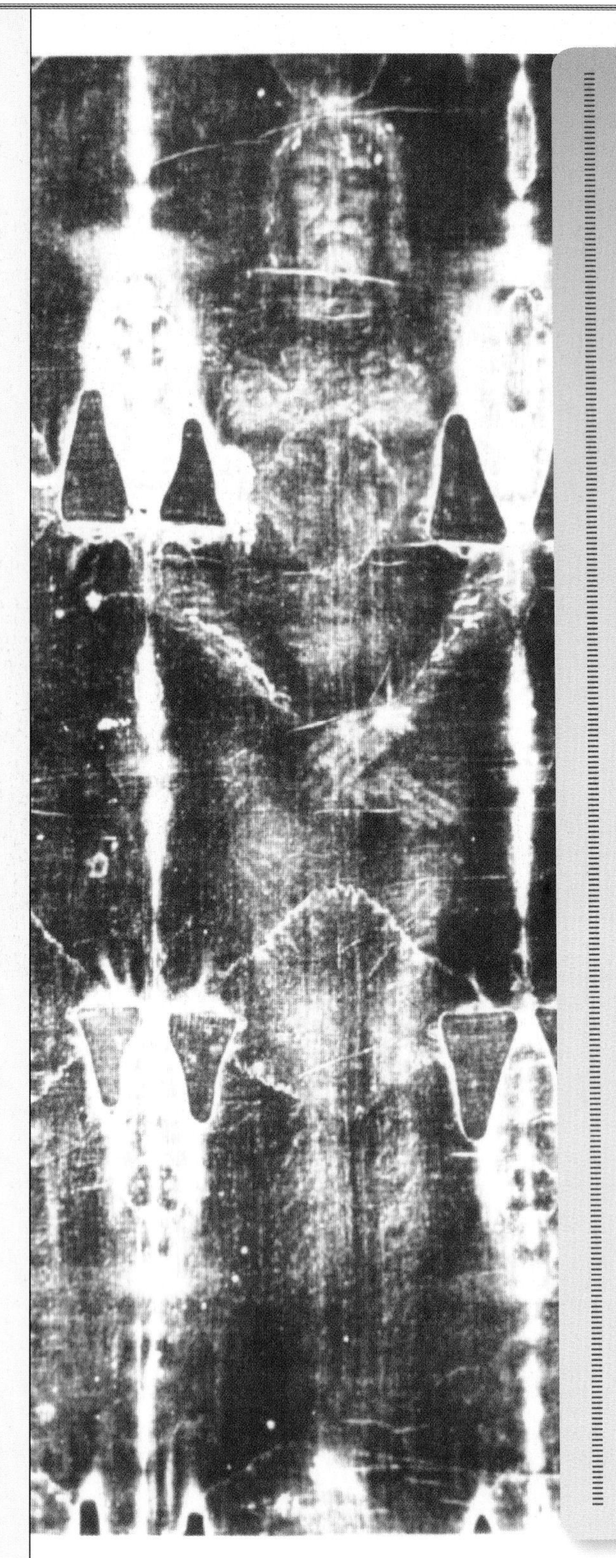

TurinShroud

Controversy continues to rage around a piece of linen which, for centuries, has been venerated as the shroud which covered Jesus Christ at his burial. An attempt made in 1988 to prove conclusively whether or not the shroud dated from the time of Christ, using radio-carbon dating, did not give the clear-cut answer so greatly desired by all parties.

The result stated that the flax from which the shroud was woven had been harvested between 1260 and 1390 – and that the Turin Shroud was therefore a forgery. However, the shroud could not be so easily dismissed, and a more recent test, made in 2005, strongly refuted the medieval dating. Raymond Rogers, a retired chemist from Los Alamos National Laboratory in New Mexico, published a research paper which demonstrated that the area of cloth used in the 1988 test had been rewoven after fire damage. 'The radiocarbon sample has completely different chemical properties than the main part of the shroud relic,' he stated. His test of another piece suggested that the shroud is actually between 1,300 and 3,000 years old – and could, therefore, have been in existence during Christ's lifetime.

The shroud is known to have been damaged in several fires since its existence was first recorded in France in 1357, and it is said to have been restored by nuns who patched the holes. Mr Roers said that the radio-carbon tested area had been dyed to match the rest of the shroud, and it was clearly of later date. Mr Rogers' micro-chemical tests focused on a substance called vanillin, which is found in material such as linen but is lost over time. The virtual absence of vanillin in his shroud sample indicated the much older date.

Incorruptible Father Paul

When the body of a saintly person does not decay after death, it is said to be incorrupt. Other mysteries associated with the death of a holy person include: unusual fragrances being smelled around the body, persisting for months or years; no rigor mortis, the limbs being as flexible as those of a living person; the bleeding of corpses weeks, months or even years after death; and the persistence of warmth for some hours after death. The photograph shows the exhumation in Belgium in July 1899 of the corpse of the Very Reverend Father Paul of Moll, a Flemish Benedictine and wonder-worker, who had died in February 1896 aged 72. The corpse was in a perfect state of preservation, and the witnesses declared that 'the skin of the face was hardened and of a [brownish] colour, the hands very white. His monastic habit was clean, and the body had preserved its original position notwithstanding the fact that the coffin had been dragged up almost perpendicularly from the tomb, from a depth of four metres.'

we know what we saw and we shared it together.' A fisherman who also saw the creature was so surprised he dropped his fishing rod! Meanwhile Abdulaziz from Kuwait believes he has seen an image of Ogopogo on Google Earth and reports: 'I stumbled upon this monster/snake/big fishing net thing that is about 280 meters long and could well be Ogopogo.' Images can be seen at http://naturalplane.blogspot.com/2009/07/has-ogopogo-been-found-on-google-earth.html (SOURCE - ENGLISH PEOPLE: 22ND JULY 2009 & PHANTOMS AND MONSTERS).

'FROSTQUATCH': Footage of what is said to be a white Bigfoot was captured by a home owner in an undisclosed location in Pennsylvania. Residents have recently reported a string of sightings and strange noises in the night. The film was taken after the home owner heard a disturbance outside. The footage shows him running through the woods and then capturing a fleeting glance of an eerie figure running away. The film can be seen via www.paranromalmagazine.co.uk/videos (Source - Phantoms & Monsters January 2010).

Experiences

My friend on the Penny Farthing

Having two new energetic dogs revived long walks along the Tyne Riverside County Park at Prudhoe, Northumberland. The banks of the Tyne were full of wildlife and it was for me a magical place in which to be at one with nature. This was 1997 and the summers in recent years had been poor. But being a northerner I was used to the cold.

Part of the walk would take me over a little wooden bridge and on to a tarmac path. Alongside lay the remnants of the industrial past: ICI waste heaps once of coal now of lime. The heaps towered high into the air and were a white-grey in colour. Sycamore and alder trees clung to its sides and grew into the sky. It was a dark and somewhat scary place at certain times of the year, but the wildlife that had taken over the waste heaps had turned it into a remarkable achievement for nature, in which it had claimed back land from humans.

This part of the route is known as the Spetchells, although the locals would sometimes say 'Spetchills', thinking it referred to the lime heaps, whereas in fact it was an ancient name for the land on which they stood.

As I would walk over the small wooden bridge and through the kissing gate approaching the Spetchells, I would often be confronted with an awesome sight. A man dressed in an Edwardian suit, chocolate-brown in colour, wearing a bowler-type hat, would go whizzing by riding a very high Penny Farthing bicycle.

He'd glance across at me, tipping the rim of his hat with his hand in acknowledgement as he passed by. I would gasp in amazement, as the bike was huge and I would marvel at his sense of balance, yet I was also concerned my little dogs may cause an accident if they suddenly ran out in front of him. He'd always be travelling in the same direction from Wylam to Prudhoe and I saw him many times in the same spot.

Although it was a strange sight, I just thought it was someone with an interest in that mode of transport and era. I must have seen him eight times in a two-year period 1997-99. Then one day in the presence of another dog walker, I remarked at the spectacle passing us by as again he acknowledged me.

'What man on what bike?' the lady dog walker asked perplexed.

'Didn't you see him?' I asked, astonished she had failed to witness such an amazing sight.

A man dressed in an Edwardian suit, chocolate-brown in colour, wearing a bowler-type hat, would go whizzing by riding a very high Penny Farthing bicycle.

'No. I only felt a gust of wind and rustling noise,' she replied.

I was amazed at this and a little confused. After that I never saw the man on the Penny Farthing again. Eleven years have now passed and I often wonder why he decided to reveal himself to me, but I also feel privileged to have shared in such a wondrous sight.

Rachel Smith, via email

Terror among the trees

I was on my way home from an old girlfriend's house. It was late and the quickest way to the taxi office was a path through the middle of Cherry Tree Woods opposite East Finchley Underground Station. It was a full moon that night and the air was thick and heavy. It was a very eerie night.

It was very dark in the woods. The only light was that of the moon which sat low in the sky. All of a sudden I felt the need to run but I said to myself, 'oh you're just being silly', and carried on walking. But I started to feel uneasy as if eyes were watching me from all around. Then I felt as if there was someone or something behind me.

The hair on my neck started to stand on end and I heard a voice say: 'Run!'

And I did run, all the way to the taxi office. Later, in the cab, I started talking to the driver. He told me that the woods were haunted by a murdered girl. I have been unable to find any proof of this.

I know the woods once belonged to the road from London to Nottingham in the Middle Ages (which may explain the statue of Robin Hood on top of the station), and Highgate Woods are just down the road.

I don't know why but I am sure the presence I felt that night was very old and dark and meant me harm. The voice I heard sounded like someone I knew but it may have been raw instinct.

'OLD AND DARK': The place in Cherry Tree Woods, London, where our reader felt a hostile presence and was overcome with panic.

I felt as if there was someone or something behind me. The hair on my neck started to stand on end and I heard a voice say: 'Run!'

I recently returned to Cherry tree Woods after 20 years. Even in daytime I feel that people are not the only things that dwell there. That night is one that will stay with me all my life.

Scott Lambert, Neasden, London

Messages from beyond?

First of all, I'm not really into the whole supernatural thing, but over a few years I've begun to notice something out of the ordinary happen in my room. I Googled it but nothing has come up about what has happened to me. This is going to sound weird...

Basically, a few years ago, I walked into my room to see a bunch of scrambled letters on my wall, white letters, like somehow projected onto it. But there was NOTHING to reflect the letters and even if something could have reflected it they wouldn't have been white.

Maybe a year later, I was in my bed (a bunk bed) and I turned around and saw there was now a bunch of huge letters. I was baffled and very scared but I took my time to read them and I'm not sure but I think it was 'turn around' backwards.

Well that happened about a year ago. Yesterday I'm just walking into my room when I see the words in small being projected on my wall. So I called my brother and said: 'Look, look and there's nothing reflecting them!'

He was all freaked out, but whilst watching it while he was there, it suddenly disappeared, so he went back in his room and I stayed there just looking at the wall. Then it came up again so I ran down stairs. I was too scared to even try and unjumble the letters this time.

Please can someone explain what this is? Any theories?

Rhiannon Evans, via email

Still rolling along

One of my very first memories as a child, of no more than four years of age, is of me sitting on my parents' sofa watching TV and out of the corner of my right eye noticing my toy dog on wheels moving slowly across the room. After two or three metres it stopped. I remember not being scared. I calmly went upstairs where my parents were putting together my new bed.

Thirty years later I was again sitting on my sofa in my house when out of the corner of my right eye I saw my son's toy truck moving across the floor slowly like it was being pushed. It stopped after two metres.

I tried to recreate this effect but could not. Do you think someone's trying to get my attention?

I have just set up my own paranormal group called Asylum Paramormal in Cheshire. Let's see who or what is there!

Lee Fletcher, via email

An unexpected guest

The following took place as recently as early September 2009, although not to me but to someone I shall call 'Dave'. The location was a guest house in Peele, Isle of Man. The weather was a howling gale, with storm-force winds and lashing rain – typical haunting weather you might say!

In a room overlooking the seafront, Dave was trying to sleep but his friend was snoring. So he took himself to an empty adjacent room (the hotel was almost empty of guests since the terrible weather of the week had taken its toll).

Dave locked the door and went into a deep sleep, only to be rudely awakened to find a figure of man in some kind of uniform standing over him. Dave watched in horror as this figure stared at him, then proceeded across the darkened room to walk through the door.

Dave then got up in pursuit. He opened the door to see the lights coming on one by one as the sensors where activated as if by someone walking under them – but the corridor on the landing was empty of anyone. Still in shock, Dave retreated back to his snoring friend!

Dave previously has never experienced anything and was very sceptical of any paranormal situation. However, this is not the only sighting or activity recorded in the hotel.

John Hall, via email

Dave locked the door and went into a deep sleep, only to be rudely awakened to find a figure of man in some kind of uniform standing over him. Dave watched in horror as this figure stared at him

Our haunted houseful

When my children were young we lived in a house which was approximately 18 years old. This house did not seem to possess a soul and was never homely. We lived in this house for eight years.

One evening I was cooking with a friend in my kitchen. We were using a work surface which faced the dining room and, onward through double doors, faced the living room. I was busy chopping onions and as I looked up I saw an elderly lady walk through my neighbour's wall, straight through my living room and through the wall of my other neighbour.

I can remember her clearly. She had grey hair pulled back in a bun, a lavender-coloured shawl and dark clothing underneath. As she walked, her feet could not be seen as they were through the floor and clearly under the foundations of the house. She was approximately 90% solid and 10% transparent. I was astounded. My friend who was cooking with me was a sceptic so I thought there was no point mentioning this apparition.

I then became aware that my friend was standing still, looking towards the area where the ghostly lady had walked. My friend said: 'Did you see that?' I replied: 'What?' She said: 'That lady who just walked through the wall!'

My friend verified the appearance and clothes of the apparition and they matched exactly with my description. I felt that this apparition was following a certain pathway that she used to walk in her life. She showed absolutely no indication of our existence or time.

Another occurrence that happened in this house was very different. Strange events began to occur. My children claimed there was banging coming from upstairs, emitting from the walls and doors. To be honest I thought that there would be a rational explanation for this. But as time went on, I experienced the banging also but only when my children were present or nearby.

The banging occurred on walls, doors, radiators, even the side of the fridge-freezer! These occurrences gradually became more frequent and the strength of the banging intensified with time. I started to think that it was time to deal with this noisy spirit but I was unsure what steps to take.

The catalyst occurred one morning when I heard my son screaming downstairs. I ran to him to discover that the downstairs toilet door was banging with such force that the door was swinging fiercely to and fro with the velocity of each blow. I pushed the children out into the front garden, closed the front door and faced the spirit. I screamed at it: 'What do you think you are doing, frightening my children?'

I told it that if it wanted to communicate with anyone, it should communicate with me. I was enraged and I remember the vigour of my fury. All of a sudden the banging stopped and I felt a 'swishing' past me. I followed the direction of the 'swishing' and opened the back door. I actually felt an energy go past me and it left the house. I shouted after it that I would not be permitting it to return and that if it ever approached my children again, it would have me to deal with!

Upon refection, I was a young woman with no real experience of banishing spirits. I think that my mother's love for my children

I ran to him to discover that the downstairs toilet door was banging with such force that the door was swinging fiercely to and fro with the velocity of each blow.

made me a significant match for this spirit. It never returned. I do not feel that it was an evil entity but a mischievous spirit who just wanted to attract the children.

Although the spirit described above vanished, several other incidents occurred within this house. In that house, I observed swirling mists that travelled from room to room, spinning around the central light fittings before moving into another room. Once in my daughter's bedroom, we watched as a mist took on a 'bat-like' appearance before dissipating into a shapeless mist again. On that occasion I asked it to leave, which it did instantly.

Spirits have always been especially attracted to my youngest daughter. One day she came running towards me and a long strand of her hair at the top of her head was sticking upright and jigging up and down. It looked very funny and I must admit I did laugh. I placed my hand over her hair and it stopped immediately. My daughter (who was very young) was indignant as she thought that the spirit was naughty for making her look silly with the top of her hair jigging around.

On a separate occasion I had a friend staying over and he was sleeping upon the settee in the living room, the area which appeared most active. The next day he told me that in the middle of the night he woke up and standing before him was the most beautiful girl he had ever seen. He was startled as she was entirely naked and just stood looking at him. Standing on either side of this young girl were two older women who were clothed in Saxon-type clothing. One woman was considerably older than the girl and the other woman was very much older with grey hair and wrinkled skin. They seemed to be protecting the young girl. My friend was so afraid that he hid his head under the quilt and stayed like that throughout the night.

This house continued to give us all strange experiences, so often that we were never shocked. I wondered if it was us as a family but when we moved to our current home, we realised that the common denominator was the house and not us. We have had a few spiritual occurrences in our current house but nothing to compare with our former home.

Recently I was talking to two previous neighbours from our old address. They told me that before we lived in our previous house; a lady lived there who had mental health problems. She used to scream often and run out of the front door claiming that people were walking through the walls. I find this very interesting and although I only witnessed this happening once, I did see it happen. Apparently nobody believed this lady because of her

psychiatric history.

I think I have this house and its spectral beings to thank for my commitment to paranormal research. I have always had a deep fascination for anything supernatural but living in this house exacerbated my interest. I personally know that ghosts exist and I am dedicated into delving into the unknown with my paranormal team Twilight Shadows Paranormal.

Maria Williams, via email

Supermarket spirit

I was doing a small bit of shopping in my local Netto store in Wolverhampton. I was looking at something, when something out of the corner of my eye caught my attention. There stood a small boy aged between 7 and 9. The only way to describe this young boy was that he looked like one of the old chimney sweeper lads (granddad's cap, white dirty shirt, dirty face, half-cut trousers, blond dirty hair). He was just standing there looking as if to see what I was doing.

I looked at this boy for a few seconds then turned away and the second I looked back he had gone. Me being me, soon after he had gone I walked around the store to see if I could see a boy wearing such clothing, but to my amazement there were no kids in the store wearing this type of clothing. Even to this very day I do believe I saw a spirit of a young boy.

Richie Bear, via email

I saw a black mass go across the pavement in front of our row of terraced houses. Thinking it was probably a shadow I thought nothing of it. But when my housemate experienced it too, I was a bit scared.

The black mass

I moved house in February and one night I was walking up our road when I saw a black mass go across the pavement in front of our row of terraced houses. Thinking it was probably a shadow I thought nothing of it. But when my housemate experienced it too, I was a bit scared.

There is a doorway a few doors down, that I've always been spooked by, I just get a horrible feeling when I walk by and so I thought I would video walking past it on my way to the shops at 9pm, the same time we both spotted the black mass.

When I got home and played back the video, the exact point at which I pointed my camera into the spooky doorway you can clearly hear a low ghostly voice saying 'Oi...you!' I didn't hear it at the time and there was nobody else around.

It wasn't until a week after catching the voice that I found out the back door leads to the Funeral Directors around the corner and that is where they take the dead bodies in and out of!

Liz Owen, via email

Phantom fun

I have had one supernatural experience. My family had just moved into a new home, the previous occupant being an elderly man who had died recently. My mother's boyfriend and his daughter had already moved in.

I went with my mother to look around the house (I was about 14, nearly 15, at the time). While inspecting my new bedroom, the room where the man had died a few months before, everyone was taking the mick about me having the room he had died in. On leaving the room, I was shoved directly in the back, causing me to stumble through the door.

I was the last to leave the room, my sister was in front of me and witnessed me falling. The shove was playful, firm but 'laddish', like you'd push around an old friend. I never experienced anything again in the room. Maybe it was just the old man having the last laugh.

Adam Upson, via email

The mystery whistler

In the winter of 1979/80 on a Friday afternoon, I made my way home through the snow from the iron foundry I worked in. We lived in an old house that had a shop at the front on the first floor, as there was a big bridge at the front of the property. This was the type of old house that had the kitchen, then the bathroom and then a coalhouse at the back.

I got in and nobody was home so I ran a bath and had a good soak. As I got dressed, I heard the crunch of footsteps on the shingle outside the garden, then whistling and the latch on the gate go clunk! The shadow of the whistler went past the bathroom window and in the back door. It must be my brother Brian home from school, I thought.

I went in to the kitchen and on into the living-room but nobody was there, so I popped up stairs, past the shop door (which was locked as Mrs Denton closed at 5pm and had gone home). I looked in my bedroom that Brian and I shared – nobody there. So I went up to the top floor that had another bedroom and guess what – nobody there!

I could feel the hair starting to stand up on the back of my neck and I made a fast U-turn down stairs. After that I sat and thought about it: Brian didn't whistle like that, he whistled through his teeth, and also we had about 6-inches of snow on the ground so I wouldn't have heard the crunching of the shingle.

A few months later I was in the bedroom on the top floor and was just about to drop off to sleep when I started to hear whispering: it was low and I just couldn't make out what was being said but it sounded like a couple of young boys. I lay for some time listening and frozen with fear too! After some 20 minutes or so, the room fell silent. That was the last time I slept in the room, as we moved.

Clive Hodge, Hunstanton

On leaving the room, I was shoved directly in the back, causing me to stumble through the door.

What is this tiny figure?

I am part of Thames Valley Paranormal Group and we were investigating the Highwayman Pub in Kidlington, Oxfordshire, when this intriguing photo was taken.

The picture was taken on a Fujifilm Finepix s1000fd camera in night mode and no flash was used, which accounts for the colours, which are created by light coming through a window to the right and shining onto a wall. The dark shadow that can be seen is a jacket hanging up, so that can be discounted.

The figure that is seen is the interesting part, as it should have been a blank wall. It appears to be a man in uniform with one hand raised and in the other hand something is being carried but it is too faint to conclude what it is (some speculate it could be a rifle). The figure is only 12 to 14 inches in height and appears in mid air. This is what we find so odd as there is nothing in the room that could have caused it.

Some other investigators were present in the room but they were all to the left of the room and not in the picture. When we zoomed in on the figure we could see it quite clearly, with distinct colour differences of the hands and head to the other colour of it. We do not actually say this is paranormal but it has so far defied any reasonable explanation.

If any of your readers can possibly come up with a reason

why this image is there I would appreciate it as we have tried to debunk it and had some people who are from outside our group try but no-one has yet been able to offer any explanation.

Simon Buckle, via email

I saw the White Lady – and she saw me

I'm 12 years old. I've had many experiences of the paranormal but this story is one of my scariest.

It was May 2007 (I was 10 years old), I can't quite remember the exact date, but I went with the school on a residential trip to How Hill, near Ludham, in Norfolk and we stayed in a 103-year-old house. I thought it was an amazing house (with a big history).

We stayed in a room marked 1 (dormitory No.1). The people in my dormitory were my brother Zack, and friends Anton, Thomas and Sebastian.

I was sitting in bed in the middle of the night (not knowing what time, possibly 1 or 2am) when I was gazing around and I saw a white figure. I think she was the White Lady of How Hill. She had long hair hanging half way down her back; she was young, beautiful and wore a night gown which looked at least 80 years old.

When I first saw her, she was gazing round the room like me. When she saw me with shock, I was very shocked too! She looked away and shook her head and she slowly faded away.

I wasn't the only person who experienced the paranormal in that house that night. Jack, one of my other friends, experienced a figure getting closer and closer to him when he blinked. And a girl who's one of my friends, Elise, experienced a figure out of the corner of her eye. Another one of my friends, Luke, looked out of his window and saw a medieval woman walking in the gardens speaking Old English and her dog was yapping beside her carrying a dead rabbit.

I'm telling you, someone or something's in that house and hardly anyone has spoken of it!

Noah, via email

When I first saw her, she was gazing round the room like me. When she saw me with shock, I was very shocked too! She looked away and shook her head and she slowly faded away.

Bedroom visitors

With reference to your article concerning 'Shadow People', I remembered an incident that happened to me about 30 years ago.

I awoke in the early hours to see a shadow crouched next to my bed. It then stood up, revealing itself to be humanoid, but just a shadow with no detail at all. As I watched, it walked along the length of my bed before disappearing into the shadow of the wardrobe next to my wall.

At no time did I feel frightened or threatened in any way, and I never saw it again.

In the same room, I woke to see a dog (a spaniel, I think) sat in the corner watching me. On a more surreal note, I once watched as the large sheet on the room's spare bed rose up and took on the shape of what appeared to be an Afghan hound!

The visions of a sleepy child or genuine occurrences? They seemed real, but who can say?

Simon, via email

The Laptop Codes

I received a telephone call from my friend, Maureen. She opened up her company laptop to do some work on it. To do this she has to go through a series of security protocols before she is allowed access. She works for a UK utility company. She telephoned me around 9.30-ish to say her laptop was typing up stuff onscreen by itself.

Both she and I are psychic but very down to earth people. I told her to either write down what the laptop was typing or try to print it off. I then went on the net to search for related articles and found that some people had either viruses or spyware which does similar things, but NOT in the way this was operating!

Most viruses (according to what I can find so far) type up certain letters, vowels or characters but do not form paragraphs of sentences. Anyway, although the sentences do not always form perfect syntax or make grammatical sense, there are quite a few linking paras or sentences containing what I believe to be certain 'key' words... the type that makes MI5/6 etc sit up and listen.

These words are for instance: ISRAELIS, 9 AND 11, (written like that... not 9-11) PLANE, ANAHEIM. There are other weird sentences like, 'I still have not been paid for a side job'.

I know my email must seem either bizzare or a tad dramatic but who is to say that this may not be some kind of 'coded' message from an unknown sender to his contact?

James Conn, via email

The hooded shadow

I have an experience relating to your article in February's magazine about Shadow People.

I live on a fairly large housing estate built around 1982. The estate is a mix of semi and detached houses in cul-de-sacs. Each cul-de-sac is connected by roads and footpaths that wind through the houses. About 18 months ago I was walking along the footpath by my house when in front of me, about 20 feet ahead, I saw a black shape come out of a garden fence as if walking through it and disappear around the corner. This happened at 3pm in the afternoon so I wasn't scared and ran after it. I found nothing and although I kept thinking about it, soon forgot about the incident until a few months ago.

I was standing outside the front of my house having a quiet cigarette and saw, maybe two or three times, this same black shadow flitting around the cul-de-sac but always in the same place. This time it was dark and although we have two streetlights close by, I didn't attempt to investigate.

Now I see it most evenings. It appears to have a human form, but a human wearing a cloak or something that covers its head down to the ground, which makes it impossible to identify if it's male or female. I'm curious to find out why it's always in the same place, moving from one spot to another as if time's replaying somehow, yet I don't get a spirit feel from it as if it's a ghost or classic haunting.

Now I see it most evenings. It appears to have a human form, but a human wearing a cloak or something that covers its head down to the ground, which makes it impossible to identify if it's male or female.

I've been on paranormal investigations in the past and have encountered spirit activity on investigations, but this feels different to anything I've encountered before.

By the way, I love reading your magazine. Keep up the good work!

Alison, Fordingbridge, Hampshire

What could Tina see?

I have never been a great believer in 'otherworldliness', but there was an occurrence that I once witnessed, when I had a part-time job at my local hostelry.

The Manager of this pub in Rainhill, Merseyside (once Lancashire), had a bitch dog named Tina. My working days were Tuesday and Saturday mornings. Tina would always come out to greet my arrival at the pub (possibly because I gave her a piece of my bacon and egg sandwich). One Saturday morning I arrived at my usual time, but there was no Tina to greet me. However, I could hear her barking quite excitedly inside the pub.

I entered to find her standing in one corner of the bar barking furiously at an empty corner. There was a doorway in this corner which led out to the street, so I presumed that something outside had disturbed her. The manager told me, however, that she had started to do this at just after midnight, when the bar staff were clearing up. The manager had eventually managed to get Tina away and upstairs to the residence, so all was well. But she had gone straight back to the corner on coming down again in the morning and, was still there on my arrival.

As I walked over to her, she would look at me for a very brief time and then return to barking at the corner. I patted her and asked her to come away, but she would not come. I decided to go over to the target area to see if I could see anything that could cause such upset. As I did so, Tina went absolutely berserk, but did not follow me and I had to come back to her. There was

absolutely nothing to see in that corner, neither was there any strange aroma.

We eventually managed to get her away from there, and it never happened again. Tina is sadly no longer with us and the manager has moved to his own pub.

Brian Winnard, via email

Light fantastic

My family and I live in a house with a rich history when it comes to paranormal goings on but what happened last night has puzzled me greatly and now I can't get it out of my head!

My husband and I were watching TV and from where we were sitting we have a clear view into the kitchen. All of a sudden I was aware of a bright flash of green from the corner of my eye. Both my husband and I both looked into the kitchen and there on the wall was quite a large mass of bright green swirling lights!

It was only there for maybe five seconds then just blinked out but it left us stunned. I haven't heard of anything like this before and the only thing remotely like it I could find on the internet was Faerie Fire...

I would be most grateful if Paranormal Magazine readers could offer up an explanation as to what this might have been?

Leanne Graham, via email

UFOs over Manchester

On December 3, 2009, I arrived home from work at 2.45 am and the first thing I did was to put the dog out in the back garden. I then switched on Sky News and made a coffee. Just after 3am, I was stood at the back kitchen door drinking my coffee and watching my dog sniff around the garden when I spotted a strange light.

It was a very bright whitish/orangish/reddish object and appeared to be a jagged triangular shape. The object was almost directly above my house and it is difficult to say how high up in the sky it was; it appeared to be several hundred feet from the ground but it could have been a lot further away. I am pretty sure that what I was seeing was the bottom/stomach of the object. It was completely silent and I could not see any movement, it seemed to be completely still.

At times the object appeared to look like it was on fire and I am pretty sure that I saw what looked like smoke or steam around the object. The light appeared to the naked eye to be roughly the size of a 5-pence piece held at arms length. I stood and observed the brightly lit object for about 45 seconds before I went inside and got my mobile phone. I took 7 still photos in total, 2 normal and 5 at full zoom (5x digital zoom). I then started to video the object on my mobile phone.

What happened next was just completely mind-boggling and quite a spectacle. After filming the light for about 30 seconds, suddenly a smaller circular-shaped light, greenish/white in appearance, appeared from nowhere. I stood and observed the second object and watched as it blinked on and off several times, whilst also disappearing and re-appearing in different parts of the night sky as well as moving around the larger triangular object. I have to say, some of the manoeuvres and speed of the moving light was just simply stunning, mind-boggling and just plain weird.

After roughly 1 minute the circular light shot off in a north-westerly direction at tremendous speed and blinked out and just simply vanished. I continued to film the main object for roughly a further 30 seconds before it just went out: it was like someone switched a light off, there was an orangish/reddish flash and the thing was gone. I am pretty sure that I saw an orangish streak dart away, but this only lasted for no more than a second and unfortunately does not show up on the video clip.

I must have gone in and out of the garden about 15 times over the course of the next hour to see if I could see the thing again, but I never saw anything else and I went to bed. I have to say, at the time and after the sighting, I never really thought that much about it, I wasn't thinking UFOS, flying saucers, aliens or anything like that. It was over the following few days that it started to dawn on me just what I had seen.

I am not saying that what I witnessed was aliens, but I would love someone to show me something man-made that can perform like the objects that

All of a sudden I was aware of a bright flash of green from the corner of my eye. Both my husband and I both looked into the kitchen and there on the wall was quite a large mass of bright green swirling lights!

I witnessed, I have never seen anything remotely close. I am more than happy to share my evidence with people but I would ask that you please withhold my name since I am a professional guy and I would not like to be subject to any kind of ridicule or unwanted attention. For the same reason I do not want to give the exact location of where I live, except to say that this sighting occurred in Greater Manchester.

'G. M', Greater Manchester

What happened next was just completely mind-boggling and quite a spectacle. After filming the light for about 30 seconds, suddenly a smaller circular-shaped light, greenish/white in appearance, appeared from nowhere.

A couple of mist-eries

These photographs were taken at about 10.45pm on 18/05/2007 at the entrance to Grimston churchyard, near Kings Lynn, Norfolk. I was visiting the churchyard on behalf of a friend and took the picture to show her the state of the churchyard.

At the time of taking the first picture I was not aware of the mist (for want of a better word). I took a second picture 2 to 3 seconds later and as you can see it is perfectly clear. The picture was in a batch of pictures that I had taken that day. I only discovered the anomaly when I downloaded the pictures later that day.

I discovered that a ley-line ends at Grimston churchyard – I don't know if this could have any significance? I am using as reference John Timpson's book Timpson's Leylines.

Some colleagues and I routinely go to a spot on the A22 road at Caterham, Surrey. It is common here for a sighting of the ghost of a girl crossing the road in the early hours.

There photos were taken around 3am on 7th Feb. I took numerous photos and most do not show this smoke/mist. About 5 photos show the smoke. At first I thought it was my breath in the cold air but trying to recreate the effect, I found it is not even similar to these photos. When I took the photos, it was clear and only when I saw the photos did the smoke effect appear.

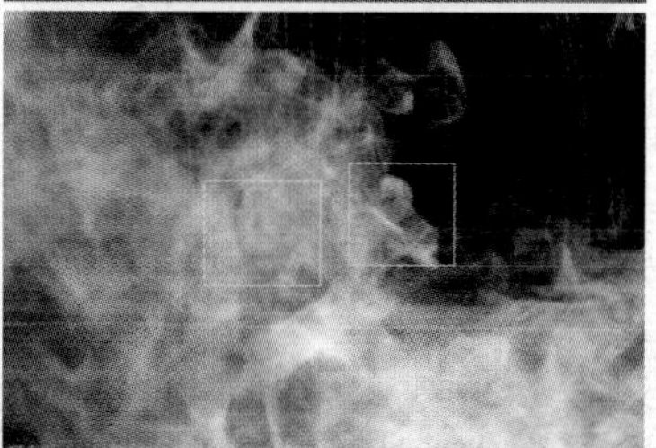

On the 'A22 Faces' photo, I was standing in the central reservation, looking to where this girl is supposed to run across the road from. I must stress, there was no smoke around me when I took this. On reviewing the photo, it appears to show an image of a bald man, head and torso, looking directly at me. Also to the left, I can make out what looks like a face breaking through the smoke. Having shown this photo to friends, others have seen other images as well, which I do not see. I have highlighted the images I see.

'A22 Stairs' is looking at the infamous stairs where the girl is also reported to be standing, looking down at the ground. A colleague is on the stairs as well, wearing a hi-viz jacket.

I am neither a believer nor disbeliever, but look for logical reasons for things. It could be water vapour, but few of the photos show this, plus the mist only appears in the area where the ghost is supposed to be – coincidence maybe?

Vivienne Moulton-Wynne (Grimston photos) and Martin Cave (A22 photos)

Experiences are continued on page 134

The existence of some reported real-life monsters is disputed because they are rarely seen – though of course the fact that they are able to live successfully out of sight of humankind is probably what keeps them alive. If their presence were accepted, their habitat would be invaded by people eager to capture a living specimen, with inevitable destruction of both the habitat and the creature.

Despite Man's best efforts to wreck the planet, there are still numerous little-visited areas where all manner of creatures are probably living unobserved. Jungles and deserts still keep their secrets, we still do not know everything that lives in the ocean depths, and many lakes also have persistent rumours of mystery residents. There are also claims of unidentified flying creatures having been seen, maybe even relics from the age of the dinosaurs.

Although we talk of 'monsters', meaning creatures both large in size and ugly in appearance, these are by virtue of their bulk and need for vast quantities of food less able to remain concealed. But they do so – though the sceptics would say that is because they don't exist! – and therefore how much easier it must be for unknown fishes, insects, small mammals, to remain unseen. Sadly very few of the possible monsters can be included here, because photographs of them just don't exist.

Monsters

A dead sea serpent?
From time to time, large carcases have been washed up on beaches around the world, often not being immediately identifiable because of decomposition, although hopes have frequently been raised that at last some proof of the existence of unknown sea monsters has been found.

This carcase was hauled up in the nets of the Japanese trawler Zuiyo-maru in April 1977, 30 miles off the coast of Christchurch, New Zealand. Because of its strange appearance and large size, one of the crew members wondered if it might be something out of the ordinary, and took several photographs before the smelly mass, masuring 33 feet long, was thrown overboard. A few samples of the flesh had also been retained, and when these were tested later the carcase was able to be identified as a basking shark, and sadly not a plesiosaur.

Sightings

Taken from the pages of
Paranormal Magazine

FLYING HUMANOIDS: What are said by some to be flying witches have surfaced again over the skies of Mexico, and have even been caught on video tape. One such video was taken by Daniel Sanchez Rosales, a resident of Mexico City, and he describes it as having humanoid features. It is said that they 'seem to infest the skies over an old cemetery'. The video was taken in February near the Mexico City International Airport, at 6.50 am in the Moctezuma district. The witness said the humanoid was facing them and seemed to be surveying its surroundings. Flying witches or the Williams X-JET? (SOURCE - PHANTOMS & MONSTERS: 29TH JULY 2009).

BIGFOOT: On July the 10th, a motorist had a near collision with a Bigfoot outside of Uniontown, in Fayette County, Pennsylvania. The witness was driving at around 35mph at 6pm when a figure ran out the side of the road on her left. She swerved to the right and missed the figure which she got a good look at, realising then that it was not a person. She describes the creature, which ran away, as 'a dark-coloured, hair-covered man-like creature, at least 6ft tall. It walked on two legs, had a big elongated head, with wild-looking hair.' The witness adds: 'The neck looked strange because the head was big and the shoulders were wide. The face was mainly covered in hair, yet the area that was exposed appeared to be very white. There was hair coming out from all over the face, like that of a dog or a wolf. The nose was flat and dark, but was also mostly covered in hair. The mouth could not clearly be seen. The ears were not seen since they were covered with hair as well. The eyes were dark, possibly black in colour, wide set, and 'wild looking'. There were 'no irises, no whites'. Meanwhile in the Sierra National Forest, Nevada, an image was caught on trail cam which many believe to be a Bigfoot. Researcher Jeffrey Gonzalez said: 'You can see features of a human face such as the nose, mouth and chin. According to the leaves and the branches that were covering the object's face, the tape measure said it was between 8 and 9 feet tall.' What is described as 'a monstrous hand print', about ten inches in length, was

Surgeon's Nessie

Loch Ness has gained a reputation for its giant resident who goes by the name of Nessie, believed by some people to be a surviving prehistoric creature, a wplesiosaur. Many photographs of something strange in the water have been taken, but analysis often proves that the 'something strange' is in fact a bird, or a wave, or a piece of wood – or a straightforward hoax. Conclusive proof in the form of a carcase is required, yet even extensive underwater exploration using mini-subs and sonar has not yet resulted in even a flipper. So the jury must remain out as to whether Nessie really exists, or is no more than a myth fuelled by publicity and gullibility.

This must be the most famous photograph of the Loch Ness Monster, allegedly taken in April 1934 by R. K. Wilson, a London surgeon. The full-size photograph shows a lot more of the lake, with the monster appearing quite small. There is now a big question-mark over this photograph, since Christian Spurling announced in the 1990s that the monster was in fact a toy submarine with a sculpted head attached.

Marmaduke Wetherell, a big-game hunter and Spurling's father-in-law, is said to have created the hoax in revenge for having been ridiculed by the Daily Mail, the newspaper that employed him. However, not everyone accepts this solution to the mystery, and Nessie is not dead and buried just yet.

Doc's Nessie

On 21 May 1977, Tony 'Doc' Shiels – artist, magician, and wizard – stood alone on the ruins of Urquhart Castle overlooking Loch Ness and tried to use his psychic powers to conjure up Nessie from the depths. He claims to have been successful, and offered two photographs in proof. They show the '4 or 5 ft long' stretch of neck that emerged from the water less than 100 yards away, though he only had time to take two shots before it submerged again. One of the original 35mm transparencies survives, but the other was accidentally destroyed, and only a black and white print survives.

As an artist, Doc was able to memorise all aspects of his brief sighting, and noted that, 'The colour of the animal was greenish brown, with a paler underside. Skin texture, smooth and glossy. The animal was visible for no more than 4 or 5 seconds. It held itself very upright, very still, except for a turning of the head and a straightening of the neck before it sank, very smoothly, below the surface. It had powerful neck muscles.'

Although, as an artist and magician, Doc has acquired a reputation over the years for surreal escapades, that does not mean that he did not see and photograph Nessie as he claimed.

© Anthony Shiels/Fortean Picture Library

found on the back of a car in N Carolina. There were no prints around the car. The witness also notes the dog was barking excessively during the night and acting strangely. (Source - Stan Gordon www.pabigfootsociety.com examiner.com July 2009).

PHANTASMAGORIA: In Pennsylvania 'giant caterpillars' about seven inches long were spotted crossing the road. The witnesses saw about seven of them at different intervals along the road. Ten tourists on Chinas Kanas Lake, Xinjiang Uygur Autonomous Region, saw a one-meter high water monster which left a ten-meter wake. A humanoid was spotted in Maine, USA, with 'skin like a salamander'. In the Ongamira Valley in Argentina, a photograph of two white figures outside a cave has been taken, said to be male and female. In Namibia locals in the Onheleiwa and Oidiva villages are suffering livestock depredations by an unknown predator that locals are convinced has something to do with witchcraft. The footprints of the animal 'are bigger than a dog' and just vanished as if the creature disappeared into the air. (Source - ParanormalNews.com, bigfootsightings.com, Phantoms & Monsters, www.newera.com)

RETURN OF THE WOLVES: A wolf seen in Polkemmet Country Park, near Whitburn, Scotland, is now believed by local wardens to have been a husky. Keith McDowell reported seeing a wolf in the park in early August. He described it as being silver in colour with a bushy tail with a black streak along its back. Police launched an investigation and warned local farmers to be on the alert. Local dog warden Pauline Sinclair said: "I think it's more likely this animal was a husky. People often use this area to let them run.' However, it is interesting to note that no one has come forward saying they own or have lost a husky fitting the above description. Meanwhile in Dorset, Latvian workers spotted a wolf in the county and thought no more of it at the time – because they're used to seeing them in their own country. Finally word got to big cats researcher Merrily Harpur, who interviewed them. (Source - Edinburgh Evening News, Merrily Harpur http://www.dorsetbigcats.org - August 2009).

NESSIE GOOGLED: A security officer believes he found the image of Nessie on Google Earth. Jason Cooke told the Sun News that the

Sightings

65ft long object was "followed by thin strands". He said: "I couldn't believe it. It's just like the descriptions of Nessie." (SOURCE - DAILY TELEGRAPH: 25TH AUGUST 2009).

FANG FOUND: A large tooth measuring 3.8 inches found in the central belt of Scotland was handed over to Big Cats in Britain Lothian's representative Sam McKeown. Workers converting an old explosives compound dug the tooth out from under concrete. Dr Andrew Kitchener said after viewing photographs: "It looks like a large carnivore's canine, but I would need to compare it with our specimens to give it a positive identification. It looks like a tooth from an old game head – the splitting is characteristic of teeth drying out indoors." The tooth has now been sent to Dr Kitchener for identification. (SOURCE - BIG CATS IN BRITAIN AUGUST 2009).

FOREIGN INVADERS: The UK is still being invaded by foreign species. An eagle owl was recently spotted in Cardiff, and local residents were warned to lock up their pets. A group of skunks are reportedly living in the Forest of Dean: one was handed into a local wildlife centre in July and another was a killed by a car. Now another has turned up in a garden in Coleford, Gloucestershire, which is thought to be one of a pair sighted a few days earlier. In the same area, colonies of Lasius neglectus, the so-called Asian super ant, has been found at Hidcote Manor, near Chipping Camden. In Rutland a motorist believes she saw a South American Capybara ambling across the road near Exton. Kate Tudno-Jones recognised the enormous rodent from zoo trips and then confirmed her suspicions on the internet. Nigel Spencer of the Rutland and Leicestershire Pantherwatch said that more reports of a capybara have come in from Exton, and Buckminster. (SOURCE - WALES ONLINE, BBC NEWS, YAHOO NEWS, RUTLAND PRESS, NIGEL SPENCER HTTP://WWW.BIGCATS.ORG.UK – AUGUST 2009).

USA MYSTERY CATS: Nicholas Dixie reported to Big Cats in Britain on the 2nd of September 'a big black cat ambling across a stubble field' at Rockland St. Mary, Norfolk, Virginia. His wife managed to get a good view of it through binoculars before it ran off. She estimated it was nearly three feet long excluding tail. Lynn Reed and his wife watched what they thought

Morgawr, the sea giant

Morgawr ('sea giant' in Cornish) is said to live in the sea off Falmouth, Cornwall, and there have been numerous sightings over the years. It has variously been identified as a prehistoric plesiosaur or a rare long-necked seal, but without a carcase to study, the identification will have to remain tentative.

A couple of photographs were taken in 1976, but they remain controversial. They were allegedly taken by 'Mary F.' who wished to remain anonymous. She sent them to the local newspaper, and in her letter she said that the monster was only visible for a few seconds, but she thought its body was 15-18 feet long.

'It looked like an elephant waving its trunk, but the trunk was a long neck with a small head on the end, like a snake's head. It had humps on the back which moved in a funny way. The colour was black or very dark brown, and the skin seemed to be like a sealion's... the animal frightened me. I would not like to see it any closer. I do not like the way it moved when swimming.'

Doc Shiels was living in Falmouth at the time, and he claimed two sightings of Morgawr himself, on one occasion when accompanied by magazine editor David Clarke. They both saw 'a small dark head poking out of the water' and, as it moved closer, they saw that 'the greenish black head was supported on a long arched neck, more slender than that of a seal'. The head was ugly, like a big snail's head with little stalks or horns. Unfortunately David Clarke's camera failed to work properly.

A live sea serpent?
On 12 December 1964, French photographer Robert Le Serrec and his wife were crossing Stonehaven Bay, Hook Island, Australia, in a motorboat when – they claimed – they noticed an enormous monster lying on the sea bed. It looked like a giant tadpole, with a large head and thin body extending to about 30 feet (9m) in length.

They said they filmed it with a cine camera and then dived into the water to take further photographs of it below the surface (which didn't come out). When the creature opened its mouth, the couple swam away – though it seems like a foolhardy action to swim close to it in the first place. By the time they reached their boat, the monster had gone.

Such was their story. The late expert on sea serpents, Bernard Heuvelmans, was unimpressed: he considered the presence of eyes on the top of the creature's head 'unlikely'. One theory put forward is that the sea serpent was in fact a deflated weather balloon that had come to grief in the bay, and Le Serrec couldn't resist dressing up his story after he had successfully photographed it.

was a black mountain lion for over ten minutes near Dublin, Alameda County, California. Mr Reed said: "He was black as can be with a head the size of a cantaloupe. It was 3 feet long, the tail 2 1/2 feet, maybe 60, 75 pounds." (SAN FRANCISCO CHRONICLE, BIG CATS IN BRITAIN – AUGUST 2009).

POLISH PRIMATE: Numerous reports of a Bigfoot or what the Polish news agencies are calling a Yeti are being taken seriously by the authorities. Piotr Kowalski filmed a "monstrous, hairy creature" while on holiday in the Tatra Mountains. He said: "I saw this huge ape-like form hiding behind the rocks. When I saw it, it was like being struck by a thunderbolt," he told the daily Superexpress. Coming from Warsaw, I never really believed the local stories of a wild mountain ape-man roaming the slopes. But, now I do." The film was handed over to Robert Bernatowicz of the Nautilius Foundation who said, "The film clearly shows 'something' that moves on two legs and is bigger than a normal man. But because the camera shakes so much it is difficult to say what it is exactly. We need to go to the site and see what traces, if any, were left." Shortly afterwards the Morningstarr reported that the Wildman had been seen again, this time ogling a bikini-clad girl. 19-year-old Justyna Folgar was swimming in the river in the same location as above, as her boyfriend video-taped her. She said: "I wandered into the river for a dip when I realised that something was on the opposite shore. At first I thought it was a bear but it appeared to be stooping and then it raised itself on to two legs and ran off. I couldn't believe it." Mountain rangers are now searching the area for the creature. (SOURCE - THEMORNINGSTARR.CO.UK AUSTRIANTIMES.AT AUGUST 2009).

FLYING CREATURES: On August 11th 2009 a man living west of San Antonio in Texas heard a "loud awful scream" and saw a large flock of birds flushed out of trees as "a giant creature swooped out of the sky and just as quickly flew back up into the rocks." The witness continues: "It looked nothing like a bird. I was about 50 yards from it and would say

Sightings

conservatively that its wing span was 15ft. or so! It was dark coloured and had a very long beak and a strange long thin tail. This sounds crazy, but it actually resembled one of those flying dinosaurs though the head was not as large and it looked like it had feathers." Meanwhile, in Arkansas a group who went camping near an abandoned Amish community say they saw a large flying creature fly 'like a large worm or snake' that wrapped itself around a tree. (LON STRICKLER PHANTOMS & MONSTERS).

ISRAELI MERMAIDS: A town council in Haifia, Israel, is receiving reports of mermaid sightings, and have offered a reward for its capture. Apparently, many people have seen the half fish, half young girl, cavorting in the waters, but only at sunset. Crowds now line the shore with cameras but as yet no photographs of the nymph have been taken. (SOURCE - SKY NEWS).

MUCK MONSTER: Video footage has been shot of a creature said to live in Florida's Lake Worth Lagoon, now nicknamed the 'elusive muck monster' by the most recent witnesses. (SOURCE - WPTV.COM, AUG 31)

ARACHNID INVASION: Emma Craven from Bournemouth was rushed to hospital after being bitten by a false widow spider (Steatoda nobilis) while cleaning her bathroom. She felt a sharp pain, her thumb turned red and then her whole hand swelled up. Two more false widows were found in the next door house. Residents of Upper Walthamstow and Bisterne Avenue in London were evacuated to rid the dwellings of an infestation of the false widow. At Fraddon, Cornwall, Craig Broad found one of the venomous spiders in his garage and Chris Lonergen found one lurking in a corner of his house in Weymouth (assistant conservation officer at Dorset Wildlife Trust Anna Muckle said it was a 'really nice' specimen!). Meanwhile, Jan Crawford, of Donegal, found 'a large jet-black spider, with very thick legs' in a bunch of bananas from the local supermarket and Donna Hopkins spotted a pair of large hairy legs in vegetables she had just bought from her local Somerfield's in Coventry. Donna's spider was later identified as the dangerous Tube Web Spider from mainland Europe. A Halifax man found a highly venomous Brazilian Wandering Spider in bananas he purchased from Asda. In Essex a couple found a nest

Wild Creek wild man

The photographs of a Bigfoot allegedly taken by a forest patrol officer on 11 July 1995 at Wild Creek in the Mount Rainier foothills of Washington State are surrounded by controversy. The story is that the officer was hiking along a ridge when he heard splashing noises and from a high bank he looked down into a swampy lagoon where, 25-30 yards away, there stood something very large and hairy. He managed to shoot 14 photographs, but because of the light conditions some of them were dark, and this is probably the best one.

The main problems with these photographs are that the Bigfoot seems strangely motionless from shot to shot; its head seems unnaturally small and pushed into its shoulders; the photographer is conveniently anonymous, and seems to have been unusually brave, for few people would have stayed around long enough to take 14 photographs of such a monster at close quarters. The general consensus of opinion is that the whole episode was hoaxed – but without a confession no one can be absolutely certain of that.

Bluff Creek Bigfoot

In North America there have been over 1,000 reported sightings of the man-beast known as Bigfoot or Sasquatch during the last 150 years, and several thousands more sightings of giant footprints. Despite all this evidence, according to science the creature does not exist because, so far, no corpse has been obtained and so there is nothing for the scientists to study.

According to the reports, Bigfoot is usually between 6 and 8 feet tall, although some reports have said 10, 12, or even 14 feet. It is covered with dark hair, and walks upright like a man, leaving giant, human-like footprints.

The most famous photographs of Bigfoot were obtained back in 1967, on 20 October when Roger Patterson and his friend Bob Gimlin were riding deep in the forest at Bluff Creek in northern California, 25 miles from the nearest proper road. They had both been searching for Bigfoot for several years, and since the creatures were said to be in the area, they had gone out on their horses to look for them. As they rounded a bend, they saw a Bigfoot squatting beside the creek. At that moment their horses saw it too and reared in fright. Patterson's horse fell and he scrambled clear and pulled his movie camera out of the saddlebag.

The creature watched them for a moment and then walked unhurriedly away. Patterson ran after it, trying to get closer and filming at the same time, stumbling and losing his footing as he crossed the shallow creek. He was 80 feet away when he stopped and obtained reasonably clear pictures as the creature strode away behind the trees. Before being lost to view, it had paused briefly, turning to look at Patterson, and its large, pendulous, hair-covered breasts are discernible on the photograph, identifying the Bigfoot as a female. Later the men made casts of the footprints the creature had left, and they were 14.5 inches long by 5.5 inches wide.

Inevitably this footage is controversial, and periodically efforts are made to discredit it, but more than 40 years later it has not been conclusively proved to be a hoax. Roger Patterson died many years ago, but Bob Gimlin is still alive and has never changed his story. It is of course possible that Patterson and Gimlin were themselves fooled by someone else, a man dressed in a fur suit, but that person would have been taking a risk, as Patterson could easily have been carrying a gun and determined to bag a corpse. Also, surely anyone planning such a hoax would not have bothered to give the Bigfoot large breasts?

of tarantula eggs attached to their Asda bananas. A Leeds couple found a tarantula in Roundhay Woods, which they managed to capture using a stick and a plastic tub. Distillery workers in Alloa were alarmed after finding five deadly black widows in the space of a week. Two venomous wasp spiders have been found in the last few weeks, one in Canterbury and the other in Norfolk. A British Airways plane bound for London was grounded at Edinburgh Airport after a passenger reported seeing a tarantula crawl under his seat. The plane was fumigated but no spider was found. Scientists say that the exotic spider explosion in the UK is due to global warming. (Source - Bournemouth Echo, October 2009).

EURO PANTHERS: Big Cats in Britain correspondent Myriam Trausch sent the group prints from the recent sightings in Europe. She reports: 'The large black cat has been seen in Belgium, France as well as in Luxembourg. It seems to wander around in the border territory of our three countries. In the past week there have been sightings of the cat in a field in-between two Luxembourgish villages called Mamer and Bertrange. According to recent news reports the cat or cats seen are 'black and as big as a deer'. One Belgian witness states that the cat he saw was 1m 20 long and 80cm in height. (Source - Myriam Traucsh and Big Cats in Britain).

BIG PRINT: Tom Dongo reports on the Church Ufology blog: 'I was out for a walk along Oak Creek above Chavez Ranch, (USA). On a sandbar I found four or five perfect, five-toed footprints deeply embedded in wet sand. My hiking boot is a size 11 and is exactly 12 inches long and 4 inches wide at the ball. My boot fitted entirely inside the larger track without touching any part of the outside of it. The track itself was about fifteen inches long and at least six inches wide. Whoever or whatever made it must have weighed between 300 and 400 pounds. I weigh nearly 200, and my boot made only a slight impression on the surface of the sand. The 15-inch track was at least 1-1/2 inches deep in the sand. The

Sightings

other nearby track was very narrow and nearly as long as the 15-inch track and had an extremely long big toe. Judging by the depth of the track, the person must have weighed about the same as I do. (SOURCE - TOM DONGO HTTP://THECHURCHOFUFOLOGY.BLOGSPOT.COM: 4TH OCTOBER, 2009).

CHAMP: Two minute mobile phone footage was taken by Eric Olsen of a creature in Lake Champlain on the USA/ Canada border. It is said by some to be the best evidence for the existence of 'Champ' to date. In mid October the witness took the footage near Oakledge Park, Burlington, and reports: 'I was just filming the water when, out of the corner of my eye, I saw something move, and I turned toward it and tried to zoom in on it. You can see that it is moving horizontally, across the water, and vertically, going under the surface and coming back up. It struck me as something that was long, that it didn't have much girth.' Cryptozoologist Loren Coleman called for 'a formal forensic analysis ... to break it down frame by frame'. (SOURCE - YOUTUBE CRYPTOMUDO.COM PHANTOMS & MONSTERS: 18TH OCTOBER 2009).

FLYING CRYPTID: Lon Strickler of the website Phantoms & Monsters received the following report: 'We were in Pacific, MO, tonight around 11:30 pm and noticed a massive flying creature, not once but three times. We were near a large cliff/mountain with some type of cave openings. We don't live in the area. I can say for sure we turned onto a road called Viaduct Road, went past a fire station and continued on for about 1 mile before we first noticed it. It was brownish/grey and the body portion was at least the size of a large adult human. This creature was tracking us in a circle pattern. The third time around we viewed it in front of the vehicle, around the driver side and around towards the rear of the vehicle. Please understand when we could see it the range must have been about 150 feet in the air, not more than 250 feet. The distance was never less than 100 yards, often much greater. We were going about 35-45 mph.' (LON STRICKLER OF THE WEBSITE PHANTOMS & MONSTERS: 26TH OCTOBER 2009).

FLYING CRYPTID: Lon Strickler of the website Phantoms & Monsters received the following report: 'We were in Pacific, MO, tonight around 11:30 pm and noticed a massive flying creature, not once but three times.

Body of evidence
The trappers and prospectors of Alaska and northern Canada in the early years of the twentieth century sometimes reported seeing hairy 'wild men' in the forests and mountains. The photograph shows an unidentified creature shot by trappers at Lillooet in British Columbia in the early 1900s, but unfortunately no further information is available and its identity must remain a mystery.

The Skunk Ape

The creature seen here was photographed near the Myakka River in Sarasota County, Florida, in the autumn of 2000. It was hiding among the palmetto plants in an elderly woman's back yard, and she sent the photographs anonymously to the local sheriff, along with a letter telling how the creature had been making night-time visits and stealing apples from the back porch. She wondered if it was an escaped orangutan, but it has since been referred to as a 'Skunk Ape', which is the Florida name for the 'swamp monsters' seen there, possibly Bigfoot-type creatures.

We were near a large cliff/mountain with some type of cave openings. We don't live in the area. I can say for sure we turned onto a road called Viaduct Road, went past a fire station and continued on for about 1 mile before we first noticed it. It was brownish/grey and the body portion was at least the size of a large adult human. This creature was tracking us in a circle pattern. The third time around we viewed it in front of the vehicle, around the driver side and around towards the rear of the vehicle. Please understand when we could see it the range must have been about 150 feet in the air, not more than 250 feet. The distance was never less than 100 yards, often much greater. We were going about 35-45 mph.' (Lon Strickler of the website Phantoms & Monsters: 26th October 2009).

DEMON CAT OR CHUPACABRA: The carcase of a cat has been found by hunters in San Carlos, Arizona. It looks like a domestic cat "but with several noticeable differences." According to local news it has "elongated fangs and possible wings," causing some to say it is the fabled Chupacabra. It is further described as "saber-toothed" because its incisor teeth are elongated into fangs, the front limbs of the creature are also longer than an ordinary cat's legs and appear to have an extra joint giving the appearance of large feet. View the pictures at paranormalmagazine.co.uk/news. (Source - The Morning Star 31st December 2009).

SUNKEN EYES: A woman who remains anonymous has had a second encounter with a strange and terrifying creature in La Pampa, Argentina. On the 20th of October at 8pm she was just entering her house when she noticed a strange presence in her living room. The being placed a hand on her arm which left scars. Various items of furniture were strewn over the floor. Her dog was found cowering under furniture. The being is described as standing nearly two-metres tall. 'Slender but very strong,' the witness reports. 'Its eyes appear sunken into its face' but that they emanate a sensation of 'tenderness'. (Source - CEUFO and Planeta UFO: 25th October 2009).

Over the past sixty years, there have been many thousands of reports of strange flying objects seen around the world. At first they were called 'flying saucers', then 'unidentified flying objects' or UFOs.

Despite the wealth of sighting reports, and claims of craft with aliens aboard crashing in the desert, it is virtually certain that hard evidence of the existence of extraterrestrial craft has not been obtained. There are plenty of photographs purporting to show UFOs, but their reliability is questionable - and indeed the more detailed the craft appears in the photograph, the more likely it is to be hoaxed!

At the one extreme are the sceptics who assert that all UFO reports are either hoaxes or misidentifications of normal astronomical events or terrestrial objects. At the other extreme are the believers who tell us that UFOs are craft from other worlds outside our solar system, or from other dimensions or parallel universes.

One thing is certain: the UFO craze has spawned an amazingly rich literature full of case-histories detailing close encounters, abductions by aliens, and even trips into space with the occupants of extraterrestrial craft. Either there are a lot of liars in this world, or many deluded or deranged individuals - or maybe even some who are speaking the truth about their otherworldly encounters...

UFOs & Aliens

Caught on camera
UFOs are usually photographed by people who have seen something strange in the sky and want to record it, but sometimes an apparent UFO just turns up on a photograph taken for some other reason. That is what happened in October 1981 on Vancouver Island, British Columbia, Canada.

Hannah McRoberts was on holiday with her husband and baby, and she was determined to prove to her husband that she could take a sharp photograph. She was attracted by the cloud and the mountain, which looked like a volcano, and she was concentrating hard on capturing this effect and keeping the camera steady when she took the photograph. The UFO is so small in the frame that it is not surprising that neither she nor her husband saw it, as they were not thinking about or looking for UFOs at the time.

Sightings

Taken from the pages of **Paranormal Magazine**

PINK JELLYFISH: A witness in Wimbledon, London, reports: 'I looked out of my flat window, over towards Merton way, and to my surprise noticed a large bright pink jellyfish-looking object surrounded by a pink haze. It appeared to be hovering over or above the pylons in the distance. It hovered for about five minutes while I frantically searched for my camera. Did anyone else in Wimbledon see it?' Could it have been an Unidentified Floating Organism as described by Dr Karl Shuker in last month's Paranormal? See Experiences on page 78-79 for more one unidentified sky beasts. (SOURCE - WIMBLEDON GUARDIAN).

BALL OF FIRE 1: A ball of flame was seen by a holidaymaker near Whitby Abbey, Graeme Edwards reports: 'It was travelling south relatively slowly, but too quick for a hot air balloon firing its burners as there was no wind in the sky. It could have been a plane with an engine on fire, or so I thought. My father thought he saw four lights but to me it just looked like a fireball. I also thought it could have been a comet or something burning through the atmosphere. It was difficult to get perspective on it to see how big or close it was as it was pitch black.' Joanne Rowe also spotted the ball of light a few hours earlier: she said it looked like some kind of rocket. (SOURCE - WHITBY GAZETTE).

BALL OF FIRE 2: Photographs of a similar UFO were taken by Michael Simpson over St Helens in Lancashire. Mr Simpson said: 'It was around the height that the police helicopter can normally be seen, so this was my first thought as to what it could be. There was, however, absolutely no sound emitting from the object. I had stopped travelling at this point and the object was moving very slowly and steadily towards me. It could not have been travelling any faster than 40-60 knots. Initially, I thought I could see a shaft of orange or red light shining down beneath the object, but as it crept ever closer it became apparent I was looking at flames. Please, let me be clear; I do not think I saw flames. I know I did.' (SOURCE - ST HELEN'S OBSERVER).

Yorkshire saucers

Stephen Pratt was almost fifteen when he took this photograph at his home in Conisbrough, South Yorkshire, on 28 March 1966. He was returning home with his mother from the fish and chip shop after 8 o'clock when she saw a pulsating reddish-orange light in the twilit sky, and they watched as it moved slowly up and down, and then faster across the sky. The rest of the family – father and two brothers – were fetched and all of them watched the strange light. Kevin Pratt said he could hear 'a low drone or whirring sound'.

Stephen's father told him to fetch his camera, a Kodak Instamatic, and Stephen took one photograph, thinking it was really too dark for photography. Kevin told how, 'The object remained motionless below the clouds, until it suddenly shot off, at a fantastic speed... and was out of sight in what seemed like a fraction of a second.'

Although only one light was easily seen, Mr Pratt thought he could make out other shapes, and in fact the photograph showed three domed objects. There have been many attempts to claim this event as a hoax, but Stephen has remained adamant over the last 44 years that his photograph shows genuine UFOs.

The Lubbock Lights

Known as the Lubbock Lights, this string of possible UFOs was photographed by Carl Hart, Jr., at Lubbock, Texas, on 31 August 1951. Hart was a 19-year-old student and amateur photographer, and he managed to take five photographs of the lights.

There were other similar sightings, and many attempts were made to explain them, the most popular being that the effect was caused by flights of birds with their undersides reflecting the street lights, especially the newly installed sodium vapour lamps. However, strings of lights in the night skies were being seen all over west Texas, including in areas without the same type of street lights.

Another suggestion by respected UFO researcher Edward Ruppelt was that the effect was caused by 'night flying moths reflecting the bluish-green light of a nearby row of mercury vapour street lights.' But somehow it seems unlikely that such an effect could be caused either by birds or moths, especially as the lead photographer of the Lubbock newspaper tried to duplicate the photographs at night from the roof of the newspaper office, and failed. He saw a flight of birds, but they were scarcely visible in the street lights, and his photograph showed only very faint images. He was convinced that whatever the lights were, they weren't birds.

HANGING OVER THE HIGHLANDS: Unidentified orange UFOs have been spotted several times recently in Ross-shire, Scotland. One witness, Mrs McDonald, was travelling to work in Alness and reports: 'I saw three bright orange lights in the sky, about 100ft off the ground. They looked like they were flickering inside. I was on the A9, just passing Rosskeen Church. I thought at first it was something to do with the oil rigs in the firth and that they had put up some new masts, but as I got nearer I realised they were just hanging there.' (SOURCE - ROSS-SHIRE TIMES).

LUFTWAFFE SCRAMBLED: A mystery object was tracked over the skies of Germany by air traffic controllers, the German Air Force was scrambled to intercept the UFO which crossed the whole of country, putting several airports on red alert. An official report is now being compiled by the Air Traffic Safety Office, (DFS) who said: 'We have ruled out all the conventional possibilities – it is a mystery. When it vanished from the radar we believed that whatever it was had crashed but there was no crash site to be seen.' The object was last seen over Grafenwoehr, which is an area used by American troops for training. (SOURCE - AUSTRIAN TIMES).

V-SHAPED: A V-shaped UFO was spotted over the Californian San Fernando Valley by a young couple on their way to dinner. They were driving in a convertible with the top down. Bush fires were raging near Santa Clarita and the smell of smoke was heavy in the sky. They then noticed 'an usually large object which frightened the hell' out of them: 'An enormous V–shaped craft, hundreds of feet across, with red lights, lumbering slowly across the sky.' The object displayed several other coloured lights and gave off an eerily red glow. After several minutes, it 'just vanished'. (SOURCE - MUFON).

TENTACLED: Soquel, California. The witness reports: 'We were working, and I was on my lunch break, when I heard my father calling my name and saying, "What's that in the sky?" I didn't think it was going to be what I saw. I got out of my truck and looked into the sky. There it was,

Sightings

a metallic object. It moved slowly across the sky, but the arms of it rotated and moved without sync. It looked like octopus arms, individually moving in different directions. The object continued to move across the sky until it was no longer visible. This object was extremely far up in the sky. I believe I saw a UFO.' (SOURCE - PHOTOS AT HTTP://WWW.COASTTOCOASTAM.COM).

UP FROM THE DEPTHS: Eight witnesses travelling in two cars spotted a UFO leaving a lake in Jemba, East Java, Indonesia. The leading car came to 'a screeching halt' as two lights, one red and one white, rose up from the lake. Suddenly, two beams of light shot up into the air from the objects and they began to change their formation. This lasted for about 10 minutes before the objects shot upwards into the sky and vanished. (SOURCE - HTTP://LEVELBEYOND.COM).

TWO TOPS: A UFO was filmed in China by an entire squadron of fire-fighters in Pan Shui City, Guizhou. One fireman said: 'We noticed an odd looking, brightly flashing star moving in a south-easterly direction and went inside the fire-fighters' barracks to get a camera.' It seemed to be two rotating top-shaped craft, 'or halves of a whole craft joined at their bases'. The slow-moving object(s) flashed purple, red, blue, orange white and gold. The fire-fighters observed the phenomenon for almost an hour before it disappeared from view. (SOURCE - AUDREY CHAN, ALLNEWSWEB.COM).

WOKEN BY ALIENS: Nestor and Sara Rivoira were asleep in their home Arroyo Leyes, Santa Fe, Argentina, when they were awakened by a loud noise which lasted for nearly ten minutes. The noise sounded like that made by a flame-thrower. They tried to get out of bed but something was keeping them from doing so. When they went into their garden the next day they were amazed to find 'strange holes' in their garden. They said: 'We thought at first that the marks could've been made by an All Terrain Vehicle, as there are many in the area. But then we dismissed this idea, since they weren't prints, but rather something created with an object that irradiates heat. If you look at them closely, there is no vegetation in the circumference, only dry, dead soil, different to what we can see around.' (SOURCE - HTTP://WWW.DIARIOUNO.COM.AR).

Over New Jersey
George J. Stock took five photographs of a UFO which hovered over his home at Passaic, New Jersey, on 29 July 1952. There had been numerous sightings in the area, and Stock spotted one travelling silently and at a leisurely speed over his property. It stopped and hovered overhead for a few moments, about 200 feet above the ground. It was about 30 feet in diameter and greyish in colour, with a large dome jutting from its centre.

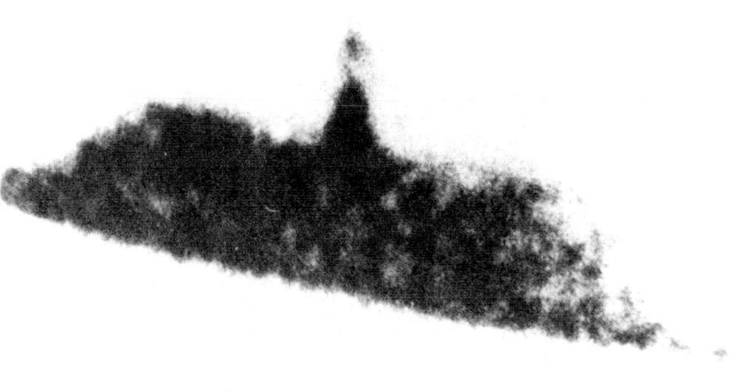

The McMinnville disc
Two classic photographs of a UFO over McMinnville, Oregon, have stood the test of time. They were taken on 11 May 1950 by Paul Trent from his farmyard, but one factor in favour of the Trents not being involved in a hoax is that they then waited several weeks before getting the film developed, and also showed the photographs only to family members. It was a friend who suggested they take them to their banker, and he alerted the local newspaper.

Since then the pictures have been subjected to thorough examination by various experts, and although some people have claimed they must be hoaxed, this may be nothing more than a natural reaction when a researcher who does not believe in the possibility of extraterrestrial craft is faced with a truly inexplicable photograph. William K. Hartmann stated in the Condon Report that 'all factors investigated, geometric, psychological, and physical appear to be consistent with the assertion that an extraordinary flying object, silvery, metallic, disk-shaped, tens of meters in diameter, and evidently artificial, flew within sight of two witnesses.'

SKY BEAST: A motorist was driving along Birfield Road, Southcote in Reading, Berkshire, on February 15 at 7pm when he and his mother 'saw a strange object in the sky'. It was moving fast in circular movements. The witness explained: 'It kind of looked like a jellyfish as it had a weird see-through film around it and hovered in the sky like one. It was lower than an aircraft and moved completely different to one and was also slower. It looked like a fireball, kind of egg-shaped but was very strange orangey, reddy and yellowy in colour.' (MUFON, FEB 16).

MULTIPLE WITNESSES: A bus driver reported a possible UFO at Stockton-on-Tees. Apparently, at about 10pm, eight orange ball shaped lights followed by a solitary one passed silently over Stockton High Street. About five drivers saw this, and they were adamant that it wasn't a known aircraft. (SOURCE - CHRIS HALL BCIB: FEB 2009).

MESMERISING: On March 3, three V-shaped UFOs were spotted over Bucks county in Pennsylvania, (see UFO Hotspots, starting on page 34). The UFOs were described as being silent 'with a plethora of mesmerizing white and blue/green lights'. One witness reports: 'I saw the lights from outside my home, they at first looked like two very bright headlights. The objects then flew over my home. The UFO was grey. (SOURCE - THE EXAMINER, MARCH 6).

FIREBALL: US strategic command reported that a shower of fireballs over Texas was not debris from the recent satellite collision which occurred over Siberia. Williamson County officials received reports from residents of orange fireballs streaking across the skies. A journalist, Eddie Garcia, from News 8 Austin caught an image of the fireballs on camera. He said: 'At the time, I'm looking in the viewfinder, and I see something flying through the sky. It looks like it could be dust, it could be something. I look up, and no, it was something burning in the sky.' (SOURCE - NEWS 8 AUSTIN: 16TH FEBRUARY 2009).

RED ALERT: Red UFOS have been seen several times over New Jersey.

Sightings

They returned again on February 17 over Morris County. Several police stations received reports from residents who reported that around ten red lights, 'moving in unison' were seen at around 8.45am to 9pm. A theory was put forward that they could be Chinese lanterns! (SOURCE - ASSOCIATED PRESS, FEB 18).

FOLLOWED: Two brothers hauling wood across frozen Millinocket Lake which sits in the shadow of Maine's Mount Katahdin, had an unnerving experience. 'They saw a low flying light, 50 feet above the tree line, shining a light to the ground. The light soon turned to three red lights forming a triangle. The brothers moved to their camp, returning a few minutes later only to encounter a single red light which appeared to follow them... while two more lights joined the first in the sky and seemed, at one point, to be surrounding them. When the brothers decided it was time to get out of there, their vehicle's engine shut down. (SOURCE - MUFON, FEB 19).

OFFICIAL: One civilian and three uniformed police officers reported seeing a UFO over Greenville, Hunt County, Texas. One witness spotted a bright object hovering above her house which dimmed, grew bright again then flew off. Sheriff Randy Meeks reported: 'Three of my officers also saw a bright light, including the deputy who first responded to the sighting. (SOURCE - HERALD BANNER, MARCH 2).

TRIANGULAR FORMATION: A video has been taken of three UFOs in a triangular formation over Huánuco, Peru. They were in the area for at least two hours before one headed north-east, the other two staying for a little while longer before disappearing. (SOURCE - UFO / OVNI, FEB 7).

BURNING UP: Argentina's Neuquén Astronomical Observatory tracked three unidentified objects entering the earth's atmosphere 'which created a tremendous flash that lit the region's skies from Alto Valle to the Cordilleran Lake region, according to witnesses'. The incident occurred around 10.15 pm. Roberto Figueroa, director of the Observatory, reported that at 'I was in the observatory with some people and we suddenly saw how the entire sky in the western part of Parque Norte become illuminated. We saw three very bright objects, unidentified, which exploded upon entering the atmosphere, producing a tremendous flash that was

Friends from Venus

According to his written accounts, Howard Menger first met alien visitors when he was ten years old, in 1932. Visiting a favourite woodland glade near his home in New Jersey, he found a woman of unearthly beauty waiting for him. She told him, 'Howard, I have come a long way to see you, and to talk to you.'

She spoke at length about his future and purpose on Earth, and told him of further visits he would have from others of 'her people', who, he learned later, came from Venus. Sure enough, by the 1950s he was claiming regular sessions with the Venusians – indeed he and his wife believed they had been reincarnated from previous lives on the planet Venus.

Menger also met Martians and Saturnians, and in 1956 was given a trip to the space people's Moon base. They all looked human, but one of Menger's tasks was to provide clothing for Venusians newly arrived on Earth, so that they could move about undetected. On one occasion he also gave a Venusian male with long blond locks a short-back-and-sides haircut so that he would not attract attention.

Menger took some photographs of his alien friends in the 1950s, and these two show Venusians, one of them silhouetted against a spacecraft. The other Venusian disappeared after touching a shiny gadget on her belt, and another spaceman standing nearby said she had returned to the spacecraft.

Costa Rica enigma
During an aerial photography mission over Costa Rica in 1971, a UFO appeared on one frame of the film. The frames were shot at intervals of 17 seconds, and no UFO appeared in the previous and following frames.

followed by a sort of smoke.' Residents from Bariloche reported seeing a light fall into Lake Nahuel Huapi. Others saw flashing lights over the lake. The Navy searched the area but found nothing. (SOURCE - RIO NEGRO, FEB 17)

OVER CHEB: Several reports of bright orange UFOs were reported from the country in February concentrated around the northern town of Cheb. Paul Beran said: 'We saw two lights and then another two, one emitting a bright orange light, the objects then shot away into the distance in a westward direction. It all lasted about a minute.' Vaclav Tondl saw the same lights buzz over the town square on February 14. Five objects circled over the town, then the church before flying off. The objects made no sound. Two nights later more UFOS were spotted by worried residents, the local police launched an investigation. (SOURCE - HTTP:// KARLOVARSKY.DENIK.CZ, FEB 20).

'CHINESE LANTERN' OVER CHINA: Physics Professor Zhang Shen spotted a fiery UFO over Kumming. His wife was standing on the balcony when she saw a 'fiery orange glowing object streak across the sky. The object was travelling at an incredible speed and crossed the sky in less than four minutes.' She called her husband who also saw the light. Mrs Zhang took a picture of the UFO on her mobile phone. The newspaper reported that the UFO pictured in China looks similar to the 'Chinese lanterns' spotted in the UK. Surely a Chinese professor could tell a Chinese lantern when he sees one? What have the British really been seeing? (SOURCE - ALLNEWSWEB, MARCH 3).

KENT: The witness was driving through Orpington when she spotted "a huge bright ball, like a fireball, falling to earth," on the 6th of March. She reports: "We watched as this spinning orange ball stopped abruptly and shot backwards in a south to westerly direction backwards very quickly. I took a picture on my mobile phone and on looking at it when I got home I noticed two small orange lights: after zooming in on them the shape changes like a triangle inside a sphere with two orange lights and a dark patch in the middle." (WWW.UK-UFO.CO.UK, 6TH MARCH).

Experiences

'Annie' clears her name

It was in April 2008 that I first realised my house was being haunted. As somebody who has had a keen interest in the paranormal since I was nine or ten years old (I'm now 44), and an out-and-out 'believer', I have had a number of encounters with spirits over the years, usually a strong smell (often of perfume or tobacco smoke), occasionally accompanied by the strong feeling of a presence, but this was the first time I had experienced anything in my own home.

At the time I had lived at my current address for over 16 years and had never experienced anything remotely paranormal. So when family photos I have lined up along a bookcase in my living room began literally flying from one side of the room to the other, despite all doors and windows being closed and the heating turned off, and I began to experience extremely loud crashing noises coming from upstairs which sounded like the wardrobe being turned over even though nothing was ever disturbed or out of place, I knew it bore all the hallmarks of a haunting.

These events went on for a couple of months, usually once or twice a day, with the occasional lapse for a short time. They did not particularly concern me since they were not aimed in my direction, but I definitely had the feeling that someone was trying to get my attention. Then one evening a friend of mine, Eddie, dropped by for a visit. Eddie is not a medium but he is interested in the paranormal and a good deal more sensitive to spirits than I am. During the course of our conversation I just happened to mention the recent activity and he immediately said, 'I wasn't going to say anything because I didn't want to worry you, but there is definitely a presence in this house.'

He went on to say he thought the spirit was a male, as it was very strong. For me, this at least confirmed what I had suspected all along, and that the activity wasn't just me misinterpreting normal phenomena. It was time to find out more.

Another friend of mine, Rodger, is an extremely gifted natural medium. I explained to him what was happening in my house and he immediately agreed to come over and try to discover the cause. When Rodger arrived the following week, the moment he entered the house he was afflicted by an intense, crushing headache. Straight away he said that the energy in the house was very negative, not evil but just a very angry female presence. After what Eddie had said about thinking it was a male I assumed this was a different spirit, but Rodger assured me it was the same one. He also said it was one of the strongest energies he had ever encountered (which would explain her ability to throw photographs and make loud crashing noises).

When Rodger first attempted to make contact with her, she was extremely agitated and kept repeating 'I didn't do it' over and over again. It took Rodger at least ten minutes to get her to calm down enough to get any sense out of her, but even then she would quickly get upset again and start repeating 'I didn't do it' once more. It took quite some time and a lot of patience to find out anything about her, but finally Rodger was able to discover who she was and why she was in my house.

It turned out that her name was Annie. She had apparently been the wife of a rabbit warrener, and one of her jobs had been to take the pelts of the rabbits to the local factory for processing. One day, she was accused of stealing six pelts that had gone missing. She was arrested and imprisoned, and subsequently tried at the Assizes (Quarter Sessions) at the nearby town of Thetford, where she was found guilty and sentenced to death. She was hanged, according to Annie, in July 1794. She was in her mid-twenties when she died.

Now that she had quietened down somewhat, it was easier for Rodger to get more information out of her. It seemed that she was so angry at being falsely accused and then executed that she refused to cross over and had remained here to try and clear her name. Of course, she had quickly discovered that no one could any longer see or hear her, and then as the years had gone by everyone connected to her trial and punishment had passed away, leaving her alone

When Rodger first attempted to make contact with her, she was extremely agitated and kept repeating 'I didn't do it' over and over again. It took Rodger at least ten minute

and trapped and not knowing how to go about crossing over.

Although she did not say so, Rodger felt that I was not the first person she had followed home in an attempt to tell her story and get help, although it seemed as if I was the first to be aware of her presence. When Rodger asked her if she wanted to cross over she said yes without hesitation, although she insisted that she wanted her story to be told and her name cleared. I promised her I would do what I could (which is the reason for me writing to you) and then with some help and guidance from Rodger she was able to cross to the other side.

Many people might think that the above is the result of an over-active imagination, but I can honestly say that since that day there have been no more flying pictures, and no more loud bangs from upstairs.

So much for all the information I had been given, but I wanted to know was if any of it could be substantiated, and, more importantly, if I could find any record of an 'Annie'. The town where I live, Brandon in Suffolk, is located within the Brecks, a vast area of sandy heath and conifer plantations, where I often go for walks. From medieval times up to the early 19th century this area had many warrens where rabbits were farmed for their meat and fur. What I didn't realise until carrying out some research was that at the end of the 18th century Brandon had been an important centre for producing felt for the hat trade, felt that was made from rabbit fur and processed at a large factory in the town. This fact seemed to lend credence to Annie's story.

Further research revealed that Assizes courts were indeed held at Thetford (another fact I did not know), but unfortunately I discovered that the records for Thetford were destroyed in a fire many years ago. A search through the lists of inmates in Norfolk's women's prisons showed plenty of 'Annes' but none that fitted the bill for my ghostly visitor. Despite this failure, I have no reason to doubt the information given to me by Rodger, and I know that what I experienced was quite real.

For now my research continues, in the hope that one day I can find proof that Annie was indeed a real person who suffered a dreadful fate for a petty crime that even now, over two hundred years later, she insists that she did not commit.

Richard J. West, Suffolk

Suddenly, I can see what they have seen, as an unknown animal comes into my view swimming towards the girls at the edge of the harbour towards the bridges and the town.

The day I sighted Storsie

I live in Östersund, which is located on the shores of Storsjön (The Great Lake), the fifth largest in Sweden. Since the Viking-era there have been many hundreds of sightings of the Storsjöodjuret, the Great Lake Monster (the animal is depicted on a runestone here!). In 2009 alone there were seven reports of sightings in the local media.

In late July 1977 (I've forgotten the exact date), I was 16 and cycling on my way home after an ordinary day of school. I am on a street called Hornsgatan on the island of Frösön, near Östersund. As I approach a crossing, I look down to the lake, which is two blocks down to make sure that there is no car approaching. For a split second I can clearly see something black, the size of a Volkswagen, rise in the water in the harbour. Within a second, since I am moving forward with some speed, a house is blocking my view. But my brain is sending me the message, 'What the hell was that?'. So I immediately turn around, and in the seconds it takes for me to do that, this black thing has gone.

So I move as fast as I can down there and as I arrive I can see nothing at all in the harbour. There is no boat whatsoever moving (and they are white or have lighter colors in any case). But I do see a few men talking excitedly about half a block from me to the left. I kick myself for it now, but I never approached them. Instead, after a few minutes, I hurried back home and told my mother excitedly of what I had seen.

At this point she tells me that my sister (Maria) and one of her friends have gone to a bridge near a hospital on Frösön a few kilometres away in the hope of spotting Storsie there – the local media had reported a recent sighting there. So my sister and her friend had been sitting there for hours, and meanwhile I had accidentally tripped over something mysterious literally just a couple of blocks from home.

Forty minutes later, I decided 

to go down there again, and this is when the real thing happened. Again, I am on my bike, and within seconds I can spot two girls about my age screaming and pointing at the pier. Suddenly, I can see what they have seen, as an unknown animal comes into my view swimming towards the girls at the edge of the harbour towards the bridges and the town.

As you can imagine, I get myself over there as fast as I possibly can, and there it is. Clear as day. I just know that this is Storsie. It is within 10 metres from us. I start to walk by the shore (which is built in such a way that it steeps down) just looking at it. It is about three metres in length, what I could see of it. First there is a head or (most likely) the back of a neck, then some water, followed by the bulk of the body. It moves along like a boat upside down. It does not move like a snake would, it just moves straight forward, and I have no idea what makes it behave like that.

After having followed it for some distance, I start to feel that I must see more and in my head I suddenly thinks that if I piss it off I may get to see it raise its head out of the water. I know it sounds crazy now, and I am not proud of it, but I picked up a small rock and threw it, but missed. I never tried a second time because I did not want to lose a second of watching this animal finding another rock. Then, after about 300 metres from the pier, it decided to dive and that was it.

Today, a small place designed for swimmers is located at the spot, but it was not there back then. As I was standing there looking out, I realized that a small boat with two or three people in it, was circling around for a few minutes closer to the bridge to my right, as if they were clearly on the lookout for something. Also, there is every chance that witnesses could have seen this from cars from the bridge itself.

For me, the story ended there. I guess I wanted to get back to my bike before somebody could nick it, so I went back to the harbour again and then onwards to home. The next day I realized that if I had jumped onto my bike and moved myself in a hurry to the smaller bridge beyond the main one, I could possibly have seen it from the bridge it had passed beneath, because on a fine summer day you can see the stones at the bottom there. Needless to say, I regret this to this day because had I seen it from that angle, I would have known much more about actual size and so on.

In my defence, I think it is safe to say that your brain is not operating properly in a situation like this. How could it? You have just seen something that supposedly should not even exist. That is one hell of an experience.

At home, my mother thought that I should report this to our newspaper, so we did. I promised them a drawing (I was making my own comics at the time, so I knew how to draw) so I grabbed a sheet and a pen and headed down to the harbour. Sadly, I do not have the exact date of the sighting, but I found out that it was in print in late July. I only wish that some of the other witnesses from that day will make a late appearance and say 'Hey, I was there.' A bit late now, but it would be interesting to meet somebody who shared the experience.

If you want to know what's going on with Storsie, please visit my blog at *www.myspace.com/storsie.*

Mike Eriksson, Sweden

'A human eye was watching me from the floor. I took a kettle of boiling water and poured it through the hole, but the eye was back several minutes later.'

Shop of horrors

My family came to England from India in 1970, and we all chipped in to buy a small corner shop. This we enlarged into another room and widened the stock and kept open 18 hours every day. We spoke good English and integrated into the Christian community in Bedford, where we were well accepted.

But problems began when we took down the wall into the room behind the shop to enlarge again in 1974. During the night the racks of tinned goods in the newly enlarged room would be thrown onto the floor; at midnight bangs and bumps and a man wailing in pain could be heard; and things from that room would go missing and turn up in strange places. These things would almost always be worse at full moon, when the large shape of an obese man could be seen wearing spectacles, and a shadow of this was easily visible many times in the newly enlarged room.

Things came to a head when my wife also reported a human eye watching her through the crack in the door, and my young son said he saw an eye through a hole in the garden fence.

Things reached fever pitch when I was at the kitchen stove

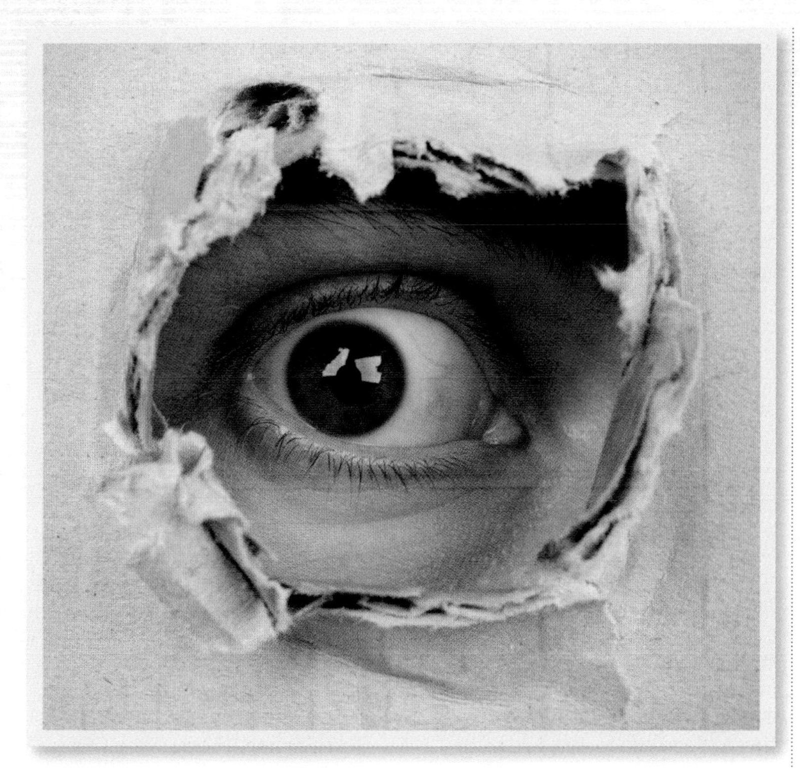

'His body is still under the floorboards here. If you dig down and clear the rubble you will first find a pair of tortoiseshell glasses.'

one lunchtime and I noticed from a knot-hole in the floorboards was a human eye watching me from the floor right by my foot, so I took a kettle of boiling water from the stove and poured it through the hole, but the eye was back several minutes later.

Several nights later while shaving I saw in the mirror an angry looking fat man's face with glasses and a black swollen eye, standing behind me.

We called in several priests, a holy man and a couple of mediums but, if anything, after their visits the night-time wailing and banging was worse and my family was getting very afraid.

On one occasion we had a lady in the shop try to sell us the Watchtower magazine [the Jehova's Witness publication], and in chatting we told her about the haunting. She organized a prayer meeting in the back room of the shop, and a bunch of these religious people came and prayed, but they saw quite plainly the shadow appear of the obese man in spectacles standing watching and they quickly all shuffled out.

We saw a magazine article about a man who had to call in an exorcist for his cottage and he gave us the address of a man he just called 'the exorcist'. We wrote to him for help, and he phoned us that night and said: 'Tell me nothing. I will come tomorrow.'

We had a sleepless night, and the man came and said do not tell me anything, and he looked from outside the shop for some while, before walking round inside. He eventually came to where we had enlarged the shop and most phenomena occurred, and he stunned us as he said: 'All this part of the shop was bombed in World War 2. The light from a full moon was ideal for bombing, and an obese man was reading his newspaper just here on this spot and ignored the air raid sirens.

'His body is still under the floorboards here. If you dig down and clear the rubble you will first find a pair of tortoiseshell glasses.'

This was all a bit of a shock, but he just asked for his train fare back to London and left. We had a builder in the next week who lifted the floorboards and sure enough found a pair of fake-tortoiseshell glasses, while moving the rubble he pulled out an old brown wartime Daily Express newspaper, then the remains of the obese man.

The police came and cordoned off the area and took away the poor man. As they lifted him, the contents of his ragged trouser pockets all fell to the floor with keys, coins and glasses case; it was all totally very bizarre. The floor was put back and no more night-time disturbances occurred.

We often talk about this and confess we did not believe in 

ghosts or hauntings until this time. My family will always be grateful to the exorcist who came to help us that day, with his penetrating intuition – Mr T Stokes – who asked that the overweight man have a Christian burial.

N. Patel and family via email

Sheerness saucer

On the evening of Sunday 14th February at 7:45pm, I saw a strange object from my kitchen window in Sheerness. The object appeared as a huge red light which changed its colour to an orange as it flew from the direction of Minster In Sheppey towards the south-west.

When the object was glowing red I could just see a disc-like shape within. The shape vanished when it was orange.

I have lived in Sheerness for a number of years and have seen many aircraft flying over during the day and a night. I have seen many aircraft with flashing lights fly over my area at night but this object appeared as a single big light changing from red to orange.

Kevin Lee, via email

Gasping for breath

Well, I think my study is haunted. It is always 5 degrees centigrade or lower, even in summer! Sure, a good explanation is that it's facing south, but I have also seen strange apparitions: an old lady lying on the floor, gasping for breath.

The first time I saw this I was SO freaked out, but it happens so often now I've got used to it. What I want to know is if it's my grandma, who died in there about 20 years ago.

Lorelei Nielson, via email

More spooky smoke

This smoky-looking picture was taken by my 6-year-old son. The vision is blurry as my son is autistic and had the camera upside down.

It was taken around Christmas. The weird part being that twice last Christmas [2008] and at no other time of the year, my wife heard her name being called behind her head, where the Christmas tree was, then several days later through the computer's speakers. Then this picture this year.

I try to look for explanations myself. If it was the camera strap then it would have to have been moving at an amazing speed as the smoky-looking lines seem to move in several directions. I can see the shape of a man looking like he is sitting on the couch; I can almost make out a lapel at what I would call the top of the shoulder.

Darren Cosgrove, via email

The weird part being that twice last Christmas and at no other time of the year, my wife heard her name being called behind her head, where the Christmas tree was, then several days later through the computer's speakers.

Attacked by the jinn

It was the summer of 1996 and I was on holiday in Azad Kashmir, in Pakistan. One night I was travelling on a motorcycle with a friend and he said to me: 'Jagga, be quiet, this place is inhabited by jinns.'

I was young and naive and did not believe in jinns. Sensing the fear of my friend, I decided to wind him up. I shouted: 'Oh jinns,

I could not breathe, no air would go past my throat because my chest was being crushed. I rolled around on the floor, fighting to get this thing off me, flailing my arms around but because I could not breathe I very quickly had no energy left.

come out and mess with me, let's see how tough you really are!'

My friend got more scared and told me to shut up which made me laugh and I continued to challenge the jinns. Little did I know that they would accept my foolhardy challenge.

Two days passed and I was out in the valleys of Kashmir with a cousin and it was late at night. We were walking back to the small village where I was staying at my aunt's house. We were walking on a cobbled path with a cliff face to my left and fields to my right. As we approached the village my cousin said he had left his walking stick in the valley where we had sat chatting. He told me to wait for him on the path while he went back to retrieve his stick, which was a long staff with metal caps on the end.

So off he went to get the stick while I waited for him on the path. After a few minutes I heard a weird noise come from above and to my left and at the same time the noise of the insects which you can hear clearly at night went totally silent. I thought, what was that noise? I knew it came from the top of the cliff to my left, which was about 20 or 30 foot high. I could not see the top of the cliff, being on the path right under it, so I walked out about twenty paces into the field on my right and turned around to see what was on top of the cliff.

It was a moonlit night and on top of the cliff I saw a black, smoky shadow about 6 foot tall and the hairs on the back of my neck stood up. As I watched this shadowy black creature it started to get taller and wider and I was frozen to the spot in amazement (I was not scared at that point). It grew and grew till it was at least 200 feet tall and 200 feet wide and it blocked out most of the sky behind it.

Then slowly it started to descend down towards me. As it got closer it blocked out everything in my vision it was so huge. It came right up to my face it was close enough to reach out and touch and then suddenly it disappeared and at the same time it felt as though my chest was crushed in a vice or a huge hand. I could not breathe, no air would go past my throat because my chest was being crushed. I rolled around on the floor, fighting to get this thing off me, flailing my arms around but because I could not breathe I very quickly had no energy left.

So I ended up on the floor and I'm saying to myself, 'Jagga, breathe!' but no air would go past my throat. Something was crushing my chest. My entire body was covered in sweat and my clothes were damp. That's when I heard a ticking noise from behind me and whatever was crushing my chest released its grip and I gasped for air.

I turned around and saw my cousin approaching: the ticking noise was the metal cap of his staff hitting the cobbled path. I stood up and as he approached me I managed to control my heavy breathing. A part of me wanted to tell him what had just happened to me but then I thought he would think I got scared for no reason and make fun of me so I decided to keep quiet.

We walked back to the village. I was silent, thinking about what had just happened to me. When we got to the village, which had small alleyways, we said goodbye to each other and he went down his alley and I proceeded up another to go to my aunt's house.

I did not get very far – there it was again waiting for me about 30 or 40 feet away on the path I had to use to get to my aunt's house. This time it was about 6 foot tall and the same black swirly smoky shadow. I stopped and it flew towards me fast, like it was carried by the wind. It hit my chest and disappeared and at the same instant my chest was crushed and I could not get any air past my throat. I tried to run to my aunt's house but after taking about ten or 15 paces I was completely exhausted, already tired by round one with this creature.

I didn't have the energy to take another step and rested my back against a wall, all the time trying to breathe but my chest is crushed. My legs gave away and I slid down the wall into a sitting position with my hands on my knees and my vision started to go.

It was like turning the brightness down on a old TV: the edges of my vision went black ☞

and the picture got smaller and smaller and then the small white dot in the middle went black. So there I am sitting there with my eyes open but no vision. Suddenly, my whole life went past me from childhood to that day: it was like flicking the pages of a book with an image on each page. That's when I thought I was about to die. That's when I recited the kalimah: 'Laa ilaaha illallaahu Muhammadur rasoolullaah.'

Praise be to Allah, as soon as I read the kalimah I was released from the grip on my chest and I gasped for air. After several minutes, my vision returned and I staggered to my aunt's house, holding the walls for support and collapsed on my bed which was outside due to it being so hot in the summer.

I awoke the following morning and found a doctor was examining me. He said I had some type of indigestion (lol) and I had a deep fear inside me that if I told anyone I would not survive. My chest hurt a lot and I did not tell anyone about what happened.

When I got back to the UK I started to catch glimpses of the same creature following me but as soon as I looked it would disappear. At first I tried to ignore it but this kept on happening for about a year and I thought, am I going crazy? Finally, I decided to confide in my mother about what happened to me. She was shocked to hear about it and said I was very lucky because other people had been attacked by jinn in the same place and had either died or gone mad.

This thing followed me for three years until I went to Pakistan and saw someone who gave me taweez and a bottle of water which he had recited the Quran on; he told me to make ablution with the water when I got home to the UK before I went to bed and that the jinn would appear in a dream and I would be able to ask it questions. He said the jinn was female and was in love with me and that if I did not get it treated, that when I got married it would sit in the nikkah and I would never get rid of it and it would harm my wife.

After wearing the taweez, I never saw it again but I never got to try the water because when I got home a visitor, who was a little girl about 3 years old, picked up the bottle and emptied its contents over the carpet.

Jagga, via email

I looked up at my husband and then at the face and was scared. It looked resigned because I was afraid and it disappeared.

Have you seen an Arcadian?

One evening in September 2003 I was reading the paper and my husband was asleep. A bright light appeared beside me. It was the shape of a Greek mask, with two eyes and a mouth [see sketch]. You couldn't see anything through, just black.

I looked up at my husband and then at the face and was scared. It looked resigned because I was afraid and it disappeared.

At first I couldn't believe what I had seen but I found out that someone I knew had seen the same shining face but with a brown body sitting in a chair watching him sleep. This happened twice, each time going when he woke up. He had also seen the face in a book, where they were called Arcadians and referred to (fortunately for us) as benign watchers. Does anyone know anything more about them?

We have a lot of paranormal activity in our home: lights, shadows, even manifestations so real that they look like a live person; cats, dogs; black balls that disappear; things move to different places; people walk past our window and go away half way across. Our dog 'talks' to someone in the kitchen, always in the same place. Although 'busy' here, nothing horrible has ever happened.

The other reason for writing is that I was very interested to read in Sightings in issue 45 about the orange lights seen from Cardiff over the M4 corridor, and also at Oldham. We live beside the M5 and on 31st December 09, my husband went outside just before midnight and saw two orange lights travelling at a great speed above the motorway. They were moving north to south. One went behind a cloud but did not reappear. The second light just vanished from the sky.

We have seen white lights in the sky moving all over the place. They move away when a plane appears and at great speed. Also, a solitary light speeding across the sky, then staying still for five minutes and then it was gone.

M A Debrick, Bartley Green, Birmingham

What happened to my uncle?

As a young child my grandparents lived way up in the mountains of Ohiopyle, Pennsylvania. Every summer my mom would take us for a visit. As the evening was getting late most of the family went off to bed. My Grandmother, Uncle and I stayed up late on the front porch watching the stars. A bright light glowed over the cow pasture about 200 yards from us. My Uncle ran up to see if something landed. I followed leisurely behind him until my Grandmother snatched me up and ran me back into the house.

From the front door I could see whatever it was had landed. Funny thing was there was no noise, just a bright light. My Grandmother was calling out for my Uncle to get back. The craft shot up into the air at an alarming speed. I ran out the door, watching it get higher and higher in the sky, until it blended into the stars. We went over towards the pasture to see if there were any marks on the ground and also to find my Uncle. He was gone.

After a few days of bewildering thoughts and no answers, along came my Uncle wandering up the dirt road. He was dehydrated and confused. He claimed the craft had taken him and he woke up on a military base some four miles away in a hospital bed. When he woke he ran out scared and no-one followed him. To this day we have no idea what really happened to him or where he was. All I know is that after this night he was never the same. My Uncle's ability to draw in detail was incredible. But something about him also changed, he no longer wanted to be around people and sat in his room for many years.

Sam Satullo, via email

'We went over towards the pasture to see if there were any marks on the ground and also to find my Uncle. He was gone.'

HAMPTON COURT: The illustration, taken from the classic work on Haunted Houses by Charles Harper (1907), shows the Haunted Gallery in the palace, where our reader may have heard the ghost of Catherine Howard.

Screaming queen

While visiting Hampton Court Palace in 1977, my friend and I were amongst a lot of other tourists in the gallery above the chapel. I heard a noise that sounded either like a child or lady screaming, but kind of in the distance. It seemed a strange thing to hear in such a formal, royal atmosphere and I looked around, but the strangers around me made no reaction, as if they hadn't heard it.

My friend, however, did. We both looked at each other, asking, 'What was that?' Then it happened again. It wasn't until later that we found out that was the 'haunted gallery' where Catherine Howard had been dragged, screaming, when being taken to the Tower.

Linda Reed, via email

Open wide for a big surprise

I awoke in the middle of the night and realised a shape was behind the curtain (and window). Before long I heard the window being forced open, then I saw the curtains being slowly pulled open. After a while the windows and curtains were wide open and I saw a horrifying faceless demon like thing on the sill.

The faceless thing leaped at me and I closed my eyes and pulled the covers over my face. I opened my eyes under the covers and realised I had been asleep and the whole thing was a dream.

I then pulled the covers off of my head and was disturbed to see the curtains and windows wide open (like in the dream), despite the fact that I have a habit of making sure they're shut every night and even IF I had forgotten to close them that night they wouldn't have been wide open, neither would have the curtains.

Adam Randall, via email

The strange au pair

This experience was about 12 years ago. I was living in Cumbria. My next door neighbour was a single dad and hired au pairs from Europe, mainly from the Czech Republic. One au pair that came to work for him wrote for a German magazine, 2000 I believe it was called. She did not speak very good English, but we managed basic communication.

She did not call strange objects in the sky UFOs. She preferred the term 'contacts'. She took me out into the back garden one clear night and pointed up into the sky at what looked like a star to me. She said: 'If it moves left it's friendly, if it moves right it's not friendly.'

I looked down at the ground for a second, stumbling on a rock, and when I looked back up into the sky the star or contact had disappeared. I was very sceptical, as you would be, and thought there would be a rational explanation to what I saw. But on another occasion she wanted to try an experiment on me and my partner.

She asked us both to drink half a pint of salt water (we pretended we had done as neither of us could stomach doing that) and turn down the lights in the living room. She sat in front of me. With my hands on my knees, she asked me to concentrate on her eyes. For about two minutes which seemed like an eternity my eyes would not blink and they started to water and strain. Her face seemed to change shape, her jaw widened and her eyes went massive and tilted dark brown, not too dissimilar from eyes we're all familiar with, those of the Grey Aliens. But for me it was the shape of her face widening underneath her nose. The best way of describing it was Desperate Dan from the comics.

Straight after that I went to sit on another sofa and my partner had a go. Afterwards when the au pair went back next door, I asked my partner to draw what she saw on a piece of paper and I would do the same. We both drew the same shape.

This was a weird experience and something I can't explain. I cannot help wondering if we had both forced down the half pint of salt water if we would have seen more or something different. She was definitely strange. Does anyone have an explanation for this? Maybe we were hypnotised, I don't know.

Andy Foster, via email

Her face seemed to change shape, her jaw widened and her eyes went massive and tilted dark brown, not too dissimilar from eyes we're all familiar with, those of the Grey Aliens.

The thing in the woods

A few years ago me and a friend were camping in Cornwall. We heard some strange noises and footsteps around our tent but thought nothing of it. About five months after this, we again went camping but this time in the Forest of Dean. We had a couple of nights with similar experiences when we decided to have a forest walk at night.

After entering the forest, a strange noise could be heard almost like a turkey, as funny as it sounds. We then walked further into the forest to see a white figure moving in and around the trees – we fled.

We returned on several occasions and the same thing happened each time: this tall, white slender figure grew closer. Now everytime we go camping or out in the woods we see the same thing. Is it an alien or is it a ghost or is this a thing that only me and my friends who have seen it are imagining?

Jacob Harris, via email

Mysterious object

I have only ever experienced one paranormal sighting, and it was on the way home from a level 1 course I attended in Hinchingbrooke [Cambridgeshire]. It was about 10 pm and I was in the car with my mum.

I was looking out the window and saw one of those red aeroplane lights, and next to it something was reflecting off of it. It's so hard to explain, but something was next to the highest light, making the red light reflect onto it. It was an object, but I couldn't explain

I feel fingers wrap around my leg and I look down to see my leg in the air. This time my leg is thrown down not dropped and my body jerks a little.

it to show my mum. And she was driving which made it harder for her to see as well. I haven't seen anything since, but hope to!

Charlie, via email

Invisible singer

Just 22 minutes ago I went to the bathroom to take a pee. The time was 03:00 am. I heard a humming [and then] a very weird sound, almost like it was trying to say a word. I couldn't actually understand but the more I listened the more the sound got louder and louder.

Eventually, after a few minutes I heard a woman singing at the bottom of the stairs. Because I live with five girls I thought it was one of them but the thing that disturbed me was that it wasn't in English, it was something close to Indian but the girls whom I share the house with are Chinese.

After this there were steps downstairs. So I went to check it out and what I saw didn't please me because there was no one to see. And now I am trying to sleep. I have a necklace with a cross on my neck while writing on this website.

Cristian, Canterbury, via email

Phantom groper

I am 15 years old and want to share my experience with a ghost. I was out for ice-cream and my mom was getting me my shake. I was sitting alone at a table and all of a sudden I feel fingers wrap around my leg and lift it up. I look down and see my leg in the air but nothing there. The fingers unwrap and my leg falls.

I scoot over and again I feel fingers wrap around my leg and I look down to see my leg in the air. This time my leg is thrown down not dropped and my body jerks a little.

Now I change tables. Now straight in front of me I see a bloody scarred-up man that is a tad transparent and he says: 'Like how I lifted your leg?'

Then he smiled a devilish smile.... then he walks away and disappears. This is the first time I have met a spirit that was not kind. I have met one at my grandpa's grave and one in church.

Chelsea, via email

The thing in the corner

I've just taken up drawing and was sat in my dining room late the other night. The room suddenly went freezing cold and my two cats started staring at the corner. So, already taking pics of my art, I took a shot of the corner with my Samsung camera phone.

When I looked at the photo below I was amazed at what I saw. But what is it? There's nothing in the corner of the room to cause a reflection. I don't have any pictures, mirrors or anything like that. My phone is new but the photo is blurred slightly as I had to get my friend to take a pic of the image on it with her camera (I can't upload it onto my computer).

It is an old cottage I live in (in the New Forest). It was an old police house. We have things happening here all the time. I often see things, hear voices and get distinctive smells, such as flowers etc.

Georgie Roberts, Hinton, Dorset

My evidence for spirit guides

I'm an Electronic Engineer with 40 years experience, working for a major company in Stevenage, UK. Over the last five years I've been designing and manufacturing ☞

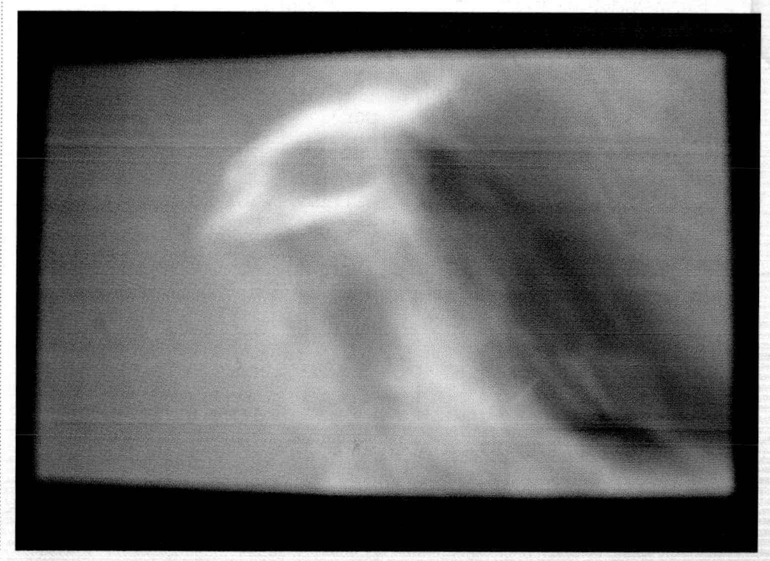

equipment for investigating the paranormal. I tend to look at most things with a scientific approach. That's not to say I don't have my own beliefs in things e.g. life after death. With over five years as a Technical-Paranormal Investigator, I've witnessed many strange and unexplainable happenings, not just at haunted locations.

This particular incident happened on the morning of Friday the 28th of September, 2007. While doing an investigation at a public library some two years earlier, a psychic medium that was present told me I had a Spirit Guide, which appeared to him as a Japanese woman. This didn't really surprise me, and might even explain my interests in Chinese and Japanese culture, which I've had for many years.

Later, while talking to Sharon (a friend who joined me on many investigations) one evening and who is also a psychic person, I asked her, while in general conversation, 'How can you tell if you have a Spirit Guide?'

She replied, 'You simply ask them questions, like do something or move something, so I know you are there. Just ask this question before going to bed.'

This seemed straightforward enough, so that night, before going to bed, I said (only in my mind, apparently you don't need to speak out aloud), do something so I know you're here, and after that I went straight to bed. The next morning I got up as usual for work (I was on shift work at that time, so I was getting up at about 4.30am).

Before continuing I'd better mention that I have an automatic (battery-operated) motion-sensing light at the top of the stairs, for safety reasons. This light doesn't come on straight away, it has a few seconds delay. Anyway, I came out of the bedroom greeted by total darkness and closed the door behind me. As I closed the door, it didn't seem to shut fully. Even pulling harder, the door just wouldn't close. At this point the automatic stair light came on, while I was still looking at the door.

The sight that met my eyes was a blue pen, which I had been using downstairs the previous night, sticking out between the door and frame, just below the door handle. When I opened the door again the pen dropped to the floor.

As I went down the stairs, the light in the lounge was set on full brightness; I have a dimmer switch that controls this light. While watching television I never have the lights on full power, only when perhaps wrapping Xmas presents and things like that.

So, two things had happened that morning. Firstly, how could a pen suddenly get placed in between the door and frame? Secondly, did I leave the lounge lights on? I was the last person to go upstairs to bed and I know I turned the lights off, and anyway, the moment I came out of the bedroom, I should have seen the lounge light shining on the wall at the bottom of the stairs, but I didn't.

Now for the twist to this story: why place a pen in the door? It wasn't until several weeks later that it all fell into place. At work we have a card entry system, even on some internal doors as well. In the past I used to take my post to work and take it to our mailroom. This room requires a card to let you back out. From laziness, I would stick my pen in the door, stopping the door from closing completely, so I didn't need to go looking for my card.

Did my Spirit Guide choose this idea to get the message over to me? As for the lights being on full, I haven't got an answer for that one, maybe it's because I never normally have them on full.

That, and one other thing that happened on an earlier date, has made me a strong believer in the fact that we all could have a Spirit Guide(s).

Nigel Brockwell,
Brotronics Paranormal Investigations

'You simply ask them questions, like do something or move something, so I know you are there. Just ask this question before going to bed.'

What this katydid did

In my backyard one night in 1995 a green katydid about 2-and-a-half inches long displayed behaviour that I can only call paranormal. On being approached, it jumped on me. When I brought it inside the house and placed it on the floor, it would face me and jump on me, in a friendly manner.

Normally, insects would either ignore a person or try to flee, but this katydid seemed to sense that I was a friend. It neither tried to flee nor bite. It was my pet and friend for some 45 minutes. I decided to release it in my yard.

After Lance expired, I went to the parking lot to unlock the car. There was nobody around. I had a strange feeling as I unlocked the doors. I heard the jingling sound of dog tags but there were no dogs around.

It's incredible because insects are not thought of as intelligent and they are mostly indifferent to people; they are very primitive. Yet this katydid showed curiosity and friendliness toward a human being, in this case myself. For some 45 minutes human and insect contemplated each other in friendship.

My favourite animals are dogs, parrots, parakeets, songbirds, pigeons, hyraxes, elephants, small goats, small antelopes, dolphins, whales and manatees. Among the reptiles I only like the friendly ones and the pretty ones. Katydids, skippers, most moths and butterflies are also endearing and there are some nice fish.

Vicken Dimidjian, NYC

The last of Lance

Last year my cousin's dog Lance, a beautiful sheltie, had to be put down. It was about 2 am, when we took Lance to the emergency vets. The vet said he had already lost his vision because of lack of oxygen in his brain and there was no way out.

After Lance expired, I went to the parking lot to unlock the car. There was nobody around. I had a strange feeling as I unlocked the doors. I heard the jingling sound of dog tags but there were no dogs around.

For about a month I heard a dog walking in the garage and my dog was behaving strangely every time that was happening. One morning about a month later my cousin asked me if I had had my dog in the back yard at 2 am that morning. I said no, why? He said that he heard jingling dog tags in the back yard. The back yard has an 8ft fence and there are no dogs around.

Was that Lance saying the final goodbye? I have not heard dog tags since.

Dean Nichols, via email

A little horror

This picture was taken by meon a preliminary visit to Fort Amherst in Chatham, Kent, prior to a Haunted Weekend event earlier this year. It appears to show a strange creature behind an iron gate.

The creature is about 3ft tall and was not seen with the naked eye, only noticed when the pic was put on the computer. It does not appear human and we believe it is an elemental entity. Although we felt it follow us around the caves it didn't reveal istelf to us. No one else has come across it in investigations to our knowledge.

Most Haunted showed it on their live broadcast earlier on the year but they couldn't explain it either. The management there have no explanation as no animals are present in the complex and there were only three people on the site at the time I took the photograph.

John Blythe, HauntedWeekend.com